T0300733

Project Management Maturity Models for Organizational Performance

Christina Chin M.M.
University of Nottingham, Malaysia

IGI Global
Scientific Publishing
Publishing Tomorrow's Research Today

Vice President of Editorial	Melissa Wagner
Managing Editor of Acquisitions	Mikaela Felty
Managing Editor of Book Development	Jocelynn Hessler
Production Manager	Mike Brehm
Cover Design	Phillip Shickler

Published in the United States of America by
IGI Global Scientific Publishing
701 East Chocolate Avenue
Hershey, PA, 17033, USA
Tel: 717-533-8845
Fax: 717-533-8661
Website: https://www.igi-global.com E-mail: cust@igi-global.com

Library of Congress Cataloging-in-Publication Data

Names: Chin, Christina M. M., 1977- editor.
Title: Project management maturity models for organizational performance /
    [edited by] Christina M. M. Chin.
Description: Hershey, PA : IGI Global Scientific Publishing, [2025] |
    Includes bibliographical references and index. | Summary: "As companies
    face increasing complexity in project execution, the need for robust and
    dynamic frameworks has become essential. Enter the Duplex Project
    Management Maturity Model (DPM3), a refined evolution of traditional
    project management maturity models (PM3), designed to address the
    growing need for adaptability, flexibility, and long-term sustainability
    in PM practices"-- Provided by publisher.
Identifiers: LCCN 2024057487 (print) | LCCN 2024057488 (ebook) | ISBN
    9798369314395 (hardcover) | ISBN 9798369350362 (library binding) | ISBN
    9798369314401 (ebook)
Subjects: LCSH: Project management.
Classification: LCC HD69.P75 P761683 2025 (print) | LCC HD69.P75 (ebook)
    | DDC 658.8/04--dc23/eng/20250206
LC record available at https://lccn.loc.gov/2024057487
LC ebook record available at https://lccn.loc.gov/2024057488

British Cataloguing in Publication Data
A Cataloguing in Publication record for this book is available from the British Library.

All work contributed to this book is new, previously-unpublished material.
The views expressed in this book are those of the authors, but not necessarily of the publisher.
This book contains information sourced from authentic and highly regarded references, with reasonable efforts made to ensure the reliability of the data and information presented. The authors, editors, and publisher believe the information in this book to be accurate and true as of the date of publication. Every effort has been made to trace and credit the copyright holders of all materials included. However, the authors, editors, and publisher cannot assume responsibility for the validity of all materials or the consequences of their use. Should any copyright material be found unacknowledged, please inform the publisher so that corrections may be made in future reprints.

Table of Contents

Chapter 7

Section 6
DPM3 Key to Organizational Performance

Chapter 8

Preface

OVERVIEW OF THE DUPLEX PROJECT MANAGEMENT MATURITY MODEL (DPM3)

The rapid advancement of industries and globalization in the modern business environment have made project management (PM) one of the most critical success factors for organizations. As companies face increasing complexity in project execution, the need for robust and dynamic frameworks has become essential. Enter the Duplex Project Management Maturity Model (DPM3), a refined evolution of traditional project management maturity models (PM3), designed to address the growing need for adaptability, flexibility, and long-term sustainability in PM practices.

The DPM3 model is based on 5 operating principles and 5 levels of maturity. It assesses the organization and the project manager using naturally occurring observable verifiable indicators along the PM life cycle processes and PM knowledge group assessment outcomes to gauge the conduciveness of the project environment (constraints), adequacy of facilitators (enablers) and the general capability of the project manager assigned. The 5 principles include (1) the need for a balanced or rounded skills sets (hard and soft skills) from the project manager, (2) matching capabilities of the project manager and the organization, (3) enhancing capabilities and maturity of project managers and organization, (4) adaptable leadership to steer the project direction in a dynamic environment and (5) flexibility to adapt to the disruptive technology of IR5.0. The 5 levels of maturity level range from accidental project manager to authority project manager. It assesses the organization and the project manager using naturally occurring observable verifiable indicators along the PM life cycle processes and PM knowledge group assessment outcomes to gauge the conduciveness of the project environment (constraints), adequacy of facilitators (enablers) and the general capability of the project manager assigned. While the maturity scores are placed under 4 component groups of PM maturity namely Environmental factors and Facilitators (Enablers), Hard-skills and Soft-skills.

These principles are essential for businesses today, as they allow an organization to refine not only the processes and tools used to manage projects but also the strategic integration of those projects with larger organizational goals. The model assesses an organization's technical proficiency and execution capabilities, focusing on processes, methodologies, tools, and performance metrics. This reflects how efficiently the organization manages individual projects, with emphasis on timelines, budget management, and quality standards.

The strategic tier of the DPM3, on the other hand, evaluates how well PM is aligned with the broader strategic objectives of the organization. It assesses factors such as leadership involvement, cultural alignment, innovation capacity, and the integration of project portfolios with the company's long-term vision. This tier ensures that the projects not only meet immediate operational goals but also contribute to the sustained success and competitive positioning of the business.

Together, these two components form a comprehensive framework that allows organizations to assess and improve their overall PM maturity, from both an operational and strategic perspective. By providing this dual approach, the DPM3 offers a unique and advanced perspective that traditional models may overlook, making it especially relevant for organizations navigating complex and multifaceted environments.

Where Does the DPM3 Fits in the World Today?

In today's globalized and highly competitive market, organizations are managing projects with increasing complexity, scope, and risk. These projects often span across multiple regions, departments, and functional areas, requiring a model that is versatile and scalable. The DPM3 fits within this context by offering organizations a framework that is both detailed and adaptable to different industries and business sizes.

In an era where agility is just as important as stability, the DPM3 helps companies strike a balance between structured processes and the ability to pivot quickly in response to market changes. Traditional maturity models often focus solely on the improvement of processes and technical capabilities, which, while crucial, may not address the need for strategic flexibility and alignment with evolving business priorities. The DPM3 fills this gap by combining the tactical with the strategic, allowing organizations to not only execute projects effectively but also to ensure that those projects contribute meaningfully to the company's long-term success.

The DPM3 is relevant in industries such as technology, finance, healthcare, and manufacturing, where rapid technological advancement and regulatory changes require both operational excellence and strategic foresight. As the pace of innovation continues to accelerate, companies must continuously adapt their PM processes to keep up with new tools, methodologies, and approaches. The DPM3 enables organizations to build a foundation of robust PM practices while ensuring that those practices remain aligned with corporate strategy.

Moreover, the COVID-19 pandemic and subsequent disruptions to global supply chains, work environments, and economic conditions have underscored the importance of resilience and flexibility in PM. Organizations are now more aware than ever of the need to manage risks proactively, make quick decisions, and pivot strategies as needed. The DPM3's emphasis on both operational and strategic maturity of project managers allows organizations to weather these disruptions while remaining focused on their long-term goals. By fostering an integrated approach to PM, the DPM3 provides organizations with the tools they need to manage projects efficiently in both stable and volatile environments.

The DPM3 is critical in today's business world because it addresses key challenges that organizations face when managing complex projects. These include:

- **Alignment Between Strategy and Operations**: Many organizations struggle to align project goals with larger business objectives. The DPMMM's dual approach ensures that PM efforts contribute directly to achieving the strategic vision of the organization.
- **Scalability and Flexibility**: In industries that are subject to rapid technological changes, scalability and flexibility are essential. The DPMMM allows organizations to adapt their PM practices as they grow or shift direction, without losing sight of operational excellence.
- **Risk Management and Resilience**: Today's business environment is filled with uncertainty, from economic fluctuations to political instability to global pandemics. The DPMMM equips organizations with the ability to foresee and manage risks while ensuring continuity in project execution and alignment with long-term goals.
- **Innovation and Agility**: The pace of innovation is increasing, and companies must remain agile to stay competitive. The DPMMM allows for the integration of new tools and methodologies while maintaining strategic focus, enabling companies to innovate without losing sight of core business objectives.

Target Audience

The target audience for the **Duplex Project Management Maturity Model (DPM3) – Key to Organizational Performance** book includes a diverse group of professionals and organizations that seek to enhance their PM capabilities and align them with strategic business goals. Specifically, the book is designed for:

- **Project Managers**: Both seasoned and emerging project managers will benefit from the practical frameworks, tools, and strategies outlined in the book. It helps them refine their operational processes and align their projects with the broader strategic objectives of their organizations.
- **Senior Executives and Leadership Teams**: C-suite executives, directors, and decision-makers responsible for strategic alignment and organizational growth will find value in understanding how PM

maturity impacts long-term success. The book offers insights into how leadership can drive PM improvements and ensure that projects support organizational goals.

- **Portfolio and Program Managers**: Those managing multiple projects or entire portfolios will gain insights into how the DPMMM can help prioritize projects, allocate resources more effectively, and ensure that project outcomes contribute to the organization's overall strategic vision.
- **Consultants and Business Advisors**: PM consultants and advisors looking to guide organizations toward maturity improvements will find a comprehensive model in the DPMMM to evaluate and implement within various industries.
- **Academics and Researchers**: Educators, students, and researchers in PM, organizational development, and business strategy will appreciate the academic rigor and real-world application of the model. The book serves as a useful reference for academic studies and teaching material for understanding the theoretical and practical aspects of PM maturity.
- **Organizations Seeking Growth**: Companies of all sizes, from small startups to large enterprises, can use the DPMMM as a blueprint for scaling their PM capabilities. Whether they are just beginning their maturity journey or seeking optimization, the book offers a flexible and scalable approach for improving both operational and strategic project performance.

This broad audience underscores the versatility of the DPM3, making the book relevant for anyone involved in managing projects, driving organizational strategy, or fostering continuous improvement in PM practices. The book is relevant to organizations of all sizes and industries that are looking to enhance their PM capabilities. Whether a company is at the beginning of its PM journey or is striving to optimize its processes, the concepts and strategies presented in this book will help guide their maturity journey.

Importance of Chapter Submissions

This book is structured to provide a comprehensive understanding of the DPM3 through a series of chapters that are built on one another. Each chapter plays a critical role in guiding the reader through the concepts, applications, and benefits of the DPM3.

Chapter 1

This chapter introduces PM background, phenomenal exponential growth trend in PM. It also examined the expanding role of project managers, misguided application of general management principles in the project environment and misuse of best practices. How the above issues cloud the clarity needed in the management of change or projects are explained subsequently and why such foundational issues prompted this research to be initiated. This chapter looks at PM3 designs to develop an alternative PM maturity model to better serve the PM community with an intuitive road map to enhance organizational performance through an improved level of PM maturity. The chapter sets the stage for understanding the comprehensive and adaptive nature of this model.

Chapter 2

This chapter is set for readers to gain the preliminary knowledge needed to better understand the purpose of PM maturity models (PM3s). It also looks at the ways in which PM maturity is assessed, how mature PM enhances organizational performance and why PM3 adoption rate had remained low despite the benefits being clearly reported by PM research in the last decade. The reasons for the persistent high project failure rates will also be examined for cause and effect. The answers should narrow the scope to those that are relevant to developing an alternative PM3. It also outlines the evolution of traditional maturity models and explains its suitability for today's fast-paced, complex business environment. Readers will learn about the levels of characteristics of PM3, and how it can be applied to assess and improve PM practices within organizations.

Chapter 3

This chapter explains the lesson learned from PM3 in the market to enable a clear understanding of what PM3 is, its objectives, the good features to adopt and pitfalls to avoid. It will assist in the initial model design to ensure target PM practitioners can gradually improve their PM practice thereby continuously enhance commercial competitiveness. As well are offering guidance and lessons learned on the constant project failure statistics for the last few decades that has created curiosity to what contributes to such high project failures.

Chapter 4

In this chapter, readers will be guided through the process designing the DPM3. It covers various tools and techniques, including self-assessment surveys, interviews and benchmarking against industry standards via the workshops and seminars conducted for the past 8 years period of data gathering.

Chapter 5

This chapter provides a comparative study of 7 well-known PM3s namely CMMi, OPM3, PMMM (Kerzner), PMMM (Crawford), PwC maturity model and P2MM PRINCE 2 to observe the common characteristics of desirable attributes of PM3s and complaints about PM3 models and to learn from it. The survey feedback consistently shows the need for PM3 models to be user friendly, using terminology commonly used by PM practitioners and descriptions of growth trends that were meaningful when seen as one maturity level to the next. Through the model analysis, it is noted that for PM3 and PM maturity assessment to be accepted in the marketplace, it is imperative that all the maturity attributes being sought should comply with or are aligned with internationally recognized recommended good practices but at the same time should also be pragmatic in application and functionally fit for purpose. This chapter recommends solutions to the identified impediments to PM performance.

Chapter 6

This chapter discusses and expands from the initial idea of the DPM3 principles and maturity level descriptively using pictorial diagram to better aid the understanding. Based on the conceptualization, a 5-level model structure was presented to show the stages of growth project managers need to go through in their career lifecycle. The respective stage in the DPM3 maturity is identified as accidental, enlightened, competent, expert and authority level.

Chapter 7

In this chapter, readers will explore the proposals for a new approach to measure organizational maturity using the Duplex PM Maturity Model (DPM3) with the objective of enhancing organizational performance. The DPM3 model and its components is illustrated using the analogy of a motorcycle with 2 wheels, with both wheels rotate to accomplish work and grow as the skill-components grow and mature with a need to always paddle and steer to keep in balance and adapt to the dynamic project environment. The front wheel represents the project manager while the back wheel represents the organization. Each wheel is supported by 10 equal spoke lengths, and each spoke represents a maturity component. This chapter will explicitly describe the operating principles, components, characteristics, level and roadmap to DPM3 maturity.

Chapter 8

The final chapter looks at the contribution of the DPM3 to the body of knowledge. It discusses the implication to the theory and practice of PM3 and what are the lessons learned to improve future PM endeavors. The theory, principles and coverage remain unchanged but the way in which the theory is applied is made fluid to enable it to be adaptable as the circumstance dictates. To ensure sufficient width of knowledge and depth of expertise, DPM3 is designed with 2-dimensional assessment (1) width of coverage, (knowing and implementing the PM maturity attribute) and (2) depth of expertise to ensure optimal use of the PM maturity attribute (maturity level). The chapter concludes with a recommendation for future research with the emerging trends such as digital transformation, artificial intelligence, and Agile methodologies, and how these developments are shaping the field of PM. Organizations can use the DPM3 to stay ahead of these changes, ensuring both operational excellence and strategic alignment in an increasingly complex world. This also provides the means for PM practitioners to advance their PM maturity as well as providing a cost-effective pathway to enhance their level of PM maturity thereby improving their chances of PM success consistently and more predictably.

CONCLUSION

This book represents a significant contribution to the field of PM by introducing and explaining the Duplex Project Management Maturity Model. By focusing on both operational and strategic aspects of PM, it offers organizations a holistic framework for assessing and improving their PM capabilities. As businesses face more complex projects and navigate increasingly uncertain environments, the need for such an integrated approach is more pressing than ever.

Throughout this book, readers will find practical insights, case studies, and tools to help them apply the DPMMM within their own organizations. The content is designed to be both theoretically grounded and practically applicable, ensuring that readers can understand not only the principles behind the model but also how to implement it effectively.

Furthermore, this book emphasizes the importance of continuous improvement in PM. It acknowledges that no organization's PM processes are perfect, but with the right tools and frameworks, they can always be improved. The DPM3's approach encourages organizations to look beyond the surface of their PM processes and consider how well those processes align with their broader strategic goals.

In addition to helping individual organizations, this book also contributes to the broader field of PM by advancing the conversation around maturity models. While traditional maturity models have served the industry well, the DPM3 takes the concept a step further by integrating operational and strategic perspectives. This integrated approach ensures that PM is not an isolated function but is woven into the very fabric of an organization's long-term success.

As PM continues to evolve, this book provides a forward-looking perspective that equips project managers, executives, and organizations with the tools they need to succeed in today's fast-paced and complex business environment. The DPM3 is more than just a framework; it is a philosophy of continuous improvement, strategic alignment, and operational excellence. By embracing this model, organizations can elevate their PM practices and contribute to their long-term growth and success.

In conclusion, this book provides a fresh and innovative perspective on PM maturity, addressing the evolving needs of modern organizations. By offering a comprehensive, adaptable, and strategic approach, it ensures that organizations are equipped to manage projects in a way that not only meets immediate operational goals but also secures long-term success. Through this lens, the DPM3 has the potential to reshape the future of PM.

Christina Chin M.M.

University of Nottingham, Malaysia

Acknowledgment

This work is the pure hard work and dedication that late Mr Robert Gan Chee Cheong has devoted himself to over the years. With his passing, I am honored to share his knowledge through this book. It is with deep gratitude and a heavy heart that I extend my sincerest appreciation for his unwavering dedication, passion, and academic prowess. This acknowledgment is a tribute to a remarkable individual who left an indelible mark on the field of project management and on my own intellectual journey as an academic, supervisor and friend.

Mr. Gan's relentless pursuit of knowledge and his commitment to excellence were evident throughout his remarkable 30-year career in the project management industry. His invaluable experiences, insights, and the wealth of expertise he amassed became the foundation for the knowledge encapsulated in this book. This work stands as a testament to his enduring legacy and serves as a reservoir of the wisdom he so generously shared.

During his Ph.D. journey, I had the privilege of being Mr. Gan's supervisor, and it was truly a wonderful and enriching experience. His passion for research, coupled with his tenacity and unyielding spirit, inspired not only me but all those who were fortunate enough to be part of his academic journey. His insatiable curiosity and commitment to academic excellence were contagious, creating an environment of intellectual growth and camaraderie.

I respect Mr. Robert Gan Chee Cheong for his never-ending hope and determination in the past 10 years to complete his Ph.D. Despite the challenges and obstacles that he faced; his resilience was a beacon of inspiration to me. The knowledge he has left behind is a lasting tribute to his brilliance and serves as a guiding light for future scholars and practitioners in the field.

As an honor to Mr. Gan, his contributions to academia and the project management industry are a celebration to all. May his legacy continue to inspire and shape the minds of those who follow in his footsteps, and to extend his research in project management.

Thank you, Robert!

Section 1
Introduction

Chapter 1
Introduction and Background of Work

ABSTRACT

This chapter introduces the project management (PM) background, phenomenal exponential growth trend in PM certification and membership. It also examined the expanding role of project managers, misguided application of general management principles in the project environment and misuse of best practices. How the above issues cloud the clarity needed in the management of change or projects are explained subsequently and why such foundational issues prompted this research to be initiated. Furthermore, this chapter relook at PM3 designs to develop an alternative PM maturity model to better serve the PM community with an intuitive road map to enhance organizational performance through an improved level of PM maturity. It highlights the research questions raised and objectives together that complements the unique contribution in this book.

BACKGROUND OF WORK

Over the last three decades, PM education and Project Management Professional (PMP) certification have increased exponentially. The number of certified PMP grew in the last 5 years by a staggering 50% from 590,416 to 887,937 PMPs (PMI Today, 2018) (Table 1) and has since swelled passed a million. PMI Today is a bimonthly newsletter circulated to PMI members in 215 countries and territories.

DOI: 10.4018/979-8-3693-1439-5.ch001

Table 1. 5-year statistics from PMI today

PMP and PMI members statistics for 5 years from Oct 2013 to Oct 2018 (PMI TODAY is a monthly PMI circular to all PMI members)							
PMP Certified PM Growth Trend					PMI Membership Growth Trend		
As per PMI TODAY	Statistics year to year	No of PMPs	Annual growth year by year (%)	5 years growth (%)	PMI Members	Annual growth year by year (%)	5 years growth (%)
Dec 2018	31st Oct 18	887,937	10.19	50.39	553150	20.33	25.31
Dec-2017	31st Oct 17	805,800	8.74		459676	-3.43	
Dec-2016	31st Oct 16	741,007	9.19		475993	0.02	
Dec-2015	31st Oct 15	678,619	6.64		475899	4.74	
Dec-2014	31st Oct 14	636,384	7.79		454379	2.93	
Dec-2013	31st Oct 13	590,416			441425		

This worldwide growth trend (*detail breakdown is only available to PMI Chapter leaders*) has also been experienced by ASEAN countries in particular Malaysia where the official statistics of PMI Malaysia Chapter membership had more than tripled from 500 to over 1791 (PMIMY, 2024) while other ASEAN chapters like Singapore, Indonesia, Philippines also enjoyed significant growth and likely that Thailand and Vietnam will follow suit.

It is unclear however if this tremendous growth trend were a direct result from the various studies showing a positive correlation between higher PM maturity level and improved organizational performance. These include the PwC global survey titled *"Boosting business performance through Programme and Portfolio Management (PPM)" that* showed *"higher PM maturity level will in most cases deliver superior performance in terms of overall project delivery and business benefits"* (Nieto-Rodriguez & Evrard, 2004). However, it is uncertain if PwC's survey on *"business benefits"* had included client satisfaction, a factor identified as a key performance indicator (KPIs) of organisational success (PMBok 6th Ed, 2017).

A study conducted by PM Solutions Centre for Business Centre for Business Practices (2006) shows a clear link between level of maturity and organizational success. The finding shows better performance was achieved in terms of improved client satisfaction (30% of respondents stated 20% improvements) and improvement in risk, procurement, and quality management (26% agreed). The impressive research resulted from this Project Management Maturity Model (PM3) however should be read with caution as it was conducted internally by PM solutions and as such, may possibly be tinted with self-interest bias.

Another study also found that the "*level of use of PM practices did indeed relate to project success*" but there was a "*substantial variation in the relative use of different methods*" (Papke-Shields et al, 2009). PM maturity should not only assess the availability of the PM tools and techniques but also verify that those tools were used in the organisation's PM practice.

A global survey of the high cost of low performance found "*89% of projects at high performing organisations meet their original goals and business intent*" (PMI, 2016). A subsequent PMI 8th Global PM survey also found "*high performance and PM maturity should go hand in hand – but many organisations are still in the slow lane*" while "*having proven project, program and portfolio management practices in place makes a dramatic difference in project performance*" (PMI, 2018). "*Some leading companies, governments, schools and universities have already embraced projects as the way to deliver their strategy and ambitions*" (Nieto-Rodriguez, 2019a).

This reveals a tremendous progress in awareness of the importance of PM when compared with a study done 12 years earlier when only 4% of the top 200 business schools in the world offer PM as part of their MBA core curriculums (Nieto-Rodriguez & Sampietro, 2017).

Since, much research have consistently attributed organisational success to higher levels of PM maturity, one would expect a corresponding increase in the demand for and use of the PM3, maturity models which are designed to measure the PM maturity and gap between where the organisations is and the level the organisation would like to be and thereby improving organisational performance. Based on market feedback however, PM3 market penetration has been low even for models that have been in the market for more than three decades. This lack of correlation merits further research to see if PM maturity models have indeed addressed the real PM practical needs and if not, what were the impediments that inhibit PM3 adoption.

Thus, this book is focused on why current PM3s have not been as successful as one would have expected and whether the following factors collected from the PM practitioners' feedback (via interviews and survey) could have contributed to the PM3 low level of implementation and if so, what lessons could be learned from the following issues such as:

- *difficulty in understanding the terminology used in the current PM3 models.*
- *lack of consensus on how PM maturity should be assessed.*
- *PM3 lack flexibility, adaptability, and scalability.*
- *PM3 lack of depth, coverage, and rigor of assessment*
- *high cost of PM3 application compared with anticipated performance gains.*
- *designs not capable of diverse industry applications.*
- *lack of senior management buy-in*

The data gathered in this book involved 10 personal interviews and surveys of 1201 project managers who attended 89 classes over an 8-year period from year 2011 to March 2019 whereby:

- *623 (52%) attended the PMP exam preparation boot camps (project managers, 90% graduates with minimum 3 years in leading projects)*
- *578 (48%) PM seniors who attended the public and in-house intermediate and advanced level PM seminars or workshops conducted in Malaysia.*

The age group from 27 to 55 years, expatriates, and locals of:

- *80% multinational companies (MNCs) from government link-companies (GLCs)*
- *20% government and small and medium-sized enterprises (SMEs) and small and medium-sized industries (SMIs).*

Participants represented were from industries, commerce, banking, insurance, management consulting, IT/ICT developers and implementers, construction, manufacturers, energy, universities (including post graduate levels), government and enforcement agencies.

Based on the result, only 2% of PM3 users had exposure to PM3, all gave unflattering feedback with the most common reasons being unfriendly terminology and difficulty in understanding the principles. Almost all participants had difficulty in using the tools which were seen as unduly complex and doubtful of the value and its contribution in increasing organisational performance (Gan & Chin, 2018, 2019). The persistent negative feedback reported about PM3s and PM in the last decade of study is an implicit call to action. There is a critical need to relook at the real purpose and imperatives of PM3s which are aimed at training project managers to be better at work and the performing organization to be better managed and more effective. PM should not be further burdened by bureaucracy at various levels of seniority nor hindered by impertinent controls, and strategies that are no longer relevant and cumbersome and worst still management myths that only served to misguide and mislead the project practitioners.

To address the shortcomings, this book seeks to develop an alternative PM Maturity Model that is user-friendly, functionally robust, adaptable, and cost-effective to give PM practitioners a head start following naturally occurring evidence of project-process work (Gan & Chin, 2018, 2019). The proposed PM3 model will be designed based on leveraging the findings from:

- *recommended PM good practices*
- *latest version of PMI's PMBok 6th Ed (2017)*
- *Agile Practice Guide (2017)*
- *PMI Talent triangle (2017)*
- *ISO 21500*
- *knowledge management*
- *data from interviews, survey, and feedback and*
- *author's two decades of international PM practices*

The information gained will be contextualised and structured to facilitate conceptual understanding of how PM3s and projects get unduly complicated by impediments to project success in Figure 1.

Figure 1. The impediments to project performance (conceptualised idea)

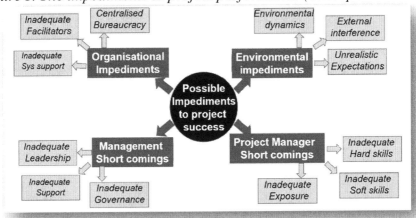

Since this research was initiated in 2010, more findings had confirmed the links between PM maturity and superior organisational performance (PMI, 2016; Gan & Chin, 2018, 2019; Nieto-Rodriguez, 2017, 2019). However, the world at the turn of the 21st Century had to face the tumultuous impact of the 5th industrial revolution. While the way projects were managed using the planned approach had contributed to much of the world's progress, new opportunities occasioned by the 5th industrial revolution pose challenges for research and development (R&D) project initiatives. These projects had to deal with project possibilities, fuzzy ideas of what can be, particularly those in medical and pharmaceutical research and those that stretch the science frontiers. They involve new ideas and extensions to harness IoT (Internet of Things) and AI (Artificial intelligence), centring the co-activity of human and machine. All these projects have short as well as long uncertain gestation periods, significant number of iterations and unplanned changes and could no longer be managed using the planned approach.

To address these new opportunities, the *adaptive approach* was first mooted in year 2000 and officially introduced when the Agile Practice Guide was published by PMI together with the PMBok 6th Ed (2017). It was an alternative approach to PM to achieve a purposeful outcome but where its final shape or form were uncertain. For example, the search for cancer cure may result in an inhibition of cancer cell growth or freezing the malignant cells to death for the natural body system to get rid of it or targeted exposure of cancer cells to certain range of ultrasound waves that kills it or hormonal treatment that suppress hormone production, the *'food'* that feeds the cancer cells thus starving the cancer cells to death. Such outcome may not be a cure but a remission likely to get sufficient cancer patients buy-in and hence considered a project success.

It must be noted however that the adaptive approach has been in practice in various forms for decades by mature project-based organisations but not formalised until PMI issued its first Agile Practice Guide in 2017. The topic was not examinable until 2021. It is therefore not surprising that participants in the survey were unfamiliar and as expected, responded with only the planned approach in mind.

To achieve this objective of developing an alternative PM3, the following questions was answered in this book to create the PM3 initial idea framework:

- *How has the PM role evolved and how would it affect the PM3 design?*
- *What are the levels of PM maturity and what are their key characteristics?*
- *What can be learned from current PM3s?*
- *What can be learned from the continuing high project failure rates?*

MOTIVATION AND CONTRIBUTION

"Three rules of work: Out of clutter find simplicity, From discord find harmony, In the middle of difficulty lies opportunity".

The above statement by Einstein illustrated why it is important for communication to be made simple, specific, clear, and void of ambiguity to be effective as well as to be keenly aware of opportunities that often exist at every turn. As such, the key motivation in publishing this book is to:

- *Emphasize the differentiation of pre-PM stages from PM stage of accountability*

The pre-PM stages take place when the initial idea is conceived, high level strategy is planned, purpose defined, alternatives considered, initial design specified, assessed to be technical and commercially feasible to procurement contracting for project managers to execute, construct or implement suing PM approaches to deliver the required outcome.

- *Identified the 2 key drivers of a project*

Project manager that leads the project team using their hard skills and soft skills maturity components to produce the project outcome. The *performing organization* that *facilitate/enablers* the project with project tools and techniques, templates, resources in the form of people, equipment and materials as well as providing the project *environment* with which it has control like the organization governance structure, infrastructure, systems, and management support.

- *Encapsulating the 5 principles of PM maturity*

It is illustrated pictorially using the motorbike to depict the 5 principles required of

PM maturity model. The description of the principles is illustrated in Figure 2 and briefly explained below.

Figure 2. The 5 principles of proposed Duplex Project Management Maturity Model (DPM3)

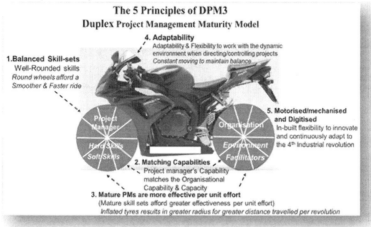

Principle 1: Need for a Balanced or Rounded Skill Set (Illustrated by the 2 Round Wheels)

Like human anatomy, every part, limb, and organs grow through various stages of maturity, progressively and in harmony. In the same way, the project manager matures by improving all their relevant skill sets (DPM3 components) simultaneously, gradually and in harmony with experience and lessons learned (Gan & Chin, 2018, 2019).

Any departure from this gradual complimentary growth will cause a distorted structure that impedes the natural smooth function, thus preventing its optimal use. Imagine a project manager having long adult hands with short children legs would be like having good PM technical skills with poor soft skills to understand people's *idinoun* (coined from Greek words for *general idiosyncratic responses, behaviours and tendencies dependent on the combination of an individual's education, knowledge, experience, exposure, perception, culture, beliefs, value system, attitude, bias and etc.*) in order to understand, lead, respond, motivate and effectively communicate their ideas and instructions.

9

It will be more productive for project managers to hone all their hard skills and soft skills gradually and functionally apply to improve their capabilities through guided experience and tacit knowledge that can only be learned and polish through actual practice. The more rounded the skills, the smoother and more efficient the performance. The same could be expected of the organization to provide their facilitators and organisational environment (*actionable aspects*) with advancing sophistication over time that is complimentary and in line with the scale of business and client expectations (Gan & Chin, 2018, 2019).

Principle 2: Matching Capabilities of the Project Manager and the Organisation

The 2-wheel sizes should be compatible to illustrate the need for compatible maturity of the project manager and the performing organisation. A mature project manager would be expected to work in a *similar but not necessarily equally* mature project organisation to optimise their combined performance potential, while the maturity levels could be different. The differences should not be so great as to hinder coordination and control and cause disconnection between the project manager, the team and their organizational structure and processes, just like the penny farthing bicycle which now exist only as a museum artefact.

While it is true in practice that mature project managers could perform without a mature organization, they can only do so for a short term but eventually will run out of steam as they will need organisational support for the long haul (Gan & Chin, 2018). This will be like the circus single wheel cycle that only experts could manage and even then, for a short period and with limited capability.

Principle 3: PM Maturity Enhance Capabilities and Maturity of Project Managers and Organization

As maturity improves over time depicting an inflated tyre increasing the wheel radius, a greater distance can be accomplished per revolution. Hence higher maturity will result in more productive outcome through greater effectiveness and efficiency meaning more productive work accomplished per unit of effort (Gan & Chin, 2018).

Principle 4: Adaptable Leadership

Need for constant moving and steering to keep the 2-wheel vehicle in motion and in balance (Gyro effect) by constantly moving forward. This emphasise the need for adaptable leadership in constant steering in the required direction depicting the constant need for alignment with strategic imperatives to achieve organizational goals while always being adaptable to the dynamic project environment (Gan & Chin, 2019).

Principle 5: Digitized and Mechanised

This principle highlights the modern project's reliance on digitization, automation and mechanization with imbued flexibility to adapt to the disruptive technology of the Industrial Revolution 5.0.

ASSUMPTIONS OF WORK

This research anticipates the following limitations should the assumptions made below not hold true in any way or form.

- The interviews are limited to project managers in contact with PMI Malaysia Chapter (PMIMY) network, a foreign university in Malaysia and ROGAN strategic advisory (RSA) business contacts only.
- The surveyed participants are drawn only from those who attended the PMP exam preparation boot camps organized by two major PMI registered education providers (REPs) in Malaysia and ROGAN Strategic Advisory (RSA) and its business affiliates' public and in-house PM boot camps.
- The surveyed senior PM participants who attended the intermediate and advanced level public PM seminars organized by REPs, public

event organizers, RSA public and in-house PM seminars and PM training classes.

- The sample of 1201 research survey participants were taken from 89 classes collected over 8 years (from 2011 to year March 2019). Attendees' compositions were:
  - 52% project managers with at least 3 years managing and leading projects and had attended the PMP exam preparation boot camps conducted by two well-known PMI's Registered Educations providers and ROGAN Strategic advisory and
  - 48% were experienced project managers (age 27 to 55 years) that attended the various public intermediate and advance level PM seminars and workshops conducted in Malaysia.
- The diversity of the PM community includes participants from commerce, banking, insurance, oil and gas (upstream), energy, IT/ICT developers and implementers, IT equipment manufacturers and suppliers, IT integrators and service providers, telecommunication infrastructure providers, PM service providers, multi-national consulting organizations, senior university academics, government departments, enforcement agencies and manufacturing industries.
- Organizations' executives, project managers and project leaders approached willingly and voluntarily to participate both in the interviews and surveys.
- The personal feedback given by survey participants will be honest and frank regarding their opinions of any or all PM procedures, tools and techniques displayed. These will include survey participants actual experiences, explanation, recommended good practices, desirable personal exposures, required competencies, personal soft skills, and vital leadership attributes.
- Survey participants will voluntarily and in confidence, reveal complaints or misgivings regarding the current or past work experiences and that they will be forthcoming about their suggestions for PM practice improvements.

CONCLUSION

This chapter has provided a picturesque of the purpose of the research was initiated. Author has found that although there's many PM3 at present in the market, yet it's success implementation and adoption rate are not to its expectation. These were raw data that was gathered through a period of 8 years of exploratory collective data from GLCs, government, SMEs and SMIs sector. To address the negative feedback reported over the last decade of study, there is an implicit call for action. There is a critical need to relook at the real purpose and imperatives of PM3 for trained project managers to better handle the organizational performances in a more effective manner. As such, this resulted a proposal to develop an alternative PM maturity model that is user-friendly, functional, robust, adaptable and cost effective for PM practitioners to head start a project-process work, that will be key contribution and value from this book.

REFERENCES

Gan, R. C. C., & Chin, C. M. M. (2018). Components of project management maturity impacting project, programme, portfolio and organisational success. In Karayaz, G., & Silvius, G. (Eds.), *Developing Organizational Maturity for Effective Project Management* (pp. 128–152). IGI Global., DOI: 10.4018/978-1-5225-3197-5.ch007

Gan, R. C. C., & Chin, C. M. M. (2019). Project management guide and project management maturity models as generic tools capable for diverse applications. In Katuu, S. (Ed.), *Diverse Applications and Transferability of Maturity Models* (pp. 269–315). IGI Global., DOI: 10.4018/978-1-5225-7080-6.ch011

Nieto-Rodriguez, A. (2019a). *The project revolution. How to succeed in a project driven world*. LID Publishing.

Nieto-Rodriguez, A. (2019b, October 3). The Project Manifesto. *Project Manifesto.*https://www.linkedin.com/pulse/project-manifesto-antonio-nieto-rodriguez/

Nieto-Rodriguez, A., & Sampietro, M. (2017). Why business schools keep neglecting project management competencies. *PM World Journal, Vol. (VI)*, Issue XI. https://pmworldlibrary.net/wp-content/uploads/2017/11/pmwj64-Nov2017-Rodriguez-Sampietro-why-business-schools-neglect-project-management.pdf

Papke-Shields, K. E., Beise, C., & Quan, J. (2009). Do project managers practice what they preach, and does it matter to project success? *International Journal of Project Management*, 28(7), 650–662. DOI: 10.1016/j.ijproman.2009.11.002

PM Solutions Centre for Business Centre for Business Practices. (2006). *Project management maturity: A benchmark of current best*. Center for Business Practices.

Project Management Institute Malaysia Chapter (PMIMY). (2024, August). *PMI MY Pulse*. https://pmi.org.my/2024/09/04/pmi-my-pulse-august-2024/ . Project Management Institute Malaysia Chapter.

Project Management Institute (PMI). (2008b). *A guide to project management body of knowledge* (PMBOK Guide) (4th ed). Project Management Institute.

Project Management Institute (PMI). (2017). *A guide to project management body of knowledge* (PMBOK Guide) (6th ed). Project Management Institute.

Project Management Institute (PMI). (2018, March). Customers- How to be the Central Point of their Success. *PMI Today*

ADDITIONAL READINGS

Project Management Institute (PMI). (2017). *A guide to project management body of knowledge* (PMBOK Guide) (6th ed). Project Management Institute.

Project Management Institute (PMI). (2024). The Standard for Program Management (5th ed.) Project Management Institute. Larson E.W. & Gray, C.F. (2017). *Project Management: The Managerial Process*. McGraw-Hill Layton. M.C. (2020). *Agile Project Management for Dummies* (3rd ed.). Wiley.

Senge, M. P. (2006). *The Fifth Discipline: The Art & Practice of the Learning Organization*. Doubleday.

Shenhar, A. J., & Dvir, D. (2007). *Reinventing Project Management: The Diamond Approach to Successful Growth & Innovation*. Harvard Business Press.

KEY TERMS AND DEFINITIONS

Adaptability: The quality to being able to adjust to new conditions or circumstances because of the constantly changing environment.

Flexibility: It refers to the responsiveness to the new situation or circumstances.

Impediments: It refers to something that hinders or obstructs the progression to attain and/or complete the tasks.

Key Performance Indicator: KPI are specific measures of performance within its specific KPAs that measure how well performance has been achieved against the given agreed target or expectation.

Procurement: This refers to the purchase of materials or consumables to meet the project activities. It may involve agreements between two parties (buyer and seller).

Quality: The outcome that meets the *"fitness for use"* criteria (Juran, n.a).

Risk: Refers to the possibility of an event, outcome or task that could have negative impact either on the project objectives, assets or individuals. However, identifying the project risk in the project planning phase will minimize the severity and impact of towards the project.

Scalability: The ability for the system to expand or grow in response to the demand without compromising the performance, efficiency or quality of the process, product or services.

Section 2
Project Management Maturity Model (PM3)

Chapter 2
The Evolving Role and Characteristics of Project Management

ABSTRACT

Literatures are carried out to answer the research questions raised in order to gain the preliminary knowledge needed to better understand the purpose of Project Management Maturity models (PM3s). The review also looks at the ways in which project management (PM) maturity are assessed, how mature PM enhances organizational performance and why PM3 adoption rate had remained low despite the benefits being clearly reported by PM research in the last decade. The reasons for the persistent high project failure rates will also be examined for cause and effect. The answers should narrow the scope to those that are relevant to developing an alternative PM3. The research objective to develop an alternative PM3 prompted four research questions. Answers to them will be used to form the basic construct needed in Chapter 3 to formulate the research approach and appropriate data collection for observation and analytical study.

INTRODUCTION

The research questions developed for this study are:

DOI: 10.4018/979-8-3693-1439-5.ch002

- *How has the PM role evolved and how would it affect the PM3 design?*
- *What are the levels of PM maturity and their key characteristics?*
- *What can be learned from current PM3s?*
- *What can be learned from the continuing high project failure rates?*

PM maturity is the state at which an organization is able to provide the e*nvironment* (controllable organizational structures, policies, procedures, infrastructures) and *facilitators* (or enablers like, tools/ techniques and resources in terms of people, equipment, materials) that are conducive for a competent PM team to engage and undertake any or all projects within its scope and capacity (Gan & Chin, 2018, 2019).

When applied it is the project manager's balanced state of competency and capability at which he/she can lead a project to accomplish the project outcome within the given project constraints of scope, schedule, cost, risk, resources and stakeholders' expectations (Gan & Chin, 2018, 2019) or within the baselines and constraints agreed with the project sponsor or executive management.

Wendler's (2012) 237 articles about PM3s found that there has no precise definition of PM3. Hence, Gan & Chin (2018, 2019) defined PM3s as "*a generic PM maturity assessment tools designed to measure the approximate level of balanced state of the organization and its team maturity in terms of its overall competencies, capability and capacity to manage projects or change initiatives, with the implicit view that more mature organizations are better able to manage projects with improved results more consistently as well as more predictably*".

PROJECT MANAGEMENT'S ROLE EVOLUTION AND ITS EFFECT ON PM3 DESIGN

The knowledge funnel (Figure 1) is used to direct the research thinking process to systematically develop the groundwork done in Chapter 1 that justify the need to develop an alternative PM3. It also addresses the research questions to be answer and the literatures review output organized to address each research question raised and the key observations that will all help in the development of the new PM3. Each research question raised is addressed in turn based on the output and key observations obtained from literatures review (Table 1).

Figure 1. The DPM3 knowledge funnel

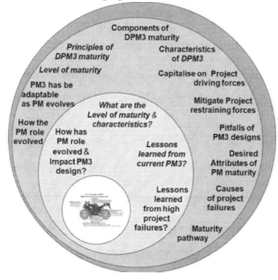

Table 1. Research knowledge funnel

Research questions	Output from literature review	Key observations
How has PM role evolved & how would it affect PM3 design?	2.2.1 How PM role has evolved the last few decades	
	2.2.2 PM3 should be designed to be adaptable as the PM role evolves	i. PM3 should allow changes in PM role/ responsibilities ii. PM3 should allow changes to PM tools iii. Fluid organization structures respond better to project dynamics iv. PM3 should assess judicious use of PM approaches v. Project purpose alignment with organisation strategy must be understood vi. PM3 should adapt as new PMO are setup or changed
What are the levels of maturity & key characteristics?	2.3.1 Levels of PM maturity 2.3.2 The attributes of each level of PM maturity 2.3.3 The Principles of PM Maturity	i. Balanced/rounded skill set ii. Maturity growth enhance capability and capacity/Matching capabilities iii. Matching capabilities iv. Adaptable leadership
	2.3.4 Maturity levels reflect seniority 2.3.5 The key Components of PM3	i. The 2 Key-project-drivers ii. The success attributes of Project Managers iii. The success attributes of the performing organisation
What can be learned from current PM3?	2.4.1 Desired attributes of PM3	i. PM3 should be designed for generic application ii. Assessment be independent of PM Methodology used iii. Imperative to use simple friendly international PM terminology iv. M3 should be designed along functional needs v. Not prescriptive in assessment approach vi. Project application software adequacy should be assessed vii. Benefit of Self-assessment option
	2.4.2 Pitfalls in PM3 design	i. Too focus on process and too little about people management ii. Too complex to understand and apply iii. Lack of internal consistency vi. Too rigid group path vii. Lack of flexible PM maturity pathway to guide users viii. Too high PM3 total cost of ownership ix. Incentives target individuals & not team work
What can be learned from the continuing high project failure rates?	2.5.1 Distorted project failure stats 2.5.2 Lack of quality leadership 2.5.3 Engaging accidental project managers 2.5.4 Fixation with best practices 2.5.5 Routine conditioning impede PM3 adoption	i. Not differentiating project failures by project stages creates Misinformation ii. Blame e-game does not help management accountability and performance iii. Command sense don't work well with random environmental dynamics iv. Routine conditioning creates expert blind spots thus hampering performance
	2.5.6 Too risky management behaviour 2.5.7 Lack of formal PM education 2.5.8 Inadequate and Unrealistic project baselining 2.5.9 Late appointment of project managers 2.5.10 Performance incentives did not target team work 2.5.11 Failure to use "project force field analysis"	v. There is a trade-off tipping-point when taking risk vi. Formal education standardise processes, communication & enhance performance vii. Inadequate and Unrealistic project baselining is a recipe for project failure viii. PM should be appointed no later than at the start of project planning ix. Need incentives to motivate Team-work to leverage from team-work synergies x. There is wisdom in harnessing driving foces and mitigating restraining forces

How has the Project Management Role Evolved?

The role of PM was of an insignificant part-time coordinator in the 1980s mainly managing project schedules. The role expanded to a full-time endeavor managing projects to deliver the required outcome within the triple constraints of scope, time and cost. With formal PM education and certification requirements in the decades that followed, the role evolved further and expanded to include responsibilities for the constraints of risk, resources, and stakeholder expectations (PMBok 6th Ed 2017).

With the organized approach over the last two decades, PM was also used to implement organization strategies to bring organization strategy to fruition. A lot of management attention was generated when studies cited the major contributions to strategy failures were attributed to projects not fulfilling project purpose or due to lack of PM resources to implement

(Candido & Santos, 2015). Indeed, the PM revolution began when management realized the benefits of PM and the potentials PM expertise can bring to the executive suite (Nieto-Rodriguez, 2019a). With the evolvement of PM role in the last 5 decades, Gan (2019) has encapsulated it in Figure 2.

Figure 2. Evolution of PM practices in the last 5 decades

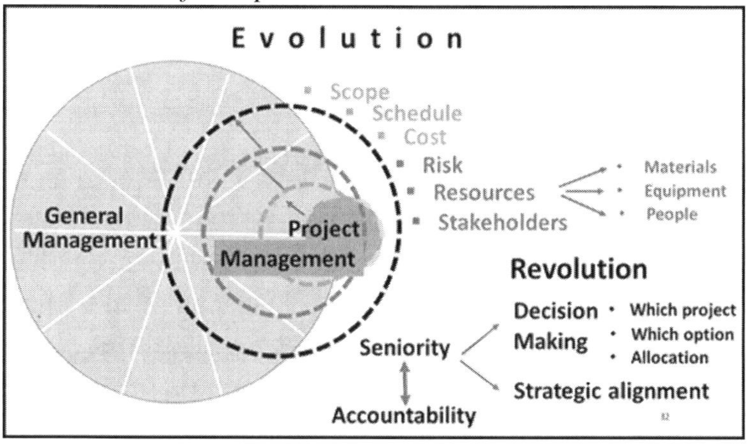

PM3 Should be Designed to be Adaptable as the PM Role Evolves

PM3s should be designed with flexibility so that they can adapt as the PM role has evolves over the last 5 decades. This flexibility should enable new responsibilities to be added, changed, or deleted. As well as allow addition and changes of PM tools and techniques, to the organization structures as well as changes in PM approaches. These details are described below.

- *PM3 should allow changes in PM role/responsibilities.*

The PM3 design should be structured to allow minimal effort to add, delete or change as PM role and responsibilities evolve (Gan & Chin, 2019). For example, the last 5 decades, many have seen the PM role expanded from an insignificant part time coordinator in-charge of project execution to a fulltime PM practitioner to deliver project outcome according to the given scope, schedule and cost baselines (known as the triple constraints). These performance responsibilities were again expanded in 2017 to include *management of project risk exposure, effective management of resources* (materials, equipment and people) and *ensuring major project stakeholders' expectations* are adequately managed (PMBok 3rd Ed 2004, PMBok 4th, PMBok 5th and 6th Ed 2017).

- ***PM3 should be adaptable to allow changes or addition of PM tools***

The PM3 design flexibility should allow addition or changes to the profession's repertoire of tools and techniques that may be adapted from general management, knowledge management, human resource management, operations-research and operation management and other sources from time to time as evidenced from the changes made to each succeeding version of PMBok over the 4 decades to 2017 and expected beyond.

- ***Fluid organization structures respond better to project dynamics.***

"Until the early 1980s, the once held assumptions of the one-right-organization-structure are now so far removed from actual reality that they are becoming obstacles to the theory and even more serious obstacles to the practice of management" (Drucker, 1999 p.5). Yet, PMI have chosen to remain prescriptive when it expanded its 5 organization-structures to 10 from which organizations could decide which structure suit their unique business (PMBok 6th ed, 2017 p. 45, 47).

Paradoxically, PMI also advocated decentralization of command and control but for projects that are being managed using the adaptive approach. This they reasoned, allow the command-and-control structure to be localized thereby maintaining the flexibility to respond and better adapt according to the project environmental dynamics. Although PMI had not given that organization structure a name, it did emphasize the point by updating its Project Management Professional (PMP) examination structure and content to include the adaptive (AGILE) approach examinable from 2021 onwards. The change gives the PM *adaptive* approach equal emphasis with the *planned* approach, that had previously been exclusively taught and used by all the major professional bodies of PM like PMI, IPMA, APM IDPM (Camb), PRINCE2, AIPM and the PM profession over the last 5 decades. Only time will tell if this new direction opens more opportunities for project-based organization to perform more effectively (AGILE Practice guide, 2017) or complicates the world of PM even further.

- *PM3 should assess the judicious use of PM approaches.*

Project performance is gauged by how well project success criteria are met. For the PM planned approach, the performance criteria are spelled out as the triple constraint baselines known before the project execution commences. However, in the adaptive approach to PM, the required outcome is unclear or hazy. Hence, the performance criteria will be a moving target because the overall outcome and scope is not definitive that directly affect the project scheduling and cost estimation process. Trying so will either be simply impossible or at best unrealistic. Such risk and uncertainties have caused a long list of multinational corporations (MNCs) to fail, and failure to comprehend the challenges that is to come from the new wave of industrialization like Polaroid (2001), Borders (2011) Compaq (2002, 2013), Nokia (2013), Kodak (2012), Toys"R"Us (2017), Thomas Cook (2019) and almost all the businesses and airlines related to the travel industry.

"MNCs decision makers may not be able to effectively learn from their prior failures because of their cognitive biases" (Sungjin, 2015), The old ways of doing business and the lessons learned then are no longer relevant in this new world. These now-defunct MNCs were not ready for the new demands of consumers who are young, fast moving, mobile, and demanding and an impatient lot. Others were unprepared for challenges brought about by global events like COVID-19 pandemic or national civil unrest. It is and remains an era in which the *"big fish eating the small fish is being replaced by the era where the fast fish that eat the slow fish"* as stated by Klaus Schwab, Founder and Executive Chairman of the World Economic Forum.

In the same way, PM has evolved and should be unobtrusively and effectively adapted using the adaptive approach to respond to the fast-changing and moving world. This adaptive approach will be better equipped to manage projects in the development of mobile applications, artificial intelligence, robotics, medical and pharmaceutical research for cures and solutions for a myriad list of human ailments. The same applies to project discoveries in material science, nanotechnology, enabling miniaturization of medical imaging tools and equipment, 5G mobile network facilitating real time integration of intelligent mobile devises, home appliances, robotic operation, national security and facial recognition applications that facilitate crime prevention and enforcement anywhere and everywhere.

Adaptive PM approach works well in internal PM service provision but in a client-vendor environment, the adaptive approach faces additional challenges. This is the common response during the author's consulting work with clients who intimidated that the clients are then heavily dependent on the trust (which the client knows can be open to abuse) that must exist, that the vendor will be professional, fair and honest in its commercial contractual dealings.

Such *trust-deficit situation* will always be prevalent and greatly impact project procurement and contracts management as observed by the author's first-hand consulting meetings. How would management maturity then be assessed when the performance target itself is a moving target? The need for management to make discreet use of the various PM approach or hybrid approach must thus also explain the discretion use and how PM performance will be measured.

- *Project purpose alignment with organization strategy must be understood.*

The 21st century has undergone a "*period of profound transition*" as predicted by Drucker (1999 p. ix). After two decades of such significant changes, one would have expected all levels of management to be well prepared for it, but management's effectiveness remains doubtful. Roughly, USD 2 trillion a year of investments or 10% collectively worldwide continue to be lost due to "*ineffective implementation of organization strategy through poor PM practices*" (PMI, 2018). More specifically, could it be "*the failings to bridge the gap between strategy design and its delivery*" as noted by Mark Langley, President/CEO PMI who retired in 2018, or was it the management inability to adequately explain the strategic intent to the PM team who are expected to execute/implement the project?

Nieto-Rodriguez (2019) declared "*the last decade has undergone a project revolution*" but has management theorist and project-based organizations realize how PM affect organizational strategy implementation? It is one thing for top management to design the strategies with the right intent but quite another to ensure the strategic intent linked to organizational goals is explained and understood before commencing project execution. While the *project economy* has arrived, PMI (2020) noted 38% still reported the *lack of active executive sponsorship in the project delivery*. In addition, 84% of executive leaders believe they are effectively prioritizing and funding the right initiatives but only 55% of PMO leaders agreed (PMI, 2018).

The disconnection between strategy and execution happens when management is unable to articulate and explain the organizational strategy objective, design, and priorities and how they link to the overall organizational goals. Until that is fully understood, the project is unlikely to accomplish the purpose for which it was initiated.

- **PM3 should be adaptable as new PMO are set-up or changed.**

What PMO (PM organization) stands for and the role they were supposed to play was not definitive until 3 years ago (PMBok 6th Ed, 2017). Mature project organizations recognized the three possible PMO roles, each higher role encompassing the role of the lower level from *Supporting, Controlling* to the *Directing* role (Figure 3).

Figure 3. PMO structures per PMBok 6th Ed (2017, p.48)

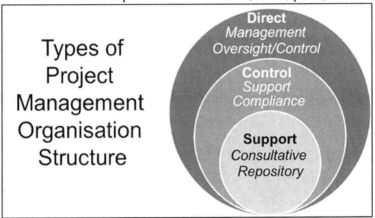

When set up to provide the *Support* role, the PMO provides consultation to the project team and serves as a central repository of project artefacts, templates and lessons learned. Those set up with the *Control* role are tasked to ensure projects are managed in compliance with organizational policies and procedures in addition to playing the project *support* role. PMO with *Direct* role are set up to maintain overall management of projects (including its profitability) under their portfolio and maintain an oversight and *control* of the project performance as well as provide project *support*. The PMO role itself could also change as the organization sees fit and the PM3 accordingly should be designed to easily accommodate the change as they arise from time to time. PMO that are set-up with *clarity of purpose*, have clear role and responsibilities and adequately supported by top management to avoid the PMO pitfall of being made defunct within 2 years of inauguration.

LEVELS AND KEY CHARACTERISTICS OF PM3

Literatures of better known PM3 implemented in the market had been studied to gauge the level of market acceptance of these models. Why some models are favored and well received while others fail to make inroads, have not really been understood by researchers in terms of both the PM theoretical framework and their applications at work.

The Level of PM Maturity

According to Gan & Chin (2018), there are 5 suitable levels of PM maturity ranging from *Accidental* project manager to an *Authoritative* project manager. The level description of PM maturity should use simple description that is intuitive to understand and appreciate for it to gain wider user acceptance, for example how the description of one stage can be seen as more mature than the one below it or less mature than those above it? (Figure 4).

Figure 4. 5 levels of PM maturity

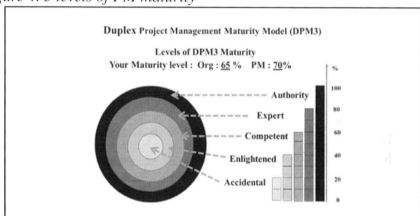

The Attributes of Each Level of PM Maturity

The attributes for each of the levels of PM maturity has been described by Gan & Chin (2018) as below:

- *Accidental project manager*

At this fundamental level, the project manager often starts their career by accidentally being there by chance/accident rather than by choice. They are chosen to lead the project without prior PM knowledge and pre-requisite skills needed to manage a project. This phenomenon happens more often in functional organization or weak matrix organization structure (PMBok 5th Ed, 2013). Project quality is often compromised, higher level of rework, unsatisfactory stakeholder satisfaction, unduly high exposure to project risk, missed deadlines, cost overruns, and missed opportunities.

- *Enlightened project manager*

They commonly work under extreme stress for long hours. With their common sense, they learn through trial and error, mistakes and look for knowledge and experience. Without sufficient exposure to the environmental dynamics and how the conflicting stakeholders' interests are managed, enlightened PM remains ignorant of tacit knowledge. They continue to seek PM knowledge from textbooks, seminars, and occasional training. The lack of success in time will prompt the enlightened project manager to seek professional help or seek PM coaches to share their tacit knowledge through demonstrating the PM practices with real-life hands-on practice. As a result, they get enlightened by their personal experience and exposure to gradually improve their project performance.

- *Competent project manager*

Through years of practice and often with formal PM education, some competent project managers can hire themselves out for a fee. Their ability to get repeat business is a testament to their ability to deliver projects to client satisfaction. They are likely to be in small and medium-sized projects that have few team members and are generally localized. Some may settle at this level of comfort and be content to seek no further in advancing their career to take on bigger and more complex projects.

- *Expert project manager*

They possess many years of knowledge, skills, and experience, recognized as industry experts so as to be entrusted with larger and more complex projects within possible cross-national boundaries. They understand the exponential impact of increasing project team members and the enormous challenges that multi-cultural teams pose. As a result, they understand the need for strict use of internationally recognized terminology and recommended good practices, the appropriate level of rigor to apply and proactively adapt to the changing environment and changing priorities throughout the project life cycle.

Expert project manager makes appropriate use of PM tools and techniques like earned value management (EVM) to track and report project progress, life cycle costing (LCC) and concepts of time value of money (NPV/IRR/Payback period) to differentiate the relative attractiveness of projects. They use constructive change to good advantage and the importance of strategic alignment to ensure all projects in their portfolio are appropriately controlled and in alignment with organizational direction and goals. In consequence, they can recognize project in distress early. Thus, they are often hired for repeat business with the ability to deliver reasonable level of client satisfaction.

- *Authoritative project managers*

They are recognized by virtue of the organization or person's pre-eminence in PM. They are often called upon for expert advice at national and international level, able to articulate a problem or issue affecting the profession and getting their case heard by the relevant authorities to garner support for action. They are called upon as *Expert Witness* in arbitration and or legal proceedings involving disputes about quality and appropriateness of PM practices. They are highly sophisticated, principled and advocates of proper organizational procedures and international standards of recommended good practices.

These managers are likely to have very broad experience across multi-industries, dealing with complex projects involving multi-culture, language, and time zones and are regularly involved with repeat invites to national, regional, and international symposiums, congress, forums, seminars and participate in panel discussions. The required effort and cost are very significant in addition to the required skill, competencies, good professional network, and natural flair for high profile jobs pose a real deterrence to many capable PMs.

The Principles of PM Maturity

Gan & Chin (2018) initially proposed 4 principles PM maturity to guide the PM3 users up the PM maturity pathway. The proposal uses the motorcycle to illustrate the principles, where the wheels are rounded to afford a smooth and hence faster rotation, the two wheels of complimentary sizes rotate to accomplish work and grow as the skill sets and maturity components grow and mature and the need to always steer and navigate depicting need for constant adaptation going forward to keep in balance (*gyro effect*). The model uses the front wheel to represent the project manager while the back wheel represents the organization. The principles of PM3 are described below:

- **Balanced or rounded skill set.**

Each wheel is round supported by 10 equal spoke lengths to illustrate the need for a *balanced skill* to enable better coordination, synchronization, and control. The attainment of maturity in the DPM3 maturity score for all the spokes is achieved through *simultaneous progressive increment*, all DPM3 component should be proportional, well-rounded to be complementary for a smoother revolution to represent a smoother workflow capability.

- **Maturity growth enhances capability and capacity.**

As the project manager and the organization *mature in PM capabilities*, the spokes/wheel sizes increase the diameter of the wheel that will accomplish a greater distance with the same number of revolution (PM effectiveness) depicting greater effectiveness and efficiency per unit of effort.

- **Matching capabilities**

The capabilities between the project manager and the organization should be of similar levels of maturity. They may be unequal but should not be so significantly different from each other to make it difficult to coordinate, synchronized and control.

- **Adaptable leadership**

The project manager's adaptable leadership maturity is represented by the handle that allow the motorcycle in motion to keep balance, directing, steering the project and navigating through the dynamic project environment.

Levels of PM Maturity Should Reflect the Seniority of the PM Role

The role of project managers at work (based on the 20 years of PM experience in 3 consulting organizations) has never been definitive nor uniform across different types of organizations, scale of operation, commerce, industries, government, enforcement agencies and NGOs. Instead, the roles are related more to organizational preferences (PMBok 6th Ed, 2017) and how the organizations remunerate their various managers based on seniority, each higher level entrusted with greater responsibilities including decision making. So, pay scales differ very significantly by more than 10 times between the highest and the lowest pay scale, revealed in confidence by managers including HR managers and statistics from managers in the Federation of Malaysian Manufacturers (FMM).

The majority also *do not know what they do not know* yet confidently they know what they were doing, a phenomenon known over the last 2 decades as the *Dunning-Kruger* effect (Dunning and Kruger, 1999). The same was observed from a group of 29 managers (half of whom worked as senior project managers) that attended a 2-day local public workshop by ROGAN Strategic Advisory on Project Risk Management from 26th to 27th Feb 2019.

However, the more mature project-based organizations have realized the strategic importance of PM. From the late 1990s, opportunities could be seen offered to high caliber project managers to move up the managerial ladder into the "C" suite of project-based organizations, an indication that the *project revolution* has begun, (Nieto-Rodriguez, 2019). From a first-hand observation, it is noted there is a growing trend of project managers being included in executive functions like:

- Pre-contract analysis and pre-contract negotiations
- Decisions between the relative attractiveness of projects on offer.
- Decision between capital equipment from disparate suppliers with different total cost of ownership or life-cycle cost.
- Effective allocation of resources relating to materials, equipment, and people
- Ensuring realization of desired planned benefits from the project
- Ensuring project objective is aligned with the overall strategic intent.
- Involved in charting the organizational direction and strategy formulation.

"In the new world, it is not the big fish which eats the small fish, it's the fast fish which eats the slow fish" (Schwab, 2018). In this new norm, organizations had to be nimble to adapt and be responsive to the fast-moving world of the 5th Industrial revolution. Project managers now need proficiency as per PMBok (2017) in the concept of:

- Life Cycle Costing (LCC) to assess relative total cost of ownership of capital assets and equipment.
- Value management involved in the creation of sustainable value through *organizational improvement, setting clear goals, improving productivity, creativity and return on investment. It is focused on value and function-oriented thinking, desired behavior, and methods, particularly dedicated to motivating people, developing skills, promoting synergies and innovation, with the aim of maximizing the overall performance of an organization* (The Institute of Value Management). Value engineering (VE) is applied at the design and engineering phase of a project. It is a creative, team-based approach

seeking alternatives to known or existing solutions with the view to eliminating *cost-added* processes while improving quality and functionality. It is focused on increasing product value or performance specification at the lowest possible cost but without compromising the required standard of safety in all its dimensions.

- Project cash flow projection
- Time value of money to evaluate the relative attractiveness of projects being considered using Net Present value (NPV), Internal Rate of return (IRR) and Payback Period to decide between the relative attractiveness of projects.
- People management. This scope has expanded to 42% of the entire new PMP examination syllabus to take effect in 2021, This is now practically more realistic and consistent with the 50% content already proposed in DPM3 by Gan & Chin (2018, 2019).

LEVELS AND KEY CHARACTERISTICS OF PM3

The PM maturity models included in this research are tabulated in Table 2 for ease of reference.

Table 2. PM maturity level and descriptions for comparative review

DPM3		Accidental	Enlightened	Competent	Expert	Authority
CMMi	Staged Representation	Initial	Managed	Defined	Quantitative Managed	Optimised
	Continuos representation	Performed	Managed	Defined	Quantitative Managed	Optimised
OPM3		Standardised	Measure	Control	Continuosly improve	-
PMMM Kerzner		Common	Common	Singular	Bench	Continuos
PMMM Crawford		Lanaguge	Processes	Methodology	Marking	Development
PwC		Initial Process	Structured	Org. Std	Managed process	Optimised
P2MM (PRINCE 2)		Unrealiable	Informed	Standardised	Monitored	Optimised

PwC's PM maturity model uses a 5-level assessment described as *initial process, structured, organization standardized, managed process* and *optimized*. It assesses the organization as a whole or for specific division, department, or any combination thereof. The model did not identify the project manager as a key project driver from the organization they serve, the latter only providing the actionable environmental factors and the facilitators/enablers to support the project. PwC's PM maturity model view the organization as the key driver of projects which arguably mean the team who lead the project including the project manager and not specifically the project manager who according to PMI should be in overall control of the project (PMBok 6th Ed, 2017).

PRINCE 2 on the other hand, holds a diametrically different view and see the project manager as being capable of managing the project with or without the organization, a view both Gan & Chin (2019) agreed but for the short term to avoid personnel burnt-out. The 5 levels of maturity are described as *unreliable, informed, standardized, monitored and optimized*.

Due to the importance of people in the management of projects, Gan & Chin (2019) research has dedicated their research model DPM3 content focused on the human side of PM endeavors. This importance is now recognized by PMI when the PMP examination syllabus from year 2021 has 42% coverage about people management.

There are many stakeholders in a project, and many play a part in the project. However, Gan & Chin (2018) have identified that there are only 2 key project drivers in the management of projects. The 2 key project drivers should possess the respective success attributes or PM key maturity components are discussed below:

- The *appointed project manager* to lead and manage a team to accomplish the project outcome. This role initiates and *orchestrates* the coordination, synchronization, and control of all the project activities to accomplish the project outcome within the agreed constraints or baselines. He/she should also be in constant alert to ensure the project focus continues to be in alignment with the assigned strategic imperatives with project risk and issues adequately managed.
- The *performing organization* that provides the *facilitators* (organizational policies, procedures, project artifacts, tools and templates, facilities, required infrastructure and resources including the subcontractors) and the project *environmental (actionable)* factors,

which the organization has control and option to act on at least in the long run.

Mature project managers are also aware that there are *environmental factors* that are *actionable)* but may nevertheless constrain the project activities. There are factors that the organization are obligated by statue to comply with statutory regulations, town council by-laws. Being certified project managers, they are also bound by professional ethical conduct or professional disciplines to uphold the relevant industry and or professional operating standards. These limit the options available, all of which can and do affect either the smooth running of the projects, impact project cost, risk, effectiveness in the management of resources and schedule commitments to stakeholders' satisfactions.

The Success Attributes of Project Managers

There are 2 main types of success attributes of a mature project manager. The types related to *hard skills* are those that can be acquired in the classroom and tacit knowledge that can only be gained through experience at work.

These *hard skills* components identified by Gan & Chin (2018) are:

1. PM approach understanding (planned, adaptive and hybrid approach)
2. PM knowledge sufficiency (know-how in applying PM Knowledge)
3. Business acumen
4. Exposure to business, industry, software applications and environment
5. PM technical domain skills in all the PMI's PM knowledge areas (as per PM technical skills as defined in the PMI Talent Triangle, 2015).

The types related to *soft skills* are skills acquired through working, exposure and networking with people. These help in the better understanding of human behavior in terms of the actions and decisions people are likely to make and the perceptions they are likely to hold. It includes human motivation arising from the different knowledge, experience, exposure, personal value system, attitudes, language, culture and bias that individuals possess.

Such skills are needed to understand, motivate, and lead the project team and stakeholders. The skills are interrelated and often interdependent with significance dependent on the role and seniority of the project manager (Gan & Chin, 2018).

The soft skills components of PM maturity are:

1. Communication skill (*horizontal and vertical levels*)
2. Leadership (*dynamic leadership in a project environment*)
3. Negotiation skills (with *various level of people, contracts, and disputes*)
4. Conflict management skills (relating to *people, schedules as well as resources*)
5. Adaptable leadership (to the *project environment and people*)

The Success Attributes of Performing Organization

There are 2 main types of success attributes of a mature performing organization. Each type has its respective components as detailed below:

- **Environmental factors (actionable factors)**

These are environmental factors that are *actionable or controllable* factors which can be acted upon by the organization and addressed either in the short or long term. Notable examples are the organization structure, general management attitude to risk, governance structure as to centralized or decentralized control, open or close communication, adequacy of organization infra structure, PM application software available, conducive work culture, a heathy level of management or sponsor's support, organizational capacity, availability of sub-contractors etc. Such actionable constraints *promote or frustrate* the project manager's efforts and are identified by Gan & Chin (2018) under the following 5 component sub-headings:

1. Project organization structure, culture, and governance structure
2. Leadership support (the level of support from top management)

3. Management attitude to risk
4. Rewards alignment
5. Organizational capacity

- **Facilitators/Enablers**

Facilitators or enablers are PM process assets provided by the organization like PM artifacts/tools, project dashboard, techniques, templates, knowhow, trade secrets, lessons learned, accounting and project status reporting applications etc.

These are classified under 5 component sub-headings (Gan & Chin, 2018, 2019):

1. Standardization (structure and level of standardization)
2. PM Operating procedures (to govern the project process work)
3. PMIS sufficiency (Project management information systems)
4. PMIS availability (Average up-time of PMIS to support the project team)
5. Sufficiency in PM tools and techniques

CONCLUSION

This chapter discusses the evolutionary roles of project managers throughout the decades that has expanded from a part time coordinator to include responsibilities for the constraints of risk, resources, and managing stakeholder expectations in a project environment. Hence, the design of the **PM3** should be adaptable as the project manager role evolves. The PM3 models should encapsulate the flexibility that enables new responsibilities to be added, changed, or deleted. As well as allow addition and changes of PM tools and techniques, to the organization structures and as changes in PM approaches.

Hence, this chapter explored the various levels of maturity, the level descriptions and how each level relate to the seniority of the PM role. It also examines how mature organizations unobtrusively use the various PM approaches to manage their projects more effectively, how PMOs are set-up to support project endeavors and if project driving forces have been or are systematically identified and capitalize on as well as restraining forces that should be avoided or the impact mitigated.

REFERENCES

Candido, C.J. F. & Santos, S. P., (2015). Strategy implementation: What is the failure rate. *Journal of Management and Organisation,* Vol (21) Issue 2. Cambridge University Press and Australian and New Zealand Academy of Management https://doi.org/DOI: 10.1017/jmo.2014.77

Drucker, P. F. (1999). *Management Challenges for the 21st Century.* Harper Collins.

Gan, R. C. C., & Chin, C. M. M. (2018). Components of project management maturity impacting project, programme, portfolio and organisational success. In Karayaz, G., & Silvius, G. (Eds.), *Developing Organizational Maturity for Effective Project Management* (pp. 128–152). IGI Global., DOI: 10.4018/978-1-5225-3197-5.ch007

Gan, R. C. C., & Chin, C. M. M. (2019). Project management guide and project management maturity models as generic tools capable for diverse applications. In Katuu, S. (Ed.), *Diverse Applications and Transferability of Maturity Models* (pp. 269–315). IGI Global., DOI: 10.4018/978-1-5225-7080-6.ch011

Kruger, J., & Dunning, D. (1999). Unskilled and unaware of it: How difficulties in recognizing one's own incompetence lead to inflated self-assessments. *Journal of Personality and Social Psychology*, 77(6), 1121–1134. DOI: 10.1037/0022-3514.77.6.1121 PMID: 10626367

Nieto-Rodriguez, A. (2019a). *The project revolution. How to succeed in a project driven world*. LID Publishing.

Project Management Institute. (2015). *The PMI Talent Triangle*. Project Management Institute.

Project Management Institute (PMI). (2004). *A guide to project management body of knowledge* (PMBOK Guide) (3rd ed). Project Management Institute.

Project Management Institute (PMI). (2008). *A guide to project management body of knowledge* (PMBOK Guide) (4th ed). Project Management Institute.

Project Management Institute (PMI). (2013). *A guide to project management body of knowledge* (PMBOK Guide) (5th ed). Project Management Institute.

Project Management Institute (PMI). (2017). *A guide to project management body of knowledge* (PMBOK Guide) (6th ed). Project Management Institute.

Project Management Institute (PMI). (2017). *Agile Practice Guide*. Project Management Institute.

Sungjin J. H. (2015). When do MNCs fail to learn from prior failure experience? *Canadian Journal of Administrative Sciences*. Vol (33), Issue 1. https://doi.org/DOI: 10.1002/cjas.1324

Wendler, R (2012), The maturity of maturity model research: A systematic mapping study. *Information and Software Technology*. Vol (52), Issue 12, 1317-1339. https://doi.org/DOI: 10.1016/j.infsof.2012.07.007

ADDITIONAL READING

Madsen, S. (2019). *The Power of Project Management Leadership: Your Guide to Making a Difference* (2nd ed). Kogan Page Kerzner, H. (2022). *Project Management: A Systems Approach to Planning, Scheduling, and Controlling*. (13th ed). Wiley.

Syrett, M., & Devine, M. (2012). *Managing Uncertainty: Strategies for Surviving and Thriving in Turbulent Times*. Wiley.

Turner, J. R. (2009). *The Handbook of Project-Based Management*. (3rd ed). McGraw-Hill. Goldratt,M.E. (2010). *The Theory of Constraints Handbook*. McGraw-Hill.

KEY TERMS AND DEFINITIONS

Accidental Project Manager: Project manager being accidentally assigned to the career by chance or accident rather than choice

Authoritative Project Manager: Project manager that are often called upon for expert advice to articulate a problem. They are highly sophisticated, principled and advocated of proper organizational procedures and international standards. They have broad experience across multi-industries, dealing with complex projects.

Decentralization: A process of delegating decision making power of command and control for projects to be manageable by lower levels.

Enlightened Project Manager: Project manager that learn through trial and error, mistakes looking for knowledge and experience.

Environmental Factors: These are controllable factors that can be acted upon by the organization either in the short or long term. For examples organizational structure, risk attitude, communication mode.

Facilitator: Refer as tools or techniques or resources that are conducive for a competent team to engage and stayed focused to achieve the project objectives.

Fluid Organization: Is a dynamic and adaptable structure of an organization that are readily responsive to change.

Judicious: Making action or decision with good judgement, wise for the best possible outcome.

Knowledge Funnel: Used to direct the research thinking process systematically to a structured and efficient solution.

Project Dynamics: Refers to various factors and interactions that may influence the progress of a project over time.

Chapter 3
Lesson Learned From Current Maturity Models

ABSTRACT

The study prompted 4 research questions in Chapter 2. Responses to these questions will narrow the scope of study required, pitfalls to avoid, enable a better understanding of the issues raised about impediments to PM, and the driving forces that motivate researchers to search for new ways to measure maturity and the restraining forces that inhibited the growth of PM3s. The knowledge gained will influence the initial design structure and identify the broad content pertinent to the construction of a new PM3. To ensure clarity of this research direction and communication, the following terms are defined in the context of duplex project management maturity model (DPM3) design objective and scope of coverage discussed in this chapter.

LESSON LEARNED FROM CURRENT PM3

Lessons learned from PM3 in the market enable a clear understanding of what PM3 is, its objectives, the good features to adopt and pitfalls to avoid. It will assist in the initial model design to ensure target PM practitioners can gradually improve their PM practice thereby continuously enhance commercial competitiveness. The following are the attributes that are desired from PM3 model:

DOI: 10.4018/979-8-3693-1439-5.ch003

PM3s Should be Designed for Generic Applications

PM3 should be design for generic application in order that it can be use in diverse applications and transferable across large number of industries, commerce, government and enforcement agencies both large and small (Gan & Chin, 2019, Katuu, 2019).

For example, CMM by Carnegie Mellon University is known to be the first PM3 introduced in the market and the only model that had been put into use in Malaysia, (Gan & Chin, 2018). The later reintroduction expanded its limited coverage (CMMi, 2002), whereby CMMi V2.0 was introduced in 2018 that focused on process-maturity, more appropriately IT/ICT process-maturity model which include support for Agile-based PM implementation (CMMi Institute, 2018). It was described as a process improvement model of software, product and systems development best practices that will elevate organizational performance stated by Kirk Botula, CEO of the CMMi Institute. This is an explicit admission that CMMi is indeed IT/ICT centric and therefore not capable of cross industry application. Despite CMMi impressive list of notable clients like Honeywell, Cognizant and Unisys, and US government agencies such as the Food and Drug Administration and National Security Agency, it remains as a maturity assessment tool for IT/ICT development and not a PM or PM3 model capable of generic application (Gan & Chin, 2019). Models like DPM3, OPM3, PMMM (Kerzner), PMMM (Crawford) and PwC maturity assessment process are designed appropriately for generic application focused on business needs. It is however unfortunate that OPM3 has since been withdrawn from the market.

PM3 Assessment Should be Independent of PM Methodology Used

PwC surveyed clients that implicitly use PwC's own PM implementation methodology. So, PwC's PM3 method of maturity assessment will rate more favorably all organizations that use its PM implementation methodology. This renders their assessment results to be inherently biased and therefore less comparable between those that use and do not use its PM implementation methodology.

P2MM maturity score is also based entirely on the adequate application of PRINCE2 PM methodology (Gan & Chin, 2019) and as a result is also incapable of cross industry application. P2MM was developed and issued by the UK Office of Government Commerce (OGC) as a framework to assess the level of adoption of PRINCE2® (Williams, 2010). It viewed maturity from a business process perspective under strategic imperatives of management controls, benefits management, financial management, stakeholder engagement, risk management, organizational governance, and resource management. As P2MM is specifically designed to assess the degree of compliance with PRINCE2 (an IT/ICT PM implementation methodology) adoption, it cannot at the same time be suitable for generic use since non-PRINCE2-adopters will be excluded in their list of mature organizations but by no means immature.

Imperative to Use Simple Friendly International PM Terminology

Clarity and simplicity are paramount to elicit PM and PM3 implementers to buy-in to the PM concepts and practices. Hence, all attempts should be made to use *"simple and intuitive terms so users can work on them on the basis of what they already know"* (Sunstein, 2013 p.1).

Hence, all industry jargon and technical terms should be avoided (Gan & Chin, 2019). This idea however is hampered by competing PM bodies like PMI, IPMA, APM, PRINCE2 and of late AGILE where each professional body uses their own terminology that can even confuse the seasoned users. Even after ISO 21500 had been issued with the view to standardizing PM terminologies, disagreement persisted in the PM profession.

Examples include PRINCE2 using project brief whereas PMI used project charter, some confuse stages with phases, deliverables which are *nouns* referring to outputs from a project process but then wrongly listed with project activities which are *verbs* that require action. All these differences serve only to confuse than elucidate but unfortunately will continue with little chance of a compromise unless enforced through an international consensus by expanding on ISO 21500 (2021) as a guide to PM.

One of the key objectives of maturity is to maintain a high standard of objectivity, consistency, and repeatability to gain the widest acceptance from the PM populace. The term configuration management is widely used in PM to mean integration management of change request (PMBOK 6th Ed, 2017) commonly referred to as *Change order* in Asia and *Change request* in USA. Why CMMi chose to treat *configuration management as identification, baselining, status accounting and interface control* is baffling, because the PM terminology use by PMI had already been widely used and have pre-existed long before CMMi came into existence. This is the main negative research survey feedback elicited from this research about CMMi that it is unduly complicated to understand and use.

In PMMM, Crawford (2007) follows the PMI terminology in common use and therefore suits PM practitioners but by doing so, the model experiences significant time lag after each release of a later version of PMBok guide before it can be kept in sync. In the interim, users need to wait to know what PM Solutions Inc. would recommend when addressing new terms and new PM processes introduced by later versions of PMBok. However, once PM standard is standardized and stabilized, this shortcoming may become less significant. With that, Crawford (2007) claimed the model contributed to widespread success in assisting organizations in improving PM processes.

PM3 Should be Designed Along Functional Needs

The foundation of an effective PM3 design should be based on clearly defined function and how it should be effectively applied. It should consider the imperatives, lessons learned from researchers, plausible assumptions and scenarios that could be anticipated and the options that might be considered under the scenarios anticipated.

Only CMMi designers explicitly state its basis for designing its PM3 when CMMi was developed from its initial CMM version designed initially to address the shortcomings of PM processes in the ICT industry. That was a period when the US government's IT department were unsatisfactorily run and mismanaged in the 1990's. In consequence, the model was structured to address the problems observed and controls designed to prevent their recurrence, an "*approach founded on the basis of a baggage of bad practices*" of the time. That is not a promising start which might have well been the reason for all the complexities that followed all later versions of CMMi (Gan & Chin, 2018).

OPM3, PMMM and PwC Maturity Models were designed around PM processes as defined in the then current version of PMBok guide, effectively based on international recommended good practices, all designed to address the functional needs of PM (Gan & Chin, 2019).

Project Application Software Adequacy Should be Assessed

Most successful organizations employ PM as a strategic tool to drive change and achieve their business objectives (Nieto-Rodriguez & Evrard, 2004). PwC global research concluded that organizations were delivering projects consistently better than others (e.g. timely projects, within budget, scope and delivering business benefits) because these organizations have a higher level of maturity in their PM3. PwC maturity model measured the strength and balance in 4 core elements that relate to *processes, structure, people* and *systems*.

In terms of systems and tools, the model focused on availability and percentage of usage. Low maturity scores were attributed to *low usage* and *long reporting turnaround time.* There was nothing in terms of enquiries to see if the systems were adequate to derive status reports by project and project phases, a routine challenge often observed at work (Gan & Chin, 2019). Comparably, CMMi is silent on the assessment of application systems adequacy to support project setup and project cost control, neither does it assess the systems availability.

Firsthand conversations with industry heads revealed a severe lack of PMIS availability (90%) for project control and project accounting support. Summaries had to be obtained from several subsystems for input to the project system before it could be used to produce project reports. Ignorance of such application availability compounds this problem further. Users who found the PMIS of strategic advantage were unwilling to share their positive opinion while others simply do not know there could be such facilities available. The inadequate project progress summary lacks vital information such as:

- Cost summary by project phases by the 5 cost types for materials, labor, subcontract, equipment and overheads
- Separate column information for change or variation orders
- Project PV (Planned value of work that should have been completed to date),
- EV (Earned value which is the value of work accomplished based on physical inspection and calculation) and
- AC (Actual cost of the project cumulated to date)
- SPI (Schedule performance index, summary view of project progress) and
- CPI (Cost Performance Index)
- Project budget balance
- Open commitment (procurement orders committed but not yet received) and
- Project profit recognized and the method used that is consistent with international accounting standards.

Without project progress accounting results, needless time is wasted on the constant routine periodic work, account reconciliation and arguments between the project and accounting team, time and energy that could be better used in managing the project. It is therefore clear that systems adequacy is integral to PM maturity (Gan & Chin, 2019).

Benefits of a Self-Assessment Option

PMMM allows self-assessment to determine PM maturity levels (Crawford, 2007) similarly to DPM3, it also allows self-assessment. Self-assessment saves cost and there is a valid argument that it allows for more in-depth assessment. However, this is then not consistent with generally accepted principles of audit and quality assurance that require auditors not only to be independent but also seen to be independent of the subject they audit to ensure objectivity and impartiality in assessment. According to OGC (PRINCE2 p.3, 2010), self-assessment of own maturity level is unrealistic for the following reasons:

Those involved with their own organization's PM process design, planning, execution and/or controls will be too close to the subject to remain objective in their maturity assessment. Such situations will likely create blind spots (Rugg & Agnese, 2013) that are likely to impair good judgement.

Management appointment of internal staff as internal PM3 assessors are unlikely to have sufficient expertise and width of experienced to make a comprehensive assessment unless they already have prior experience that are broad in terms of scope and types of industries. Having managed projects formally from project initiation to closeout is vital to see the big picture requirement. It is unlikely the PM of clients have such high caliber staff in their team to undertake such responsibility.

PM maturity assessors should not be remunerated by the senior management organization seeking their independent assessment. Instead, their appointment should be appointed by most shareholders, so that they are not only independent but can also be seen to be independent in a neutral position to maintain objectivity in their audit process. It can be seen how the lack of independence can impair good judgment and become so wrong with catastrophic consequences. As a result, the Sarbines-Oxley Act (2002) was introduced to remedy such a defect.

In addition, when organizations are self-assessed, the summary results cannot realistically be relied upon for intercompany comparison purposes due to the differences in assessors' degree of impartiality, competence, rigor of assessment, personal values, and personal standards. Yet, if the purpose is for organizational self-improvement, and self-assessment is done objectively and periodically it will be helpful. Such low-cost options the market seeks could then be used to reveal valuable organization trends, year onwards whether the maturity growth is going according to plan or if intervention is needed.

Pitfalls in PM3 Designs

There are many pitfalls to PM designs, the significant ones are detailed below:

- **Too focused on process and too little about people management.**

"In the realms of managing people, everything we do is aimed at application, helping people do the work they need to do" (Senge et. al, 1999). "There is also a strong correlation between the "soft" stuff and shareholder returns" noted in McKinsey Quarterly (Sep 2014).

"Project managers spent 90% of their time in communication and typically identify communication-related issues as the problem they faced most frequently in project" (Mulcahy, 2015, p.45) while "the top 2% of successful project managers spent more than 90% of their time in communication" (PMBok 6th Ed, 2017). APM viewed all project-based work relies fundamentally on the ability of people to work together, (APMBok 7th Ed, 2019). All these are a clear statement of the critical importance of people in project performance.

Despite all these known facts, the human side of PM maturity did not feature in 3 of the six PM3s studied in this research. Instead, the focus was almost exclusively on processes and how well the organization provides the project enablers and facilitators, tools, techniques, artefacts and how conducive the environment is provided to support the PM effort.

Another obstacle was the *"one right way to manage people"* described as *'a practice having outlived their usefulness'* (Drucker,1999 p.5). Leadership styles whether from the trait school, behavioral school, contingency school, visionary school, relationship school or transformation leadership schools did not adequately explain how the theory in isolation would apply and work in practice.

People in projects are drawn together (many for the first time) to work on a project with varied groups of stakeholders, or idiosyncratic responses arising from conflicting interest, different levels of knowledge, experience, exposure, belief systems, bias, different languages and culture, work habits, attitudes, and varying levels of seniority.

How could any leadership style lead this myriad groups of people effectively are open to question as it would be like proposing to have one size fit all fallacy?

Each leadership style proponent suggests a mutually exclusive use of their approach. Instead, the management of people should be more inclusive, using a combination of leadership styles and experience to progressively manage each target group as they evolved through the progress of the project. It is only when people are recognized as of critical importance in project performance will management pay more attention to selecting the right people, coach them with the right skill sets and extend them with the appropriate level of management support. Those that do are those that have matured.

- **Lack of a flexible maturity pathway to guide users.**

CMMi's prescriptive approach to maturity improvement measure compliance with preset standards and predefined sequence to ensure consistency of practice. This requires standardization to ensure consistency and predictability. However, the downside of strict compliance stifle project team's imagination and creativity, attributes that are needed for both the planned and adaptive PM approach to adapt to the vagaries of changing management priorities, dynamic project environment and schedule dynamics (Gan & Chin, 2019).

As a result, many research reports of CMMi success in the market have been questioned. *"If CMMi were so successful as shown by the many research reports, it would contrast against the relatively low CMMi penetration in the marketplace"* (Gefen et. al, 2006, p.11). Based on interviews with 30 project managers of a large high-tech world leader in software development, Gefen found at the corporate level, the company had the highest CMMi maturity score of 5 and by definition *compliant with strict centralized procedures* and therefore is a mature PM organization. However, contrary, many projects with low CMMi maturity scores *for not being compliant with strict centralized procedures* performed just as well. Gefen's research team learned that the team with poor CMMi scores *had to deal with complex algorithms and poorly defined requirements.* That required the team to develop applications *iteratively and incrementally,* a flexibility when applied then violate strict procedural compliance requirements and consequently will achieve a low CMMi maturity score. Gefen's research concluded that instead of a rigid compliance with CMMi prescription, the teams that had low CMMi scores had relied on their PM experience to remain *flexible and adaptable* thus allowing them to move forward with their development (Gan & Chin, 2018, 2019). As good performances were produced irrespective of whether the team had a high or low CMMi score, the prescriptive strict procedural compliance to achieve high CMMI score, and ostensibly better organizational performance is thus proven to be irrelevant.

PMMM (Crawford) model explicitly required *"that for each succeeding PMMM level, the assumption is that all criteria for the preceding level for that knowledge area have been (or are being) fulfilled"* (2007). While this view appears logical, it is inconceivable for an organization to follow the discrete steps that are defined, then fully completed before moving to the next maturity level going forward. PM processes for immature PM organizations are more likely to be all encompassing (best effort basis), although may not be so organized, comprehensive nor in depth but they mature, although in a disorganized fashion. The maturity will likely be enhanced progressively, iteratively and in tandem to include other advanced processes within that knowledge area. Other theoretical problems with the PMMM (Crawford) model includes the following:

PMMM (Crawford) level 3 maturity is described as *"organizational standards and institutionalized process"* but can be seen as inconsistent when one attributes is listed as *"Informal analysis of project performance"*, (2007, p.7). How could organizational standards that are supposedly institutionalized be based upon informal analysis of performance in the first place? In addition, PMMM (Crawford) level 3 maturity is described as *"Institutionalized process"* but the best practices require that *"Management use data to make decisions"* listed at level 4 as *"Managed Process"*? A question arises, how could a business process be institutionalized, if their management does not use data to make decisions?

How could an organization with a PMMM (Crawford) level 4 maturity score *"Managed process"* not have documented lessons learned for risk related matters but only to be documented at level 5? Other than the *Accidental* maturity level, organizations do document lessons learned with various approaches as they mature progressively in practice (Gan & Chin, 2018). Project managers commonly scribble their lessons learned as they happen and file them informally while most others record them way after the event and as a result many of these cases are forgotten altogether.

The PwC's 5 maturity levels begin with *unreliable processes to informal processes, standardized processes, monitor processes to optimized processes*. The model expects all core elements within each maturity level to be fully satisfied before the next level becomes relevant. This is unrealistic in practice since many successful project organizations have their own preference as to what should be standardize (like scheduling, procurement, risk and cost management) while leaving others to be implemented gradually (Gan & Chin, 2018).

PwC maturity model will classify organizations at level 2 having informal processes and therefore expect to perform poorly in projects. In reality, quite the opposite can be true due to experience but not necessarily diligence in the documentation process and hence achieve a low PwC PM maturity score but a successful project, nevertheless.

Projects are unique endeavors operating under many constraints facing a dynamic environment, changing schedules, conflicting stakeholders' interest, and vagaries of managerial priorities. Unlike operation management, these challenges require varying levels of skill, tenacity, and experience to navigate to succeed managing projects of any significant value. So, PM3 models that are prescriptive in application may have missed the point. Instead of emphasizing a central command and control structure to maintain order and consistency it should recognize that decentralization with a *fluid organization structure* enables greater adaptability at the local level. In other words, not more rigidity that serve to stifle creative thinking but follow the form or principle but exercise discretion at the content level,

Maturity models allow "*the freedom to fail*" so project teams are encouraged to experiment and continuously improve and refine. Management should "*drive out fear*" of mistakes which Deming (n.d) saw as sorely needed, discretion to effect change, recalibrate, adjust and experiment to make things happen (AGILE implementation guide, 2017).

Adaptability is required in PM and any PM3 requiring prescriptive compliance will more likely stifle team creative use of PM3s to improve organization maturity. Tailoring to adapt should be allowed, if reasons are adequately documented (PMBok 6th Ed, 2017).

Projects for the 5th industrial revolution face significant uncertainties, from changing strategies designed to handle the unpredictable unknowns to changing tactics and experimentation to circumvent unexpected challenges. For such projects, significant iterative processes and frequent changes to scope and deliverables are expected throughout the project. As a result, too far forward plan for scope, schedule and cost estimates become wholly unrealistic. So, the adaptive approach was designed as an alternative, with weekly short sprints (work schedule) and short daily "*stand-up*" project meetings to review the previous day's progress. Large deliverables are broken down into smaller and more manageable functional deliverables that could be delivered earlier to show delivery results more frequently and in weekly spurts. Thus, PM3s that are rigid and prescriptive are likely to face market rejection in both the predictive and more so in the adaptive project environment.

- **Too high PM3 total cost of ownership**

CMMI implementation needs consulting support from CMMI certificates from Carnegie Mellon University, an explicit indication of its complexity. Such requirements are freely available from CMMI websites. As a result, it is seen as cost prohibitive to implement for the wider market. CMMI thus struggled to gain inroads in the Malaysian marketplace. OPM3 needs consulting support for PM practitioners to use and since been withdrawn by PMI in 2015. There is not much publicity to date for the other PM3 models like PMMM (Kerzner), PMMM (Crawford), PwC and P2MM nor are there research studies as to why this may be so. As a result, the cost of ownership for these models was not available for comparative study.

LESSON LEARNED FROM CONTINUING
HIGH PROJECT FAILURE RATE

The constant bombardment of project failure statistics for the last few decades has created curiosity as to what contributed to such high project failures. The following details derived from literature review provide useful lessons to be learned.

Distorted Project Failure Statistics

Mature project organization continuously manage projects of significant value and scale and are familiar with early project development stages, from the entrepreneur's vision of what can be, identification of purpose, strategy formulation on how best to accomplish the goal, feasibility study to design for purpose (Figure 1). Each stage is managed by a different group of expertise with performance and statistics clearly differentiated. It is in the early stages when business management approaches are used and finalized before it reaches the construction or execution stage when PM methodology will be used.

Figure 1. Project development stages in large scale projects

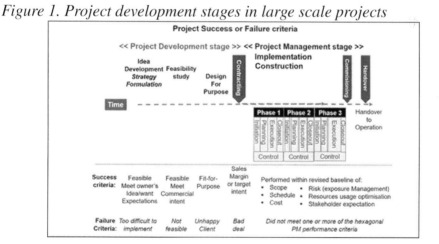

As "*how we interpret our observation depends on our paradigm* (Kuhn,1962), so project failure statistics must differentiate failures at the respective stages to enable remedial action by cause of failure which Candido and Santos (2015), illustrated in Figure 2, call a "*failure of the strategy*" attributed to:

- Business strategy implementation failure
- Strategic planning systems implementation failure
- Strategic projects are being abandoned, rejected or shelved.
- Competitive improvement does not result from new technology adoption.
- Business process reengineering failure
- Unsuccessful implementation of the balanced score card
- TQM's initiatives do not meet its target objectives.
- Business acquisition and mergers that fail.
- Corporate mergers not achieving the synergy anticipated, etc.

It can be seen from the dozen type of project failure studies, only research by IBM focused on PM failure which showed 41% having fully met their objective and 59% had met 2 of the 3 goals (quality, time, budget). The statistics shown *formulating the wrong organizational strategies* as the top management problem, a responsibility which according to Drucker (1999 p. 43) must in essence be *accountable* for the results of their project development relating to:

- The quality of decision
- Strategies defined.
- Clarity of purpose statement when initiating a project
- How would the project purpose align to which strategic imperative?
- How the anticipated project benefits can be realized?

Figure 2. Business strategy implementation failures rates

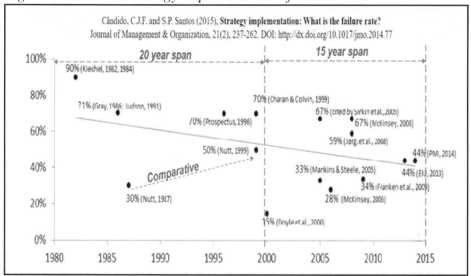

In Carlos (2015) study, the strategies did not accomplish the project purpose or put in another way, it did not fulfill the *fitness for use* criteria (Juran, n.d). These had nothing to do with the project implementation or execution which are about meeting scope, schedule and cost baseline, effective management of project risk exposure, effective use of resources (*people, equipment and material*) and management of stakeholder expectations (PMBok 6th Ed, 2017).

So, if the project purpose is ill defined, the project begins on the wrong track and from then on, no amount of PM effort will help alleviate the management error in "direction", assigning PM to solve the wrong problem. The responsibilities of "C" suite executives should not be confused with PM responsibilities that implement, execute, or construct as directed. Not differentiating project development failures from project implementation or execution failure create an *expert blind spot,* (Rugg & D'Agnese, 2013) that can result in unintentional misinformation, misleading or giving conflicting messages leading to wrong conclusions, that projects failed and by extension a PM failure. That is misleading as can be seen from the details listed in Figure 2.6 from Carlos and Santos study which would have likely confused the whole PM community and even the PM profession for decades.

Lack of Quality Leadership

It was aptly described as "*acknowledging the root of the problem: attitudes of management*" when Tom Peters (1987) quoted Deming (n.d) as insisting that "*the management is merely 90% of the problem*. Peters questioned "*the quality of direction being given to the team*", which he saw as "*wholly inadequate resources to get the job done efficiently and the lack of opportunity for the team to contribute their ideas on how to do their job better*". In short, quality leadership was sorely lacking, and detriment to project performance that should show up during the PM maturity assessment.

Folly of Engaging Accidental Project Managers

Project managers (invariably all) start their career by accident rather than by choice. Gan & Chin (2018) term these as *accidental project manager*. At this most fundamental level, the project manager (including the author) was often there by chance when the position was vacant, or a project opportunity arose, and he/she happens to have the technical domain knowledge/skill (instead of PM knowledge). Being the most senior person available, such candidates are given the chance to lead the project without prior prerequisite PM skills.

Although the cost is low employing accidental project managers, the project suffers from trial-and-error basis of PM, causing harm to the project itself in terms of lack of quality delivery, lost time due to project delays, cost over-runs, high cost of mistake and rectification and undue exposure to project risk. Such costs are seldom if ever recorded and so management run the risk of not realizing the high hidden cost of using untrained project managers.

Project managers from SMI/SMEs vary in their degree of PM maturity and are unfamiliar with the benefits of formal PM practices and habitually engage untrained project managers (Gan & Chin, 2018). Such organizations are not clear about the importance of clarity of purpose, why projects are initiated and how formal PM enhance PM performance. The tendency is then to focus on producing deliverables according to technical specification without reference to *"fitness for use"* criteria. Variation orders are acted on without any reference to strategic imperatives nor with prior business justification. Trial and error approach with non-standard PM terminology and tools results in inadequate or ineffective communication, miscommunication, and unclear project instructions (Gan & Chin, 2019). Worst, the general fear is that PM3 assessment might highlight those inadequacies.

MNC and GLC surveyed participants on the other hand are more likely to be graduates with good attitude and communication skills and familiar with multi-language and multi-cultural team challenges. Unlike their peers from SMI/SMEs, these participants welcome PM3 assessment as they understand the values and benefits of PM maturity (Gan & Chin, 2019).

Fixation With Best Practices

The importance of *"constant and relentless iteration"* (Peters, 1987) is a continuous improvement mindset diametrically opposite of *"doing-it-right-first-time"* (DIRFT) advocated by Phil B. Crosby (a famed Management Guru) in response to the quality crisis faced by industries in the late 80s. "Best practices" are largely used in operations management where there is mass production with high levels of automation and operating in a very controlled or mechanized environment. The term *"best practice"* connotes the highest level that can be achieved thus deters expert users from ever thinking of other possibilities even though it might be obvious to do so.

Best practices are therefore not appropriate in managing projects since projects invariably operate in a dynamic environment and are largely accomplished by people, (Gan & Chin, 2018). After the keynote address at the PMI 2014 Leadership Institute Meeting in Phoenix, Tom Peters (2014) agreed on the sideline that "best practices" tended to create mental handicaps, especially when they operate in a dynamic environment of constant and rapid change where much was beyond the control of the project manager (Gan & Chin, 2018). Thus, management should not be fixated with best practices but instead promote use of recommended good practices, the terminology that is more open and motivating and it encourages a thinking and continuous improvement mindset useful in all project endeavors.

Why then do so many PM practitioners routinely follow best practices and faithfully listen to what management gurus tell them, often without questions nor context and thus prone to "blindly" follow without adequate understanding and reasoning? Greatbatch and Clark (2005) opined it was *"how the gurus spoke instead of what they wrote and their extraordinary ability to attract large audiences through live performances"*.

It was *"the gurus"* manner of speaking than writing, an effective communication technique that make them far more convincing than the substance of their message (Jung, 2006). He also surmises that the authors seem to take an ethnomethodological approach that emphasize the process of real-life interaction, the use of verbal and non-verbal techniques of volume, tone, pitch, prolongation of sound, gestures, facial expressions etc. To create situational impressions and the importance of the construction of a sense of social reality, a sense that actors share the same lifeworld using 3 effective oratorical techniques, which are:

1. Rhetorical services such as contrast, emphasis, pauses, lists, funny expressions and puzzle-solutions.
2. Humor accompanied by a range of verbal and non-verbal practices.
3. Storytelling.

All these, the authors highlighted would actually:

- Heighten audience attentiveness.
- Strengthen the gurus' emotional bond with their audiences.
- Make message more memorable.
- Enhance their star status.
- Generate a huge income for the gurus.

Jung (2006) concluded that Greatbatch and Clark's (2005) analysis were thoughtful and presented very effectively in public speaking contexts and while the authors concluded *"what set the gurus apart from less accomplished speakers is their ability to use these techniques effectively in public speaking contexts"*. *Jung* cautioned (due to the small sample of 4 being studied) that it was quite another to conclude that effective use of those techniques made the gurus highly ranked since the *"causal claim required analysis of variations between the successful and the unsuccessful speakers in addition to the analysis of the commonality between the successful speakers".*

All these however do not adequately explain how PM practitioners who are trained and experienced to make tough decisions in the face of dynamic environment, often with very limited resources to produce results, could have been so easily misled to follow "best practices" without contextual understanding (Gan & Chin, 2019). Even PM3 organizations, leaders in PM maturity assessment like OPM3, PMMM (Kerzner) and PMMM (Crawford) continued to be entrapped in this *expert blind spot* syndrome.

How could PM maturity be assessed against adherence to best practices that simply do not exist from an international practice viewpoint when large organizations have their own proprietary best practices? P2MM to assess PM maturity being compliance with PRINCE2 implementation methodology, which it is assumed to be a best practice which is itself contestable and debatable. How could a PM implementation methodology like PRINCE2 be a best practice when its use is limited to IT development, IT implementation and government related projects when the subject is about project management, a subject for general application (Gan & Chin 2019)?

PM bodies like PMI, IPMA, APM, OGC UK, AIPM and large PM organizations like PwC, KPMG, Accenture and Deloitte do refer to best practices, when in fact each only refers to their respective proprietary best practices, tacitly showing there is really no globally accepted best practice. ISO did not really have a standard for PM until the publication of ISO 21500 (Legerman et.al., 2013). Even then, ISO 21500 was only issued as a guide to PM, not a statement of best practice. PMI too flip flop between the used of *"Best practices"* and *"Recommended good practices"* for 3 successive editions to 2017, an implicit admission that best practices is not such a good idea.

The use of the phrase "best practices" also tends to create the phenomenon of an "*expert blind spot* that often results from *routine conditioning*" (Senge et al,1999, Rugg & D'Agnese, 2013). Routine conditioning also creates brain-barriers that hinder project performance (Black & Gregersen, 2002) as well as stifle *TeamThink* when there is a need to look for fresh insights, ideas, and possibilities.

Thus, it is not about best practices but how best and appropriate to use each of the recommended good practice tools like the project dashboard, project S curve, logical framework analysis, force-field analysis, barriers to communication, RACI chart, RAM Chart, force field analysis, control charts, checklist, project risk register, stakeholders register, power interest grid, Delphi technique, Pareto chart and principle etc.

Routine Conditioning Impedes PM3 Adoption

Over 80% of surveyed participants in this research were inexperienced beyond their own industry and unexposed to formal PM education. More than 20% of the project managers (senior level above age 40 years) hold entrenched views of their role and scope of work. With decades of experience managing projects but only from the client's viewpoint, these project managers were entrusted to oversee contractors to ensure project deliverables are handover in accordance with project specifications, schedule and payment as agreed in the fixed-price contract. These surveyed participants were bogged down with industry jargon, technical details and entrenched views borne out of *routine conditioning*. Unsurprisingly, many were unwilling to let anyone encroach into their territory nor hear any argument contrary to their point of view, that PM and PM3 are indeed for generic application (Gan & Chin, 2019).

Routine-conditioning is a human tendency that "*lead us to be blind to critical features of the living world that shape whether or not we ever have any success in actually sustaining it*". It was described as "*our personal history in institutions starting with school, has conditioned most of us to see a mechanical world – a world of measure (largely meaning KPIs), plans and programs, a world of people "in control" and leaders who "drive" change* (Senge et al,1999).

Not much seems to have changed, judging from the output of a recent research that suggested 26 KPIs to gauge the performance of projects (Montero et.al, 2015). Would focusing on so much detail not lead the project manager to miss the forest for the trees? Even more surprising is the suggested KPI for revenue generation, a responsibility that has never been under the project manager's purview nor privy to it. Researchers conditioned by routine tend to do research for research's sake resulting in expert-blind-spot and hence likely to overlook the test of relevance and implications in practice. In addition, KPIs, while useful for operation management with stable operating environment to produce repetitive output are wholly inappropriate to measure project performance which operates in a dynamic environment and largely by people.

The use of recommended good practice is an effective way to speed PM initiation, planning, execution, close-out and control. Critical thinking is however needed to think through before using them appropriately. In the PMBok 5th and 6th Ed, it specified enterprise environment factors (EEF, internal and external) as *conditions not under the control of the project team that influence, constrain or direct the project,* (PMBok 6th Ed, 2017 pg. 38) per (Table 1) below.

The critical thinker can observe *organization systems, employee capability, commercial database, academic research and financial considerations* are classified under EEF but could equally be classified under organization process assets (OPA) defined as *plans, processes, policies, procedures and knowledge specific to and used by the performing organization* (PMBok 6th Ed, 2017 pg 39). This is confusing to research participants as observed during participants' attendance in PM seminars.

Rightly, management should only be concerned about environmental factors that can be *actionable* and whether to work on it either in the short or long term. In this way, non-actionable environmental factors can be noted separately as constraints for mitigating measures to be prepared expeditiously. Such display of maturity in managing projects may prove to be a daunting challenge and deter others from taking on the maturity improvement challenge.

Table 1. Reclassification of PMBok (2017) enterprise environmental factors

Project management Enterprise environmental factors		Project management Organisational Process Assets	
P M I	Organisation Vision	P M I	Plans
	Organisational Mission		Processes
	Organisational values		Policies
P M B o k	Organisational Beliefs	P M B o k	Procedures
	Cultural norms		Knowledge base
	Hierarchy		Templates
	Authority relationships		Information from previous projects
	Organisational systems PMBok 6th Ed p. 37		Lessons learned repositories
	Organisational governance		Change control procedures
	Geographical distribution of org assets		Internal infrastructure available
	External infrastructure available		Internal IT OS/Application software available
	Resources availability		
	Employee capability		

Project management Enterprise environmental factors		Project management Organisational Process Assets	
P M I	Market place conditions	P M I	
	Social norms		
	Legal restrictions		
P M B o k	Commercial Database	P M B o k	
	Academic research		
	Government and Industry standards		
	Financial considerations		
	Physical environment		

Too Risky Management Behavior

Risky management behavior in projects is more prevalent with SMI/SMEs. Project risks are not systematically identified nor are risk management strategies planned, a critical element for successful projects performance (PMBok 6th Ed, 2017). As a result, risk contingencies are often not factored in the overall project cost estimation, the basis on which project proposal are priced. Others inflate service charge-out rates based on three times the consultant's gross pay to provide the overall pricing that includes project contingency cost, a counter-productive approach in a project tender or competitive bid situation.

The lack of systematic risk identification, risk strategy planning and disclosure of project contingencies will not yield vital lessons that could otherwise be learned of what works and what did not. Such laidback management attitude is detrimental to the mature organization's continuous performance improvement initiative and should be avoided.

Lack of Formal PM Education

Responses as to what role a project manager plays were predictable but diverse depending on where the survey participants came from, a small, medium or multinationals organization or government departments. All too often, answers should be made but no reference to the role associated with their level of seniority in the PM department (Gan & Chin, 2019).

PMI explicitly recognizes that the organization and the way they are structured determine the project manager's role and responsibility (PMBok, 2017). With a blurred view of their roles, it is challenging to imagine the scope of PM work and how they are applied across multi-industries and disciplines and much less about the use of PM3s to gauge their organization's general level of PM maturity.

All these reflect a lack of formal PM education in international PM recommended good practices and thus adversely impact organization performance. Many project managers do not have prior exposure to formal PM education and when they eventually did, half had trainers who had never been in senior management roles. Invariably, only project managers engaged in large organizations with full fledge internal PM training really understood the varying levels of PM maturity where each level has their defined role and scope of work responsibilities. With such diverse background, it is common to see the lack of consensus of what the PM role should be.

Lack of formal PM basics foundation knowledge and skills make it more difficult to understand how PM skills apply generically (Gan & Chin, 2019). The PM roles and responsibilities have now been explicitly defined depending on the organization structure and the management's preferences (PMBok, 2017). So, it pays to ensure project managers have formal PM education so that they know the global recommended good practices, the international PM lexicon, internationally recognized tools and techniques and multi-cultural ideas of how people are generally managed.

Inadequate and Unrealistic Project Baselining

Projects are often assigned with budgets and timelines that are wholly inadequate and misguided. As a result, the projects are already *"dead on arrival"* since there was no hope of successfully managing those projects due to the wholly inadequate timeline and budget given the scope committed. Common feedback received from participants in the past 8 years survey conducted in this research, often reveal no basis were shown on how the baselines were arrived at except the excuse *"that was the prospective client maximum allocation, else we lose the deal"*. The sad truth is that a *"bad-deal is often far worse than a no-deal"* (Gan, 2006 to 2007).

Why then do the project managers not raise the issue to management before accepting the assignment? Common participants responses cited were:

1. Management invariably retorts "If you cannot, let others who can".
2. "That was the prospective client maximum allocation, so do we lose the deal?".
3. "The sales team frequently complaint our project service cost is too high".
4. "If we are too conservative in our rates, we will be unable to compete".

Project managers surveyed intimated that they did not have the guts to raise the pertinent question due to sheer lack of experience in various project cost and schedule estimation techniques to arrive at their independent estimate that could be used as a test of reasonableness.

When an organization has done all its best and consistently loose in bidding for project work, the difficult question should then be raised *"could the organization be in the wrong business?"* (Gan & Chin, 2018).

Late Appointment of Project Managers

This contributes to the high incidence of project failures. It should be noted, the reason for timely appointment of project managers is to enable project managers to gain a foundational understanding of the project purpose. This is vital to ensure the reasons for every project change request are in alignment with organizational and strategic goals (PMBok, 2017). Surveyed participants from large reputable organizations agree.

Two project directors even intimated that they did all the planning and gave project managers no say in the project baseline, an obvious ignorance and serious departure from PMI recommended good practice that require projects manager to be appointed in a timely manner, at early as is feasible but latest at the start of the planning. This is to ensure the project baselines are realistic and achievable (PMBok, 2017).

Performance Incentives Target Individual Performance and Not Teamwork

This mainly to motivate the performing organizations' sales team and little to incent teamwork. So, the sales team finds it easier to sell when there are no personal financial consequences to over-sell and over-commit since it is the project team that had to face the consequences of carrying the project to completion. These were observed from 20 years personal experience at PM work and common feedback from the surveyed participants (Gan & Chin, 2019).

Management stress teamwork at management meetings and how it creates organizational synergies and of its strategic importance to organizational goals. When it came to motivational incentives, these are conveniently overlooked or even forgotten, a simple case of management not walking their talk (Gan & Chin, 2018),

There are organizations that have begun a rethink of how the project people should be rewarded for team work to enhance organizational performance. These include sharing a portion of sales revenue placed into a project incentive pool from which bonuses were shared proportionately based on project service revenue earned. Others payout 50% sales commission on sales revenue actually paid by the client and the other 50% released on successful completion of the project (Gan & Chin, 2018). Although this creates additional paperwork, the performance incentives are more effective when targeted at both individuals and teamwork.

Failure to Recognize and Capitalize on "Project Force Field Analysis"

Mature PM organizations perform more effectively using *force field analysis* to systematically identify the project *driving forces* and project *restraining forces*. Until recognized, it is unlikely any action will be taken to mitigate these restraining forces that are impediments that hold back project progress. In the same way, opportunities are lost when organizations do not know project driving forces exist and when they do, no effort is made to capitalize on the benefits of project driving forces in a timely and more effective manner.

CONCLUSION

Although PM has been in existence and evident from the pyramids in Egypt and the Great Wall of China, its formal global acceptance was only initiated in the 1960s by APM in the UK but only got its royal charter in 2017. PMI was only inaugurated in 1969, and interest generated when the world witness US and Russian space program being launched and worldwide growth of large civil and building works. In the last six decades, PM has evolved and gained traction from the many successes in mega projects. It grew from an insignificant functional group of "experts" entrusted with coordination and control of construction, development, and implementation of change to become a respectable professional service offered by global consulting organizations with significant value and prestige. While the last 2 decades witnessed PM increasingly engaged in organizational strategy formulation, program, and portfolio management decision making to the "C" suite level management, a PM revolution indeed. What then are the implications for the profession? How can project managers and their performing organization keep pace with the developments taking place and at the same time avoid the impediments to PM? Are PM3 providers aware and have taken note of these developments? This is imperative to enhance their level of maturity to remain relevant in this fast-moving era of the disruptive 4th Industrial revolution. Those questions are addressed in the forgoing chapters.

REFERENCES

Association of Project Management. (2019). *APM Body of knowledge* (7th ed.). Association of Project Management.

Black, J. S., & Gregersen, H. B. (2002). *Leading Strategic Change: Breaking Through the Brain Barrier*. Pearson.

Candido, C.J. F. & Santos, S. P., (2015). Strategy implementation: What is the failure rate. *Journal of Management and Organisation*, Vol (21) Issue 2. Cambridge University Press and Australian and New Zealand Academy of Management https://doi.org/DOI: 10.1017/jmo.2014.77

Crawford, J. K. (2007), Project Management Maturity Model (2nd Ed). Auerback Publications, Drucker, P.F, (1999), *Management Challenges for the 21st Century*. Harper Collins.

Gan, R. C. C., & Chin, C. M. M. (2018). Components of project management maturity impacting project, programme, portfolio and organisational success. In Karayaz, G., & Silvius, G. (Eds.), *Developing Organizational Maturity for Effective Project Management* (pp. 128–152). IGI Global., DOI: 10.4018/978-1-5225-3197-5.ch007

Gan, R. C. C., & Chin, C. M. M. (2019). Project management guide and project management maturity models as generic tools capable for diverse applications. In Katuu, S. (Ed.), *Diverse Applications and Transferability of Maturity Models* (pp. 269–315). IGI Global., DOI: 10.4018/978-1-5225-7080-6.ch011

Gefen, D., Zviran, M., & Elman, N. (2006), What can be learned from CMMI failures? Communications of the Association for Information Systems. 17. (pp. 36). https://doi.org/DOI: 10.17705/1CAIS.01736

Greatbatch, D., & Clark, T. (2005). *Management Speak: Why We Listen to What Management Guru Tell Us*. Routledge. DOI: 10.4324/9780203087718

International Standard Publication 21500 (2021), *Project, programme and portfolio management: Context and concepts*, (2nd Ed). International Standard Publication

Jung, D. (2006), Reviewed work: Management Speak: Why we listen to what Management Gurus tell us by David Greatbach, Timothy Clark. *Administrative Science Quarterly,* Vol (51), 4, pp.669-671. https://www.jstor.org/stable/20109897

Kuhn, T. (1962). *The structure of scientific revolution*. University of Chicago Press.

Legerman, A., Zandhuis, A., Silvius, G., Rober, R., & Stellingwerft, R. (2013). *ISO 21500 in Practice A Management Guide*. Van Haren.

McKinsey, Q. (2014, September 1). Tom Peters on leading the 21st - century organization. McKinsey & Company. https://www.mckinsey.com/capabilities/people-and-organizational-performance/our-insights/tom-peters-on-leading-the-21st-century-organization

Montero, G., Onieva, L., & Palacin, R. (2015), Selection and Implementation of a Set of Key Performance Indicators for Project Management. *International Journal of Applied Engineering Research*. Vol (10), 18, pp.39473-39484. https://www.ripublication.com/Volume/ijaerv10n18.htm

Mulcahy, R. (2015). *PMP Exam Prep Book* (8th ed.). RMC Publications Inc.

Nieto-Rodriguez, A., & Evrard, D. (2004). *Boosting Business Performance through Programme & Project Management*, PricewaterhouseCoopers. https://www.mosaicprojects.com.au/PDF/PwC_PM_Survey_210604.pdf

OGC. (2010), *PRINCE2 Maturity Model (P2MM) Self-Assessment*, Office of Government Commerce.http://miroslawdabrowski.com/downloads/PRINCE2/Maturity%20models/PRINCE2%20Maturity%20Model%20P2MM%20v2.1%20-%20Self%20Assessment%20.pdf

Peters, T. (1987). *Thriving on Chaos*. Harper Perennial.

Project Management Institute (PMI). (2013). *A guide to project management body of knowledge* (PMBOK Guide) (5th ed). Project Management Institute.

Project Management Institute (PMI). (2017). *A guide to project management body of knowledge* (PMBOK Guide) (6th ed). Project Management Institute.

Project Management Institute (PMI). (2017). *Agile Practice Guide*. Project Management Institute.

Rugg, G., & D'Agnese, J. (2013). *Blind spot*. Harper Collins.

Sarbines-Oxley Act. (2002), Senate and House of Representatives of the United States of America in Congress. chrome-extension://efaidnbmnn-nibpcajpcglclefindmkaj/https://www.govinfo.gov/content/pkg/COMPS-1883/pdf/COMPS-1883.pdf

Senge, P., Kleiner, A., Roberts, C., Ross, R., Roth, G., & Smith, B. (1999). *The Dance of Change*. Crown Currency.

Sunstein, C. R. (2013). *Simple-The Future of government*. Simon & Schuster.

Williams, G. (2010). *PRINCE2 Maturity Model*. Office of Government Commerce.

ADDITIONAL READING

Backlund, F., Chonéer, D., & Sundqvist, E. (2013). Project Management Maturity Models – A Critical Review. *Procedia: Social and Behavioral Sciences*, *119*, 837–846. Advance online publication. DOI: 10.1016/j.sbspro.2014.03.094

Crawford, J. K. (2014). *Project Management Maturity Model (PM Solutions Research)* (3rd ed.). Auerbach Publications.

Karnatak, A. (2023). *Project Management Maturity Model*. Notion Press Appleby, T., Cabanis-Brewin, J., Crawford, J.K., Cruz, F., Pennypacker, J.S., West, J.L., White, K.R.J. (2007). *Advancing Organizational Project Management Maturity*. Center for Business Practices.

Liao, R., Chen, H., Sun, C., & Sun, Y. (2022). An Exploratory Study on Two-Dimensional Project Management Maturity Model. *Engineering Management Journal*, *35*(4), 445–459. DOI: 10.1080/10429247.2022.2154093

Silvius, G., & Karayaz, G. (2018). *Developing Organizational Maturity for Effective Project Management.* IGI Global. DOI: 10.4018/978-1-5225-3197-5

KEY TERMS AND DEFINITIONS

Configuration Management: In a project is a systematic process for controlling and tracking changes in the project's deliverables, documentation etc.

Generic: It can be use in diverse applications and transferable across large number of industries, commerce, government and enforcement agencies both large and small

Methodology: It refers to systematically describe the 'how' of the conduct in performing the task in a project.

Pitfalls: It refers to hidden or unexpected problem or obstacles that can cause a project to fail, delay in attaining its objectives hence potentially may derail a project's progress to completion.

Project Baseline: It is a fixed reference point to measure and compare the project planned against actual progress. There are scope baseline, schedule baseline and cost baseline that are used in the project environment. The baseline helps in tracking performance, deviation and deciding what adjustments are necessary for the project to be on track and on time for delivery.

Project Failure: It occurs when a project does not meet its intended goals or objectives in many ways

Project Force Field Analysis: Refers to systematically identifying the project driving forces and restraining forces that are holding back the project progress

Routine Conditioning: It refers to regular process of maintaining the repeated condition or stimuli on the specific matter, activity or task.

Self-Assessment: In this context, it refers to the process where the organization evaluates their own level of maturity. This option saves costs before allowing for in-depth assessment.

Terminology: It refers to a set of terms or words that are specific to a particular subject, activity, or field.

Section 3
Methodology

Chapter 4
Methodology and Rationalization of Work

ABSTRACT

This chapter discusses and explains the mixed method research approach being used and outlines the rationale for the adoption. The study was conducted in 8 stages. Each stage explains how the samples were collected to adequately represent the PM practitioner population in terms of the industries, commerce or government departments and age groups they represent. It also elaborated the new model to be functionally more robust and user friendly or intuitive to use to attract user buy-in. Based on the analysis, the most desirables attributes of PM3 were identified, in terms of the maturity level description, maturity growth path and practicality of use.

INTRODUCTION

PMBok (2004, 3rd Ed) in circulation and all subsequent updates made through PMBok 4th, 5th and 6th edition (2017) were used as the main knowledge guiding post to ensure completeness, consistency and accuracy in coverage. Literatures about PM3 models, detailed scrutiny of selected PM3 tools, research statistics available of project performance and project failures were used to supplement the knowledge gained from this 8-year research effort. This study includes feedback from 1,201 participants that were either seasoned PM practitioners from various levels of seniority who between them have attended 89 PMP exam preparation boot camps

DOI: 10.4018/979-8-3693-1439-5.ch004

and surveyed participants who attended the intermediate and advanced level public PM seminars/workshops conducted by ROGAN Strategic Management's (RSM) (Table 1).

The knowledge gained were used to conceptualize the new model design to avoid the known impediments that plague the PM3s already in the marketplace, The initial idea used was to construct a Malaysian PM3 (MPM3) structured to cover only the PM practices and PM3s implemented in Malaysia. Such scope limitation was quickly found impractical as most survey participants came from multinationals, local conglomerates, government linked corporations/organizations (GLCs) all of whom have significant number of foreign team members with differing exposures, cultures, and languages. The same was experienced even for the small medium enterprise (SMEs) and small medium industry (SMIs) which goes to show that PM is truly global in scope.

The study as a result was extended from local to a global research effort, wherein the model was renamed as Duplex PM3 (DPM3) to de-limit its local scope and emphasize the duplex nature of the model that encompass both the project organization that support the project manager as the project driver.

RESEARCH PLAN AND DESIGN

The PM practitioners' population studied encompasses business owners involved in PM, performing organization employee project managers and client project managers. Projects in the study involves change initiative, big and small, all with identical characteristics but managed with different levels of seniority, rigor, and emphasis.

Since studying the population will take too long and impractical largely due to budgetary and schedule constraints, sampling was used as an effective alternative approach (Saunder et el., 2000) where the study involved 1,201 participants from 89 seminars/workshops and PMP exam preparation boot camps representing all the top 10 significant industry sectors involved in PM (Table 2).

Table 1. Data sampled from surveyed participants

| Data from 5-day PMP exam preparation Boot camps and 2-day or 3-day Intermediate & Advanced level PM seminars/workshops All classes were carried out from 9am to 5:30pm daily | | | | | |
| Participants in survey attendance | | | | | |
Year Conducted	PMP Boot camps	PM seminar Intermediate Advanced	Total Number of participants	Number of Classes	Duration/dates/ Course titles /locations
2019	15	29	44	2	Appendix 1
2018	35	66	101	7	Appendix 2
2017	39	98	137	10	Appendix 3
2016	25	74	99	6	Appendix 4
2015	68	130	198	11	Appendix 5
2014	138	103	241	18	Appendix 6
2013	128	45	173	15	Appendix 7
2012	121	8	129	10	Appendix 8
2011	54	25	79	10	Appendix 9
Total	**623**	**578**	**1,201**	**89**	
	52%	**48%**	**100%**		

Test of significance was used to ensure:

- The top 10 industries involved in PM services in Malaysia were included.
- Inclusion of 2 main significant organization sizes which are large and international like MNCs/GLCs/Government and smaller entities like SMIs/SMEs
- Inclusion of the 4 main seniority groups representing 4 levels of PM seniority or PM expertise level -*Enlighten, Competent, Expert and Authority* level experience (Gan & Chin, 2018).
- The age group ranges represented were under 30, 30 to 40, 41 to 50 and above 50 years old.

Table 2. Industries represented in the PMP boot camps & seminar/workshops

	Industry/Commerce/Government	Selected	Represented	MNC/GLC	SMI/SME
1	IT/ICT/Integrators & HW suppliers	✔	✔	✔	✔
2	Application & Systems developers	✔	✔	✔	✔
3	Telecommunication infra	✔	✔	✔	
4	Building and Civil Construction	✔	✔	✔	✔
5	Building Developers	✔	✔	✔	
6	Energy, Oil and Gas	✔	✔	✔	
7	Banks & Finance companies	✔	✔	✔	
8	Insurance	✔	✔	✔	
9	GLCs/Government Agencies/Ministries	✔	✔	✔	
10	Manufacturers/ETO	✔	✔	✔	✔
	Top 5 Consulting companies		✔	✔	
	University PM Professors & Lecturers		✔	✔	
	Enforcement Agencies/Anti corruption		✔	✔	
	Government Special projects		✔	✔	

RATIONAL OF APPROACH

The interdependencies of multi-factor variables most of which involved human behavior which are not always consistent nor predictable, often influenced and impacted by survey respondent's state of mind at the time of the survey and vagaries of the human spirit all make rational quantitative study difficult.

The use of the DOE (Design-of-Experiment) was not possible as the project work environment, unlike in the science lab, could not be subjected to any controlled environment to enable quantitative observation of results from variation of one variable at a time while all other variables are held constant. As a result, a more pragmatic mixed research method was used that utilizes both qualitative and quantitative analysis (Creswell, 2003).

The richness of open-ended questions for surveys and interviews were used to solicit participants' opinions, experiences, and possible "*feelings*" about desirable attributes of PM3. It is also noted that their opinions could be subjective as to what user friendliness means and what they entail. Qualitative research method was also used even though it was time consuming and with some level of subjectivity. They are unlikely to be significant enough to void the conclusions that could be drawn from them through the use of repeated survey of subsequent groups.

To gauge the general ranking of PM3 attributes, the quantitative research methods was used with weighted average feedback scores so that the Pareto principle could be applied to focus the research study on the vital few but without losing touch of the trivial many.

Data Collection Methods

Since there was no ISO standard for PM until 2008, this study was benchmarked against PMI's PMBok 3rd Ed (2004), the de facto industry standard at that time and adopted by most fortune 500 organizations that undertake projects.

The survey data were validated against each new release of PMBoks as they become available beginning with PMBok 3rd Ed (2004), then updated by reference to each of the 4th, 5th, and 6th Edition (2017) as well as feedback from surveyed participants (Figure 1).

Figure 1. Data collection plan

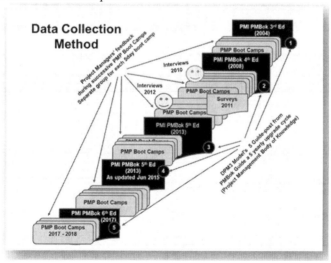

PROCESS AND WORKFLOW

This study was initiated to develop a PM3 model, designed to avoid the many PM3 pitfalls in general and those observed from shortcomings of the 7 more commonly known PM3s. The new model would have to be functionally robust and more user friendly or intuitive to use to attract user buy-in. The study was conducted in stages.

Stage 1: Literatures Review of Well-Known PM3 Models

A comparative study of 7 well-known PM3s namely CMMi, OPM3, PMMM (Kerzner), PMMM (Crawford), PwC maturity model, P2MM and PRINCE 2 was carried out to observe the common characteristics of desirable attributes of PM3s and common complaints about PM3 models and to learn from and avoid those enumerated pitfalls.

Stage 2: Interview to Determine the Project Success Criteria

The initial idea was to limit the scope of research to develop the *Malaysian Project Management Maturity Model (MPM3)* model. As indicated later in this research, it was quickly found impractical to limit the scope to Malaysian PM practices as almost all participants were managing projects that were multinational and multicultural. So, the scope expanded and was refined and renamed as *Duplex Project Management Maturity model (DPM3)*. The renaming was to reflect the *dual nature of the model* that recognized the *project manager* and the *performing organization* as the 2 key drivers of all project endeavors.

Stage 3: Preliminary Face to Face Interview With Experienced Project Managers

The research was initiated using a preliminary face to face interviews using open-ended question of what constitute project success in a pre-scheduled face-to-face interview of two and a half (2 ½) hours per interview. The interviews were conducted locally (Klang Valley, Malaysia) in May 2010. The interviews revealed the following:

Definition of project success depends on level of people interviewed:

i. **Owner Project Managers** of performing organization state project success as:

    - Meeting project profitability or ROI (Return on investment)
    - Adequate major stakeholders' satisfaction
    - Creating opportunities for repeat business

ii. **Employee Project Managers/Project Directors** of the performing organization

    - Fulfilment of scope, time and cost
    - Purpose fulfilment
    - Organization strategy alignment

iii. Employee Project Managers of the client

    - Ensure deliverables meet quantity/performance specifications.
    - Ensure progress of delivery within baseline/approved time-extension
    - Authorize progress payment as per contract subject to retention sum
    - Authorize release of retention sum after expiry of the warranty period
    - Ensure defects listed in the NCR (Non-Conformance Report) were all rectified before the project can be fully accepted and signed-off

All interviewees in the face-to-face survey have intimated they have not undergone any formal PM training. No interviews were conducted after 2017, which otherwise would have included the additional responsibilities included in PMBok 6th Ed (2017) relating to:

- Effective management of project resources
- Adequate management of project risk exposure

- Ensuring major stake holder's satisfaction

Another notable feedback revealed from the survey was:

Project managers were delegated often only after scope/time/cost commitment.

Project managers were appointed only after the initial scope, time and budget had already been committed to the client. This was the predominant practice in SMEs PM organization who uses business owners and senior directors background experience to make the ballpark estimates to bid for projects.

Project managers were not involved in overall planning before contract commitment.

Project managers delegated with the project were not given opportunity to review the budget or when given, no one dared to "*challenge*" the feasibility of the budget and timeline given. This was the prevalent practice in SMEs. Estimates carried out by owner PMs who were former quantity surveyors, construction managers or IT professionals in project integrations were more likely to be better at their estimates. The other half make their "*gung-ho*" "*can do*" guesses often with painful cost consequences.

Project managers were not given discretion on choices of resources.

Project managers were responsible to deliver the projects within the given baseline but no options or rights to choose their resources, team development budget nor able to remove or sideline any team member for lack of performance (this was the prevalent observation throughout this study).

Project managers were seen more as doers than planners and controllers.
- Little if any discretion was allowed to vary the project plan.

- Merely do progress reporting without use of project dashboard nor earned value management (EVM). They were entirely those working in SMEs.
- No questions were asked of the project managers' own seniority level/salary scale and experience except that they were all seasoned project managers in their mid-thirties to forties.

Stage 4: Survey Participants for Desirable Attributes of PM3

Due to the small sample size of face-to-face interview, more research was deemed necessary to gauge the current PM situation in the country.

The first basis-data was drafted from PMI's PMBok 3rd Ed published in 2004 together with the researcher's 20 years of PM practice and supplemented by literature review. The basis-data was then used to solicit verbal feedback from attendees (average 15 attendees per class) at ROGAN Strategic Management's (RSM) monthly 5-day PMP exam preparation boot camps (for graduates with at least a minimum of 3 years post graduate supervisory experience in PM practice), PM training classes, seminars, and workshops for intermediate and advance level PM personnel.

Verbal questions on significant factors affecting project performance were asked for YES/NO answers after the end of each of the 11 chapters taught and whether they have indeed used them or otherwise would use them. Factors with high YES votes were ranked higher after each successive class.

Where logical, factors with similar characteristics were merged for simplicity and clarity's sake. Hence, communication skills included subskills in presentation skills, brevity, eloquence, skills in negotiation and conflict management, active listening, and emotional intelligence. Leadership skills included skills relating to strategic outlook, self-awareness, purpose driven, articulate communication and presentation skills, negotiation skills, emotional intelligence, and conflict management.

It was obvious at the time that project managers were handicapped by their lack of hard skills such as business acumen, lack of exposure to business, industry, application and the project environment all of which were not in the PMBok then but have since been included in PMI's PM talent triangle (2017). However, it became obvious after some months of observation that these lack-of-skills were more of individuals from SME/SMIs than those from MNC/GLCs who were of high caliber individuals with formalized training and exposure. Hence, PMBok 4th Ed published in 2008 was then used to cross check on the PM recommended good practices that could be used to further improve PM3 maturity factors.

Verbal questions on significant factors affecting project performance were again asked for YES/NO answers after the end of each of the 12 chapters taught (successive versions of PMBok tend to change and expand in scope). The feedback was then used to refine the factor ranking. It soon became clear from end-of-class feedback forms of the importance of negotiation and conflict management when they were frequently ticked for follow up workshops.

Negotiation and conflict management skills workshops were from then on conducted as public programs with high turnouts and very positive feedback. As a result, negotiation and conflict management skills were treated as independent factors worthy of their own separate headings.

The big leap forward in PM knowledge came with the publications of PMBok 5th Ed (2013) and its later update in Jun 2015. This was more in-line with PM practices that the author was accustomed to in the four preceding years while engaged in PM global consulting practices in East Asia offices of KPMG and PwC consulting.

Verbal questions on significant factors affecting project performance were again asked at each of the 5-day PMP exam preparation boot camps conducted for a YES/NO answers after the end of each of the 13 chapters taught. This version confirmed what were already anticipated that project managers not only need the exposure but also the business acumen to understand and appreciate how decisions were made, how to differentiate between alternatives available and the leadership quality that was so badly needed to lead and motivate the team to perform at their highest potential.

The publication of PMI latest research work on the PM talent triangle (2017) is discussed and feedback obtained to gauge its market acceptance level.

Stage 5: Ranking of Desirable Attributes of Project Managers

A survey was conducted with both PM lecturers and final year PM undergraduate students from the Faculty of Industrial Management of a local university. This survey group was chosen by virtue of their under-graduate specialization in PM, final year and fresh from their theoretical studies and hence untainted by the vagaries of industry practice. Hence, seen as best to gauge and rank the PM3 attributes advocated by vendors, PM researchers and PM practitioners.

The list of desirable attributes obtained from literature reviewed were displayed on the screen and explained to the 56 final year PM undergrad-uates. Participants were asked to rank their 10 most desired attributes of PM3 models. Of the 56 who attended, 53 responded. The number of counts per score and the weighted average score recorded calculated for each attribute were tabulated.

Using the Likert scale, participants were asked to rank 10 relatively sought-after attributes of PM3 by a score of 1 to 5 for each of the 10 attributes displayed on the screen. A score of 5 is given when they are a *"must have"* attributes, score of 4 if they felt it was *very important*, score of 3 if it *was important*, score of 2 if they think it's a *maybe or unsure* and score of 1 if the attribute was *irrelevant*.

The number of scores were weighted by the number of participants who gave the score and the total summated (Table 4.3).

The weighted score is calculated as the sum of all (score x count)

E.g. User friendliness score = (5 x 19) + (4 x 24) + (3 x 10) + (2 x 0) + (1 x 0) = 221

Table 3. Survey results for desirable attributes of PM3s

	Desired attributes in a PM3	Number of persons scoring for the desired attributes					
		5 Must have	4 Very Important	3 Important	2 Maybe	1 Irrelevant	Total Weighted Score
1	User friendliness	19	24	10	0	0	221
2	Flexibility	12	25	16	1	0	210
3	Adaptability &practicality	9	19	20	5	0	191
4	Scalability	6	16	19	7	1	167
5	Robustness/rigor in assessment	7	17	20	9	1	192
6	Degree of use of good practices	5	26	14	6	0	183
7	Standardization of processes	5	20	20	7	2	181
8	How organization & project managers are assessed	12	32	5	5	0	213
9	Fitness as an PMM assessment	14	25	12	1	1	209
10	Affordability	7	26	15	4	1	197

The list of desired PM3 attributes was then reorganized according to the ranking results where the highest score was listed first (Table 4).

Table 4. Ranking of top 10 PM3s desirable attributes

Desired attributes of a PM3 Model	Number of persons scoring for the desired attributes					
	5 Must have	4 Very Important	3 Important	2 Maybe	1 Irrelevant	Total weighted Score
User friendliness	19	24	10	0	0	221
How organizations & project managers are assessed	12	32	5	5	0	213
Flexibility	12	25	16	1	0	210
Fitness as an PMM assessment	14	25	12	1	1	209
Affordability	7	26	15	4	1	197
Robustness/rigor in assessment	7	17	20	9	1	192
Adaptability	9	19	20	5	0	191
Degree of use of good practices	5	26	14	6	0	183
Standardization of processes	5	20	20	7	2	181
Scalability	6	16	19	7	1	167

The top 3 most **desired attributes of PM3** were:

1. User friendliness
2. How organization and project managers are assessed
3. Practicality, flexibility, and fitness for use as a PM maturity model

Affordability appeared to have much lower votes than the results of a previous survey. The difference is likely due to the former survey involving working project managers while the later survey involved only final year PM students who have not yet been in the workforce.

Stage 6: Survey Market Acceptability of PM3 Maturity Level Descriptions

As the top reason for low uptake of PM3 in the marketplace has been users' difficulty in understanding of PM3 maturity level description, what each level entail and how each level relate to its next higher level, a survey was conducted on the PM3 descriptions used to understand why they were not easily understood and to relate.

The five PM3 models available were listed as model A to E to conceal the identity of the model being surveyed. This limit possible bias that may occur when survey participants have prior knowledge of any of the models displayed for feedback. The PM3 models coded A to E were listed in rows with their respective advancing maturity level description in columns 1 to 5 (Table 5).

Table 5. PM3 maturity level descriptions for feedback rating

PM3 Models	Tabulation of PM3 Level description					
	Maturity Levels >	1	2	3	4	5
Model A		Standardize	Measure	Control	Continuously Improve	
Model B		Unreliable processes	Informal processes	Standardized Processes	Monitored Processes	Optimized Processes
Model C	Staged	Initial	Managed	Defined	Quantitatively Managed	Optimizing
	Continuous	Incomplete Performed	Managed	Defined	Quantitatively Managed	Optimizing
Model D		Initial Process	Structured process	Org standards Institutionalized	Managed Process	Optimizing Process
Model E		Accidental	Enlightened	Competent	Expert	Authority

In the 1-day PM3 workshop conducted, participants were shown and given explanations of the five models (four well known PM3 Models + DPM3 model) coded as Model A, B, C, D and E as shown in Table 5. The models' advancing levels of maturity level description displayed were explained and how those maturity levels and its maturity growth path measure up to the 3 most desired attributes of user friendliness in terms of the PM3 maturity level description, maturity growth path and practicality of use.

The 56 final year PM undergraduates who attended the survey were asked to show and explain their scores as each model score were called. For some models, several participants did not give any score as they did not understand the maturity level descriptions displayed. The survey scores were recorded (Table 6). The real model identity was then displayed. A low score of 1 would represent a low desirability score and a score of 5 representing a high desirability score or meet the market desired attribute.

The number of participants per score is tabulated by the respective column. The total score is then weighed by the number of responses, summated, and average to enable comparison. The score for each desired attribute is calculated using the total weighted average score. The top 3 desirable attributes of user friendliness, fitness for use and adaptability/ flexibility are not directly comparable but given equal weightage and average into a single score to facilitate comparison only.

When Model C (CMMi) score was called, very few raised their hands, displayed uncertainties and a bit confused as to what the level description were supposed to mean. It was revealed at the vote count that they did not understand the maturity level as was described. This is represented by the low counts in row 1 for CMMi.

Table 6. Feedback score counts for PM3 user friendliness.

PM3 Models Surveyed Feedback score	PM3 top 3 desirable Attributes	Feedback score where 5: Excellent 3: Good 1: Poor				
		User friendliness	Fitness for use	Adaptability or Flexibility	Total score/ responses	Weighted average score
OPM3 By PMI 3.459	1.Level description	3, 4, 5, 2	3,3, 5, 2	3, 4, 4, 2	143/40	3.575
	2.Growth path description	3, 5, 4, 2	3, 4, 4, 3	3, 3, 5, 3	148/42	3.523
	3.Practicality	3, 3, 5, 3	3, 4, 5, 2	3, 3, 4, 2	141/43	3.279
Maturity Model PwC 3.568	1.Level description	4, 3, 3, 3	4, 3, 2, 3	4, 3, 1, 2	160/35	3.174
	2.Growth path description	4, 3, 1, 3	4, 3, 3, 3	4, 3, 1, 3	129/35	3.686
	3.Practicality	4, 3, 2, 3	4, 3, 2, 4	4, 0, 2, 4	124/35	3.543
CMMI Carnegie Mellon 3.015	1.Level description	0, 0, 1, 0	0, 0, 1, 1	0, 0, 1, 1	13/5	2.600
	2.Growth path description	0, 1, 1, 1	0, 0, 1, 1	0, 1, 1, 1	23/8	2.875
	3.Practicality	0, 0, 1, 1	1, 1, 2	0, 0, 1, 0	25/7	3.570
PMMM (Crawford) PM Solutions 3.411	1.Level description	1, 3, 2, 4	1, 0, 2	1, 2, 2	65/18	3.611
	2.Growth path description	1, 1, 2, 4	1, 1, 2	1, 1, 2	53/16	3.313
	3.Practicality	1, 0, 2, 4	1, 0, 2	1, 0, 2	43/13	3.308
DPM3 3.679	1.Level description	0 52 54 0 0				3.679
	2.Growth path description	0 52 54 0 0				3.679
	3.Practicality	0 52 54 0 0				3.679

Stage 7: Ensuring DPM3 Alignment With International Good Practice

To ensure the DPM3 model comply with globally recognized terminology and internationally recommended good practice, the following PMI's PMBok were used as general PM knowledge guidepost unless better clarity could be obtained using alternative definition, explanation, illustration and then included in the glossary.

   Guidepost 1: PMBok 3rd Ed (2004)
   -   PMI first definitive statement of recommended good practice
   -   adopted by IEEE and Australia
   Guidepost 2: PMBok 4th Ed (2008)
   Guidepost 3 & 4: PMBok 5th Ed (2013 and 2015 update)
   Guidepost 5: PMBok 6th Ed (2017)

Stage 8: Continuous Survey Conducted at Public PM Seminars and Workshops

This survey involved 578 participants (Table 4.1) from 22 public PM seminars and workshops from world class organizations, GLCs, government and enforcement agencies, local conglomerates, and 10% from SME/SMI sectors. The industries included IT/ICT, application developers and implementers, telecommunication providers, oil and gas (upstream), banking and finance, construction, developers, insurance, government linked companies and enforcement agencies, engineering institute and institute of finance. The age group ranges from under 30 years, 31 to 40, 41 to 50 and those above 50 years old. There is an even distribution of attendees who had PM certification and those who did not. This is due to the classes being carried out at intermediate to advanced levels.

This feedback was used to continuously refine the DPM3 model being developed. The final version was published as a book chapter titled *Components of Project management maturity impacting Project, Program, Portfolio and organizational success* (Gan & Chin, 2018) Chapter 7 in the edited book "*Developing Organizational Maturity for Effective Project Management*" published by IGI-Global. Another research was also published as Chapter 11 titled *Project Management Guide and Project Management Maturity Models as Generic Tools Capable for Diverse Applications* (Gan & Chin, 2019) in the edited book "*Diverse Applications and Transferability of Maturity Models*" also published by IGI-Global.

Ethical Considerations

In the context of this study, ethics refer to the appropriateness of the researcher's behaviors in relation to the rights of the subject of their study including any or all effects that might adversely impact the subject (Saunders et al, 2000). This ethical code of conduct expected from researchers in the survey activities has been strictly observed to ensure respondents rights are observed, nor will they be in any way or form suffer physical harm, discomfort, pain or personal embarrassment or even loss of privacy. Disclosures of any kind or form are protected using cross referencing whereby the respondents' records are maintained only as a number and identity kept separately in a cross-reference file separate from the project file. This allows factual verification later when necessary.

The official request to potential respondents were as laid out in a formal survey invitation letter where potential respondents were solicited specifically without monetary rewards, totally voluntary and their discretion freedom to opt out at any point in time. The ethical principles and practices have been strictly observed and in compliance with the institution ethics protocol.

CONCLUSION

The study was designed and conducted in stages to better understand the views about PM3s and gain a deeper understanding as well as reasons for the persistent project failure statistics despite the significant growth in PM education and certification. In addition, what could be learned from the identified impediments to project success as well as what could be done to improve the PM3s design so that project-based organizations could perform more effectively.

REFERENCES

Creswell, J. W. (2003). Research Design: Qualitative, Quantitative, and Mixed Methods Approaches. *Sage (Atlanta, Ga.)*.

Gan, R. C. C., & Chin, C. M. M. (2018). Components of project management maturity impacting project, programme, portfolio and organisational success. In Karayaz, G., & Silvius, G. (Eds.), *Developing Organizational Maturity for Effective Project Management* (pp. 128–152). IGI Global., DOI: 10.4018/978-1-5225-3197-5.ch007

Gan, R. C. C., & Chin, C. M. M. (2019). Project management guide and project management maturity models as generic tools capable for diverse applications. In Katuu, S. (Ed.), *Diverse Applications and Transferability of Maturity Models* (pp. 269–315). IGI Global., DOI: 10.4018/978-1-5225-7080-6.ch011

Project Management Institute (PMI). (2013). *A guide to project management body of knowledge* (PMBOK Guide) (5th ed). Project Management Institute.

Project Management Institute (PMI). (2017). *A guide to project management body of knowledge* (PMBOK Guide) (6th ed). Project Management Institute.

Saunders, M. N. K. Lewis, & P., Thornhill, A., (2000). *Research methods for business students*. Prentice Hall.

ADDITIONAL READING

Fetters, D. M. (2020). *The Mixed Methods Research Workbook: Activities for Designing, Implementing, and Publishing Projects*. Sage Publications, Inc. DOI: 10.4135/9781071909713

Kerzner, H. (2019). *Using the Project Management Maturity Model: Strategic Planning for Project Management* (3rd ed.). Wiley.

Mertens, D. M. (2023). *Mixed Methods Research*. Bloomsbury Publishing. DOI: 10.5040/9781350273191

Venkatesh, V., Brown, S., & Sullivan, Y. (2024). *Conducting Mixed-Methods Research: From Classical Social Sciences to the Age of Big Data and Analytics*. Virginia Tech Publishing., DOI: 10.21061/conducting-mixed-methods-research

KEY TERMS AND DEFINITIONS

Data Collection: It is a process of systematically conduct of gathering, measuring and analyzing information from various sources (e.g. mixed method approach) to answer the research question.

Data: It refers to raw facts gathered from the mixed method approach that will later be used for analysis, interpretation and decision. Another word, it is aimed to extract meaningful insights and knowledge from the research investigation.

Earned Value Management (EVM): This is a project management technique used to measure project performance and progress in an objective manner. The key components in measuring EVM are planned value, earned value and actual cost. With EVM, project manager can make accurate to assess project health and performance to ensure timely project completion.

Ethics: Refers to the appropriateness of the researcher's behaviors in relation to the rights of the subject of their study including any or all effects that might adversely impact the subject (Saunders et al, 2000)

Government Linked Companies (GLC): Are businesses in which the government holds a stake hence having more influence over its strategic decisions, policies and management. It is common in many countries.

Mixed Method: It is a research approach that combines both quantitative (e.g. numerical data) and qualitative (e.g. descriptive data) method to provide a comprehensive and validity on the research output. Using this approach able researcher to cross validate the findings obtained from the research.

Multi-Factor Variables: It refers to variables that are influenced by multiple independent factors or conditions which involves human behavior which are not always consistent or predictable at the time the research was conducted.

Multinational Companies (MNC): These are larger business e.g. corporations that operates in multiple countries for example Apple, Toyota, Unilever.

PMP Boot Camp: This is an intensive training program carried out typically in 5 days to focus on the Project Management Body of Knowledge (PMBOK) theories and methodology that will prepare candidates to sit for the Project Management Professional (PMP) certification exam.

Research Design: This is an overall roadmap or framework used to plan and conduct how the research will be conducted in a systematic way. A well-structured research design plan will ensure research objectives are attained to produce meaningful results.

Sample: It is a subset of a large population selected for the purpose of the study. There are various types of sampling that can be used for research e.g. random sampling, purposive sample, stratified sample and convenience sampling.

Small-Medium Enterprises (SME): These are businesses that fall within a specific size range of employees, revenue etc defined by government regulations.

Section 4
Analysis and Discussion

Chapter 5
Success Criteria and Attributes of Maturity Models

ABSTRACT

A comparative study of 7 well-known PM3s namely CMMi, OPM3, PMMM (Kerzner), PMMM (Crawford), PwC maturity model and P2MM PRINCE 2 was carried out to observe the common characteristics of desirable attributes of PM3s and common complaints about PM3 models and to learn from it. The survey feedback consistently shows the need for PM3 models to be user friendly, using terminology commonly used by PM practitioners and descriptions of growth trends that were meaningful when seen as one maturity level to the next.

PROJECT SUCCESS CRITERIA FROM PM PRACTITIONERS' ROLE

The Malaysian PM3 (MPM3) model was subjected to a preliminary test using open-ended question of what constitute project success in a pre-scheduled face-to-face interview of two and a half (2 ½) hours conducted locally (in Klang Valley, Malaysia) in May 2010. The survey revealed the following that definition of project success depends on level of people interviewed:

DOI: 10.4018/979-8-3693-1439-5.ch005

1. **Owner Project Managers** of performing organization stated project success as:
   - Meeting project profitability
   - Managing stakeholders' satisfaction
   - Creating opportunities for repeat business
2. **Employee Project Managers/Project Directors** of performing organization stated project success as:
   - Fulfilment of scope, time, and cost
   - Purpose fulfilment
   - Organization strategy alignment
3. **Employee Project Managers of the client** stated project success as:
   - Ensure deliverables meet quantity and performance specs.
   - Ensuring vendor progress of delivery within baseline/time-extension
   - Authorize progress payment as per contract subject to retention sum.
   - Release of retention sum after expiry of the warranty period.

All interviewees intimated they have **NOT** undergone any formal PM training.

The survey was conducted with both lecturers and final year PM undergraduate students from the Faculty of Industrial Management of a local university. The group was chosen by virtue of their undergraduate specialization in PM, final year and fresh from their theoretical studies, untainted by vagaries of industry practice and hence seen as best to gauge and rate the PM3 attributes advocated by PM researchers and PM practitioners. The list of desirable attributes obtained from literature review were displayed on screen and explained to the 56 final year PM undergraduates. Participants ranked their 10 most desired attributes of PM3 models. Of the 56 who attended, 53 responded. The number of counts per score and the weighted average score calculated for each attribute in Table 3 in Chapter 4.

The results clearly show high scores *for user friendliness, flexibility, adaptability, and fitness for use* as a PM maturity assessment tool and how the organization and its project managers were assessed. These factors appear to dictate the level of user buy-in and by extension, its level of PM3 adoption. The top desirable attributes were consistent throughout the study period. The same result pattern appears consistent throughout the subsequent years of surveys conducted at public PM seminars and workshops.

DPM3 is the Top PM3 When Ranked for Top 3 Most Desired PM3 Attributes

Using the Likert scale, the number of scores obtained for each of the 5 models displayed A to E when weighted and tabulated in Table 1, with the model's name attached. This comparative study in terms of the user friendliness of the maturity level description, the growth path description and practicality of use as basis to rank the PM3 reveal the rankings as follows:

Table 1. PM3 ranking in terms of user-friendly level description

Ranking	PM3 Model name	Weighted Average Score	Total Score
3	OPM3	: 3.575 + 3.523 + 3.279	10.377
2	PwC	: 3.174 + 3.686 + 3.543	10.403
5	CMMi	: 2.600 + 2.875 + 3.570	9.045
4	PMMM (Crawford)	: 3.611 + 3.313 + 3.308	10.232
1	**DPM3**	: 3.679 + 3.679 + 3.679	**11.037**
-	PMMM (Kerzner)	No documentation available for study	
-	P2MM	No documentation available for study	

The top 3 ranking obtained were:

  1: DPM3
  2: PwC
  3: OPM3

Almost all (more than 90%) responded that high scores were given for the clarity of description that they described as easy to understand, advancing maturity level description and the growth path they represent. The feedback appears consistent with researchers' feedback who have consistently lamented that the PM3 maturity assessment process and terminology were unduly complex and hence an impediment to PM3 adoption (Kasse, 2004, Gan & Chin, 2018, 2019). This survey result remains consistent throughout the 8-year period of survey.

It should be noted that CMMi achieved a weighted average score of 3.570 because of the low score with a count of 7 votes out of a possible 56 votes. Feedback showed many participants did not vote for it because the model was too complex and technical for them to understand. It was thus no surprise that CMMi had to set up a CMMi university to bridge this knowledge gap to assist in its application, thus showing a tacit admission of its complexity. P2MM too had terminologies that were at times alien to those not familiar with IT/ICT and PRINCE2 applications (Gan & Chin, 2018, 2019).

The lessons learned from mistakes of past models and feedback from PM practitioners allowed the new model design to avoid the pitfalls of past models and the opportunity to capitalized on the known desirability of PM3 attributes. This allowed DPM3 to score higher on users' feedback and ranked first in terms of its total weighted average score.

MITIGATING IMPACT OF IMPEDIMENTS TO PM3

For PM3 and PM maturity assessment to be accepted in the marketplace, it is imperative that all the maturity attributes being sought should comply with or are aligned with internationally recognized recommended good practices but at the same time should also be pragmatic in application and functionally fit for purpose. The following are the recommended solutions to the identified impediments to PM performance identified in the literature review.

Misuse of "Best Practices"

Best practices are indeed useful, well-intention procedures and practices design for repetitive production, stable environment, and organization structures with familiar stakeholders. "*Best*" generally connotes that it cannot be bettered, improved nor improvised under any circumstances but when used in a project environment that is dynamic, it will likely stifle independent thinking and even curtail well considered discretion (Gan & Chin, 2018, 2019).

Best practices are thus often seen as rigid prescriptive directives out of touch with realities in the dynamic project environment, with ad hoc organization structure that are almost always set up for the purpose with very different stakeholders who may be positively and negatively impacted by the project process and project outcome.

It is far more professional to use *recommended good practice* as this will create the shift in the team thinking paradigm or mind-set to the "*get better*" mindset as Halvorson & Higgins (2013) puts it. This will motivate the team to perform better than they did, in small steps of improvement that encourage the team along the way. This enables team agility to be more flexible, agile, and better adapted to the dynamic project environment thereby enhancing their chances of PM success. This change is also consistent with continuous improvement mindset (Kaizen) that has been practices very successfully over the last three decades since 1986 (ISO21500, 2015). It is an international practice statement where team discretion is expected in terms of choice of processes, their appropriate application and rigor of use. Recommended good practices just like best practices are specified at a high level and it therefore is imperative that project team members are mentored and coached in the proper use of PM tools/ techniques at work.

This study observed that more than 900 participants (close to 75% of 1,201 surveyed) were mostly from the GLCs, SME/SMIs and a handful from MNCs admitted they simply *do not know what they do not know* until they were exposed to more effective ways of managing different aspects of a project management process. These relates to the preparation and presentation of the *project dashboard, project S curve, logical framework analysis, RACI chart, RAM Chart, forcefield analysis, communication barriers, project risk register, stakeholders register, power interest* grid to prioritize management of different type of stakeholders, *Delphi technique, Pareto principle* etc. Mentors share their work experience in applying the tools and how they use them under varying circumstances is critical to accelerating team performance.

Break Free From Routine Conditioning
That Causes Brain Barriers

Processes and procedures are laid out when all structures and operational matters are stabilized and calibrated for optimal performance in a static environment. These processes and procedures should be followed as they were designed for optimal performance as long as processes, structures, facilitators, and environment remain constant.

Over time, the processes followed become routine and they become second nature, and habitual, just like what experienced drivers do when driving their car using the subconscious mind, habits that tend to create *brain-barriers*. It is a condition that prevents the team members from thinking nor seeing the obvious, the need to change when circumstances change right before their eyes. When project situations change, what was appropriate then may not be appropriate now and so it pays for top-management to introduce a mandatory procedure to conduct an independent review of the processes or set of procedures every time there is a change to continually ensure its continued relevance or else what could be done about it. This prevents brain barriers becoming a PM impediment.

Imperative to Differentiate Project
Purpose Failures From PM Failures

Project purpose failures and PM failures should be differentiated so that each stage is separately identified with the assigned management responsibility. In this way, all project stages at the idea development that involves strategy formulation, feasibility study, design for purpose are segregated from the construction or implementation stage where PM approaches are applied. The PM stage where the PM expertise is applied to manage the initiative in accordance with the given scope, schedule, cost, risk exposure, effective resource usage and ensuring stakeholder expectations are met (Figure 5.1).

The stages before construction/implementation are largely management functions that rarely involve PM services. They relate to setting the organizational vision, strategic formulation, problem statement and imperatives to overcome or fulfill a strategic intent.

These purposes are summarized in a project charter as a mandate for the project manager using PM approach to lead and produce the required outcome in alignment with the organizational goal but not responsible for the effectiveness of the purpose in meeting that organizational goal.

Figure 1. Development stages for large-scale projects

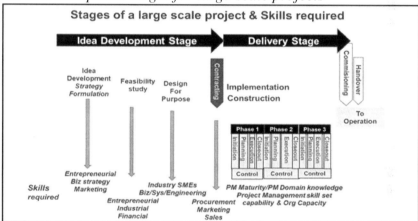

In this way when projects fail, the failures can be separately attributed with cause and effect isolated so that lessons could be learned to continuously reduce the number of project failures thus improving organizational performance. In essence, top management should accept responsibility for the results of their project development relating to:

- The quality of their decision,
- Strategies they defined and
- Clarity of their purpose statement when initiating a project
- How the project purpose would align to which strategic imperative
- How the anticipated project benefits would and can be realized

By this way, the project manager is made *accountable* specific to the PM responsibilities like:

- Ensuring project baselines are realistic and achievable
- Delivering the project outcome in accordance with project specification,
- Ensure project purpose alignment with organizational strategy,
- Delivering the project within approved baseline of scope, schedule, and cost,
- Effective management of project risk exposure
- Effective management of project resources
- Ensuring key stakeholder expectations are met

More Attention Should be Given to the Human Side of PM

The human factor is critical in management of projects. It has been observed that *"project managers spent 90% of their time in communication and typically identify communication-related issues as the problem they face most frequently in projects"* (Mulcahy, 2015, p.45). Since people are at the heart of PM, it is of critical importance to understand human behavior, how we tend to respond to given stimuli, what motivate or demotivate us and the people we manage, how people decide the way they do and what drives their action so that the mature project managers is better enable to use the more effective approach to motivate and manage their team and engage with all pertinent stakeholders more effectively.

"In the realms of managing people, everything we do is aimed at application, helping people do the work they need to do" (Senge et. al,1999). *"There is also a strong correlation between the "soft" stuff and shareholder returns"* (McKinsey Quarterly, Sep 2014). *"The top 2% of successful project managers spent more than 90% of their time in communication"* (PMBok, 2017).

So, although it seems obvious that people are the key drivers of projects, the human side of PM maturity did not seem to feature in 3 of the 6 PM3s studied in this research. Instead, they seem to just focus on processes and how well the organization provides the project facilitators, tools, techniques, artefacts and how conducive they provide the environment to support their PM effort.

Another obstacle to PM practices was the notion of the "*one right way to manage people*" which Drucker (1999 p.5) described as *a practice having outlived their usefulness*. The familiar theory of leadership styles whether from the trait school, behavioral school, contingency school, visionary school, relationship school or transformation leadership schools, all did not adequately explain how their theory in isolation would apply and work in practice especially in a project environment.

People in projects are drawn together (with many for the first time) to work on a project with a varied group of stakeholders often with conflicting interest, different cultures, languages, work habits, attitudes and varying levels of seniority and experience. How each leadership style could lead this myriad groups of people effectively is open to question as it would be like proposing to have *one size fits all* fallacy.

Each leadership style proponent seems to suggest a mutually exclusive use of their approach instead of being more inclusive preferring to use the leadership style that is more appropriate for each target group and subgroup.

PM practitioners in the larger PM consulting organizations recognize leadership as a two-way street. While recognizing the need to know their target audience personality profile, they also recognize they themselves also have their own natural behavioral style. Hence, they need to adapt their behavioral style to suit the situation to be more effective in communicating with clients and stakeholders. The common use of Dominance, Influence, Steadiness and Conscientiousness (DISC) personality profiling tools and dozens of others are tacit recognition of the complexity of our personality and human behavior that challenges effective communication that (Sigmund Freud, n. d) explained as driven by our innate drives and needs.

In addition, the project teams assembled to undertake the project will have develop their team and mature over the project duration. Will standard leadership style proposed be relevant for all stages of the team level of maturity or will it be more appropriate to use the Tuckman Ladder (1965, 1977) approach where the team at each advancing level of maturity from *forming, storming, norming, performing* to *adjourning* stages be better led by the corresponding role of a *leader, facilitator, coach, collaborator* or *reviewer* as described in PMBok 6th Ed (2017, p. 338) or should it be best left to the project manager on how best to utilize the various combination as they deem appropriate ?

Balanced Skill Sets Tend to Outperform Imbalanced Skill Sets

The need for a balanced skill set that progressively improves over time is preferred over strength in one but ignorance in others (Gan & Chin, 2019). This view is prevalent as project managers are often seen as a specialist in PM but otherwise a generalist with the main function of coordinating and planning with a team of technical and subject matter experts, a skill sometimes referred to as the "*T*" skill. PMI acquisition (9th Aug 2019) of "*Disciplined Agile*" is a testament to PMI strong belief in balance skill sets between the predictive to the adaptive or hybrid approach to the management of change and it is based on the belief that Mark Lines said, "*every organization is different and within each organization, there are different ways of working*" (PMI, 2019). In short, a balanced skill set is needed to be able to adapt and be flexible to manage the project and its environmental dynamics.

The complexity involved in measuring PM maturity, the evolution of the PM profession and the impediments to project performance drawn from the literatures review and survey feedback collected over the 8 years to Mar 2019. It suggestive to relook at existing PM3 designs that pay more attention to understanding of people behavior and people management, their approach and structure together with its assessment tools, terminology and definitions that provide more people orientation, understanding and usage but without compromising the PM3 functionality, meaning and purpose.

Project Managers Should be Appointed as Early as is Feasible

Project managers should be appointed as early as is feasible, preferably during the project chartering but latest at the start of the project planning (PMBok 6th Ed, 2015) so that they can gain a foundational understanding of the project before they commence with the overall project plan. This also enables them to be in a better position to manage and control the variation order requests that are likely throughout the project progress.

The project managers should be involved and in control of the overall PM planning process since they are accountable for the eventual overall PM outcome. Accountability should commensurate only with the level of authority given. For instance, should the budget allocated to the project be inadequate, the project managers should be allowed to *"challenge"* the feasibility of the budget allocated with facts and figures to justify their rationale or otherwise to revisit the scope of work for scope reduction and consequential timeline adjustments.

While it is acceptable for project managers to be allocated a team, it should also be reasonable for them to recommend removal of specific team members for lack of performance in accordance with the organization's competency framework. Unless reasonably refuted, the recommendations should be followed through without undue delay so that the project is not unduly burdened by incompetence that inevitably results in quality issues, cost and schedule overrun.

Project Managers Should be Vetted for Prerequisites Before Assignment

Many projects failed often because of multiple factors. More than half of PM participants surveyed were handicapped by their own lack of hard skills such as business acumen, and lack of exposure to business and industry. With computer applications being used and the dynamic project environment, which unfortunately will impact the project managers overall approach to the project plan, time management, sense of urgency, failure to understand the gravity of impending issues, inadequate attention to project risk, inappropriate or inadequate engagement of key stakeholders, and failure to foresee impending crisis. Hence, unprepared when they happened and worse still when several were to happen at the same time.

To succeed in projects, there is unfortunately little room for shortcuts. Mature project managers ensure they personally meet the project prerequisites before accepting the project engagement or else seek additional management support to mitigate their shortcomings. The major management consulting organizations and MNCs engaged in project deliveries provide project prerequisites checklist and some include this in their RAM chart. Mature program managers or project directors ensure the prerequisites are met before the project manager is involved.

The big leap forward came with the publications of PMBok 5th Ed (2013) and its later update in June 2015. Verbal questions on significant factors affecting project performance were again asked at each of the monthly 5-day PMP exam preparation boot camps for Yes/No answers after the end of each of the 13 chapters taught. This version confirmed what were already anticipated that project managers not only need the exposure but also the business acumen to understand and appreciate how decisions were made, how to differentiate between alternatives available and the leadership quality that was so badly needed to lead and motivate the team to perform at their highest potential. The publication of PMI latest research work on the PM talent triangle will be discussed and feedback obtained to gauge its market acceptance level.

CONCLUSION

The results surveyed clearly show high scores *for user friendliness, flexibility, adaptability, and fitness for use* as a PM maturity assessment tool and how the organization and its project managers were assessed. These factors appear to dictate the level of user buy-in and by extension, its level of PM3 adoption. The top desirable attributes and patterns appear consistent throughout the subsequent years of surveys conducted. With the lessons learned from mistakes of past models and feedback from PM practitioners allowed the new model design to avoid the pitfalls of past models and the opportunity to capitalized on the known desirability of PM3 attributes. It suggestive to relook at existing PM3 designs to have more emphasis in understanding people behavior and management, approach and structure with its assessment tools, terminology and definitions that provide more people orientation, understanding and usage but without compromising the PM3 functionality, meaning and purpose.

REFERENCES

Crawford, J. K. (2007), Project Management Maturity Model *2nd Ed*, Auerback Publications, Drucker, P.F, (1999), *Management Challenges for the 21st Century*. Harper Collins.

Gan, R. C. C., & Chin, C. M. M. (2018). Components of project management maturity impacting project, programme, portfolio and organisational success. In Karayaz, G., & Silvius, G. (Eds.), *Developing Organizational Maturity for Effective Project Management* (pp. 128–152). IGI Global., DOI: 10.4018/978-1-5225-3197-5.ch007

Gan, R. C. C., & Chin, C. M. M. (2019). Project management guide and project management maturity models as generic tools capable for diverse applications. In Katuu, S. (Ed.), *Diverse Applications and Transferability of Maturity Models* (pp. 269–315). IGI Global., DOI: 10.4018/978-1-5225-7080-6.ch011

Halvorson, H. G., & Higgins, E. T. (2013). *Focus, use different ways of seeing the world for success and influence*. Penguin Group.

Kasse, T. (2004). *Practical Insights into CMMi*. Artech House Computing Library.

McKinsey, Q. (2014, September 1). Tom Peters on leading the 21st - century organization. McKinsey & Company. https://www.mckinsey .com/capabilities/people-and-organizational-performance/our-insights/ tom-peters-on-leading-the-21st-century-organization

Mulcahy, R. (2015). PMP Exam Prep Book (8th Ed). RMC Publications Inc. International Standard Publication 21500 (2021), *Project, programme and portfolio management: Context and concepts*, (2nd Ed). International Standard Publication

ADDITIONAL READING

Kerzner, H. (2019). *Using the Project Management Maturity Model: Strategic Planning for Project Management* (3rd ed.). Wiley.

Zwikael, O., & Smyrk, J. (2011). *Project Management for the Creation of Organisational Value*. Springer.DOI: 10.1007/978-1-84996-516-3

KEY TERMS AND DEFINITIONS

Accountable: It refers to individuals who are ultimately responsible for ensuring the deliverables and completion of the project successfully. For example, in a project environment, project managers are made accountable for specific responsibilities such as ensuring project baselines are realistic and achievable, delivering project outcome in accordance with project specifications etc.

Best Practices: Refer to the most effective and widely accepted methods, techniques or processes for achieving the desirable results.

Brain-Barriers: Due to the routine processes followed over time, it become second nature and habitual creating it. These barriers can impact project success, preventing effective observation on the circumstances or adapting to changes.

Fitness for Use: It is the degree to which the model or tool meets the requirements and expectations of its intended purpose.

Imbalance: This refers to where a team member or project manager lacks the necessary combination of skills required to execute the project. Hence, it may lead to weak project management knowledge, skills gap in critical areas, inefficiencies etc.

User Friendliness: It refers to how easy for users of the tool (such as team members, stakeholders) to understand, navigate, apply the model effectively. The model needs to feature aspects such as ease of use, flexibility and adaptability, simple and clear.

Chapter 6
Conceptualization of Duplex Project Management Maturity Model

ABSTRACT

Upon leveraging the desirable attributes of PM3 from Chapter 5, this discussion continues to describe the conceptualization of DPM3. This chapter explains each evolution of the DPM3 principles that was initially depicted using the pictorial diagram of a bicycle. Followed by describing a 5-level model structure to illustrate the stage of project manager maturity level identified as Accidental, Enlightened, Competent, Expert and Authority. Concluding the chapter with explanation of the operating principles that includes having balanced skills, matching capabilities, maturity, adaptability as a leader and flexibility for a dynamic environment. There are also two major drivers identified that are the organization with constraints in terms of environmental and facilitators and project managers skills in terms of hard and soft skills.

DOI: 10.4018/979-8-3693-1439-5.ch006

CONCEPTUALIZATION OF DPM3

The MPM3 (Malaysian PM3) model originally had more than 360 PM maturity assessment questions largely based on PMBok 3rd Ed (2004) and supplemented by 15-years PM experience that the author gained implementing projects and 3 years as principal consultant and consulting manager in two of the then big 5 PM global consulting organization.

The PM3 model, MPM3 had an initial 383 response requirements but was renamed DPM3 for two reasons:

1. *To reflect the expanded scope covering not only Malaysia but also the countries in the ASEAN region (Association of Southeast Asian Nations) due to the international nature of staff composition of organizations surveyed.*
2. *Almost all organizations surveyed, whether large or small and medium size had project teams that were either multi-culture, global or regional in scope or had members with international experience and exposure making it impossible to isolate attributes that were truly Malaysian.*

The search for duplication of ideas carried out resulted in some reduction in the number of assessment questions. It was again refined, after conclusion of an expert-witness program (independent subject matter expert engaged by the respective parties to the litigation, to show relevant information that have a reliable foundation and admissible in arbitration and court proceedings) and in an in-house training program conducted for government linked company (GLC) involved in government special projects with 22 participants tasked with:

- Reviving abandoned projects of the private sector that involve many buyers.
- Rescue of troubled projects related to government initiatives.
- Lead/oversee public infrastructure projects to mitigate traffic jams & ease traffic flow.

It was discovered that organizations with failed projects were too ambitious by undertaking too many projects far beyond their means even during the boom period. This was also consistent with Dr Syed Naguib Syed Abu Bakar's (2016), a known Malaysian expert in project rescue who made the same assertions during his keynote address at the PMI Malaysia Chapter International Symposium in Oct 2016. According to him, the causes were attributed to weak financial skills such as:

- Unrealistic cash flow projections
- Unrealistic schedule baselines
- Weak financial capacity to withstand the recession (late 1990s)
- Poor financial planning
- Over stretched team creating stress over too long periods.

Dr. Syed (2016) also found causes due to poor PM which he cited as:

1. Unclear, ambiguous, or incomplete scope statement
2. No client expectations were set or agreed at the project start.
3. No clear role delineation.
4. RACI chart were not used to record who were responsible, accountable and when needed who could be consulted and who should be informed
5. Client's roles and responsibilities were not clearly understood
6. Performing organization role were not adequately explained
7. Client team commitment to the project were unrealistic in view of their routine commitments
8. Timing of their respective individual's availability were not adequately planned out
9. Client team expectations were not adequately managed through the project life cycle
10. Project contingencies were not planned for inclusion in the project cost baseline

The above resulted in an expanded DPM3 survey questionnaire.

Pictorial Representation of DPM3 Principles

The initial idea was how best could the PM process be depicted using a pictorial diagram which communication experts recommend are much more effective than written or spoken words, or use of a common object that could illustrate the concept of PM, a time-bound initiative to move from an **AS-IS** status to the **TO-BE** status. Transportation seems the most obvious, but transportation could be accomplished by 2 wheelers, three wheelers or four-wheel-drive or even a long truck or trailer.

There were also many stakeholders in a project but a careful study using the test of significance resulted in focus on the prime movers of the project. Who were the real significant players that lead and drive a project? There were in essence two key players, the performing organization that provides the facilitators and environment and the project manager who leads and manages the project. The simple artwork of a bicycle was seen as a good fit to illustrate the desired conceptual framework but eventually the idea of a real bicycle was more complete to use as an illustration (Figure 1).

Figure 1. Pictorial diagram to illustrate DPM3 model development

The bicycle model with spokes in the first-year report remain unchanged but the spokes were limited to 2x5 to depict the 2 types of attributes (hard skill and soft skill), each type limited to the top 5 significant attributes required of a mature project manager and 2 types of attributes (environment and facilitators) of the performing organization.

More clarity was derived from further reading and refinement of thoughts made possible by self-reflection and internal arguments focused on explaining a complex subject where project dynamics were always at play and do often derail the unsuspecting project manager. The focus was on how the idea could be simplified further so that it is made easier to understand and relate wholly thereby bringing more value to the business and PM community.

The samples to be surveyed were better stratified to give more representation to significant industries like power and energy and include not-for-profit organizations and the government sector.

The name changed from Malaysian to Duplex PM Maturity model was also to avoid country fixation with extreme limitation of scope as well as giving the model a prefix "Duplex" to reflect its core identity of a two-entity contribution of project success, the organization that provides the resources and environment to the project endeavor and the project manager who drives the project.

The inappropriate imbalance maturity between the organization and the project manager that could lead to eventual failure was best illustrated by the Penny farthing bicycle (on the left) that has been totally replaced by the common bicycle (on the right) with 2 balanced wheel set (Figure 2).

Figure 2. Pictorial diagram on the need for wheel balance

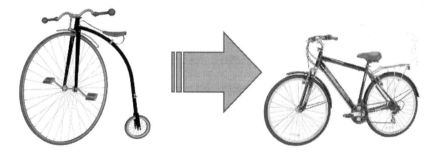

The model was again changed from a *manual bicycle to a motorized version* (Figure 3) to illustrate the modern day need for technical enablers, digitization, and automation and imbued flexibility through modular designs that could minimize the impact of an era of disruptive change.

Figure 3. Pictorial diagram from a bicycle to a motorized bike

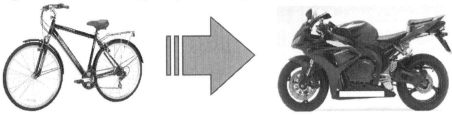

The 5 Fundamental Levels of DPM3 Maturity

A 5-level model structure seems appropriate as seen from the stages of growth project managers go through in their career lifecycle. Then the choice of the description of the maturity level was needed but had to be easy to understand to gain market acceptance, an easy common understanding of each level, intuitive in differentiating each level and their possible capability and how each level would relate to the level below or level above it.

The search for simplicity and clarity of terms easy for the layman to understand each stage of maturity was refined and respective stage identified as **Accidental** project manager, to **Enlightened, Competent, Expert** and at the epitome of PM career as an **Authority** about PM (Figure 4).

The level improvement for each level to the next was pitched to be an approximate equidistance between the levels so that scores between zero to 20 = Accidental level, 21 – 40 = Enlightened, 41 to 60 = Competent, 61 to 80 = Expert and 80 + score as being an Authority about PM.

Figure 4. The 5 levels of DPM3 maturity

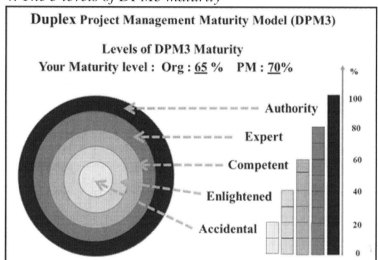

The 5 Principles of DPM3

DPM3 Maturity Model's 5 Operating Principles

1. ***Need for a Balanced skill sets*** where rounded skill sets like a wheel provides a smoother ride. Each wheel is supported by 10 equal spoke lengths where each spoke represents a maturity component.

Figure 5. DPM3 maturity 10 spoke wheels

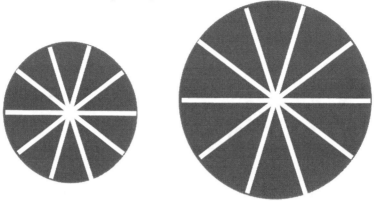

DPM3 uses a 2-wheel model with 10 spokes that lengthens with corresponding wheel size to depict maturity growth. One wheel representing the project manager (front wheel) and the organization (back wheel) as per Figure 5. As the components mature, the spokes lengthened increasing the wheel parameter that travel a greater distance (effectiveness, efficiency and capacity) per revolution.

2. ***Need for matching capabilities***.

Matching capabilities of project manager and their organizational capability and capacity. Their relative maturity may be unequal but should not be so significantly different to make it difficult to coordinate, synchronize and manage just like the Penny Farthing of old which was very quickly phased out.

3. ***Maturity increases capabilities***

Growth in maturity should be targeted based on the organizational need and preference and all done as a gradual process where all components are nurtured to grow at the same time to achieve a balanced growth that allow the maturity to enlarge but remain rounded along the way.

A larger wheel travels a greater distance for every wheel rotation and hence increases in general capability and capacity. The attainment of maturity should be proportional so that the maturity components are well rounded and complementary thus facilitating coordination, synchronization and control.

4. *Adaptable leadership*

One of the key success ingredients is for the project manager to be able to continuously lead and adapt to the ever-changing environment and situational dynamics expected in a project work by adapting and constantly moving forward and steering to navigate the project in the desired direction, negotiating turns and circumventing bums along the way to eventually accomplish the project purpose alignment with strategic intent and organizational goal.

5. *Digitized/motorized/mechanized model*

DPM3 use of the digitized/motorized motor bike (Figure 6) was added in the latest version to depict the need for resilience in ideas, innovation, capability to evolve and adapt with in-built flexibility to adapt to the dynamic project environment and be in tune with the disruptive technologies of the 5th industrial revolution, an era where the "*fast fish eats the slow fish*" stated by Klaus Schwab, Founder & Executive chairman of the World Economic Forum (2018).

Figure 6. The 5 principles of DPM3

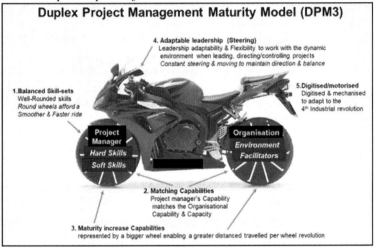

The 2 Key Drivers of DPM3

There are 2 major drivers in PM are (see Table 1):

1. **The Organization** with **5 Environment constraints** and **5 Facilitators**
2. The **Project manager** is the key driver of the project and to be successful they need to possess the **5 main Hard skills** and **5 main Soft skills.**

Table 1. The components of DPM3 maturity model DPM3 components of PM maturity

	Project Manager's Components		Organization's Components
Hard Skills	H1: PM Process Understanding	Environmental	E1: Project Organization Structure / Culture / Governance
	H2: PM Knowledge Sufficiency		E2: Leadership Support
	H3: Business Acumen		E3: Management Attitude to Risk
	H4: Exposure to Business / Industry / Application / Environment		E4: Reward Alignment
	H5: Technical Domain Skill		E5: Organizational Capacity

continued on following page

Table 1. Continued

	Project Manager's Components		Organization's Components
Soft skills	S1: Communication Skill	Facilitators	F1: Standardization
	S2: Leadership Skill		F2: PM Operating procedures
	S3: Negotiation Skill		F3: PMIS Sufficiency
	S4: Adaptability & Flexibility		F4: PMIS Availability
	S5: Conflict Management Skill		F5: Sufficiency in PM Tools & Techniques

Environmental Components of DPM3

These are 5 environmental components that are related to the organizational environment that may impact the project manager's performance and affect decision drivers and motivation of the project team. These are:

E1: Project Organization Structure / Culture / Governance
E2: Leadership Support
E3: Management Attitude to Risk
E4: Reward Alignment
E5: Organizational capacity

Facilitating Components of DPM3 That are Organizational

The 5 facilitating components that the performing organization provides may be adequate thus facilitating the project work or inadequate thus frustrating the project manager's performance at the workplace. These are:

F1: Standardization
F2: PM Operating procedures
F3: PMIS Sufficiency
F4: PMIS Availability
F5: Sufficiency in PM Tools & Techniques

The Project Manager's Hard-Skill Maturity Components

The 5 hard-skill components that the project manager should possess and how they can be built up from Accidental level to be one of authority are:

H1: PM Process Understanding
H2: PM Knowledge Sufficiency
H3: Business Acumen
H4: Exposure to Business / Industry / Application / Environment
H5: Technical Domain Skill

The Project Manager's Soft-Skill Maturity Components

The 5 soft-skill components the project manager should possess and how they can be built up from Accidental level to one of authority are:

S1: Communication Skill
S2: Leadership Skill
S3: Negotiation Skill
S4: Adaptability & Flexibility
S5: Conflict Management Skill

These are the pathways to hone the essential skills needed to better understand the human aspects of managing projects. A summary of the top 10 desired attributes of PM3s were used to measure how well the current PM3 met the desired attributes and tabulated for easy comparison and as a basis to refine DPM3. The comparatives below (Table 2) serve as a guide.

Table 2. *Comparative review of PM3 models (for user friendly attributes)*

	Comparative review of the PM3 models :												
	Desired PM3 attributes	PM3 Attributes being studied and assessed					PM3 Model scores where 1 = Low and 5 = High score						
		Low desirability ------------------------------------ High desirability					DPM3	CMMi	OPM3	KPMMM	PMMM		P2MM
		1	2	3	4	5			PMI	Kerzner	Crawford	PwC	PRINCE2
1	PM3 Maturity level desciption												
	Is intuitive & User friendly	Accidental	Enlightened	Competent	Expert	Authority	5						
	Staged	Initial	Managed	Defined	Quantitative Managed	Optimised		1					
	Continuos representation	Performed	Managed	Defined	Quantitative Managed	Optimised			1				
		Standardised	Measure	Control	Continuosly improve	-				1			
		Common Lanaguge	Common Processes	Singular Methodology	Bench Marking	Continuos Deveelopment					3		
		Initial Process	Structured	Org. Std	Managed process	Optimised						1	
		Unrealiable	Informed	Standardised	Monitored	Optimised							1
2	Maturity growth path/progression	Prescriptive		Step approach		Appropriate gradual progression	5	1	3	3	2	3	3
3	Independent of PM Methodology	Dependent				Independent	5	3	4	3	3	1	1
4	Maturity impact Org performance	Possible negative correlation				Positive correlation only	5	1	5	5	4	5	5
5	Capable of generic application	Specific	Limited			Applicable across all industries	5	1	5	5	5	5	2
6	Easy to understand & apply	Technical & Complex				Easy & intuitive to understand	5	1	3	3	3	5	4
7	Follow naturally occuring evidence	Do not follow natural work flow				Follow natural work flow	5	3	4	4	4	4	4
8	Use of common PM terminology	Little commonality			Follow ISO21500/PMBok 6th Ed		5	1	5	4	4	5	4
9	Affordable cost of implementation	High cost				Low cost	5	1	1	3	4	3	4
10	Assess People/Process/System	Assess 1 only		Assess 2	Assess all including people skills		5	2	2	5	2	4	5

CONCLUSION

DPM3 illustrate this user-friendly terminology by showing how *accidental* project managers can move up the PM3 maturity scale first by themselves being *enlighten*, then becoming *competent* in managing projects, before becoming an expert and if they wish to and capable, become an *authority* in the PM profession capable of representing the interest of the PM profession at all levels of industry, commerce, society and government. The lessons learned from the literature review and survey results and incorporated in the DPM3 model has led it to achieve top score in comparison with the other 7 PM3 models reviewed.

REFERENCES

Gan, R. C. C., & Chin, C. M. M. (2018). Components of project management maturity impacting project, programme, portfolio and organisational success. In Karayaz, G., & Silvius, G. (Eds.), *Developing Organizational Maturity for Effective Project Management* (pp. 128–152). IGI Global., DOI: 10.4018/978-1-5225-3197-5.ch007

Gan, R. C. C., & Chin, C. M. M. (2019). Project management guide and project management maturity models as generic tools capable for diverse applications. In Katuu, S. (Ed.), *Diverse Applications and Transferability of Maturity Models* (pp. 269–315). IGI Global., DOI: 10.4018/978-1-5225-7080-6.ch011

Project Management Institute (PMI). (2004). *A guide to project management body of knowledge* (PMBOK Guide) (3rd ed). Project Management Institute.

Schwab, K. (2018). *The Global Competitiveness Report*, World Economic Forum 2018. https://www3.weforum.org/docs/GCR2018/05FullReport/TheGlobalCompetitivenessReport2018.pdf

ADDITIONAL READING

Avença, I., Domingues, L., & Carvalho, H. (2023). Project Managers soft skills influence in knowledge sharing. *Procedia Computer Science*, *219*, 1705–1712. DOI: 10.1016/j.procs.2023.01.464

Crawford, J. K. (2021). *Project Management Maturity Model: Providing a Proven Path to Project Management Excellence* (4th ed.). Auerbach Publications. DOI: 10.1201/9781003129523

Müller, R., Drouin, N., & Sankaran, S. (2019). Modeling Organizational Project Management. *Project Management Journal*, *50*(4), 499–513. DOI: 10.1177/8756972819847876

Sohi, A. J., Bosch-Rekveldt, M., & Hertogh, M. (2020). Four stages of making project management flexible: insight, importance, implementation and improvement. *Organization, Technology and Management in Construction: an International Journal,* Sciendo, Vol. 12 (Issue 1),) pp. 2117-2136. DOI: 10.2478/otmcj-2020-0008

KEY TERMS AND DEFINITIONS

Business Acumen: It refers to the ability to understand and apply business knowledge effectively in strategic decision making. The kills of business acumen include financial literacy, market awareness, operational insight and problem solving in the project environment.

Project Management Information System (PMIS): This is a centralized system to help project manager to plan, execute, monitor and control project activities. It provides real time information for ease of monitoring on the project execution activities and support decision-making among stakeholders. There are many examples of PMIS in the market such as Primavera, Asana, Jira, MS Project etc.

RACI Chart: This is also known as Responsible, Accountable, Consulted and Informed chart that is a project management tool used to define roles and responsibilities for tasks, activities and deliverables within a project. Within a form of a matrix chart, it helps clarifies each team member's roles and responsibilities, minimizing task ownership confusion, miscommunication and improves project performance and execution.

Section 5

Duplex Project Management Maturity Model (DPM3)

Chapter 7
Principals, Components, Characteristics, and Levels of DPM3

ABSTRACT

By leveraging on the literature reviews, interviews and survey data collected throughout the last 8 years, this research proposes a new approach to measure organizational maturity using the Duplex PM Maturity Model (DPM3) with the objective of enhancing organizational performance. The DPM3 model and its components is best illustrated by using the analogy of a motorcycle with 2 wheels, with both wheels rotate to accomplish work and grow as the skill-components grow and mature with a need to always paddle and steer to keep in balance and adapt to the dynamic project environment. The front wheel represents the project manager while the back wheel represents the organization. Each wheel is supported by 10 equal spoke lengths, and each spoke represents a maturity component.

OPERATING PRINCIPLES OF DPM3

The DPM3 model is based on 5 operating principles and 5 levels of maturity (Gan & Chin, 2018, 2019). It assesses the organization and the project manager using naturally occurring observable verifiable indicators along the PM life cycle processes and PM knowledge group assessment outcomes to gauge the conduciveness of the project environment (con-

DOI: 10.4018/979-8-3693-1439-5.ch007

straints), adequacy of facilitators (enablers) and the general capability of the project manager assigned.

The maturity scores are placed under 4 component groups of PM maturity namely Environmental factors and Facilitators (Enablers), Hard-skills and Soft-skills. The following section in this chapter elaborates in detail the DPM3 model and its components. The two motorcycle wheels rotate to accomplish work and grow as the skill-components mature and become more effective to accomplish more with the same effort and the need to constantly use the handle to steer, keep direction and balance thus depicting the need for adaptability as the circumstances dictate.

The front wheel represents the project manager while the back wheel represents the organization, and each wheel is supported by 10 equal spoke lengths and each spoke represents a maturity component. As the components mature, the spokes lengthened and increase the wheel radius that will travel a greater distance per revolution depicting greater effectiveness and efficiency per unit of effort.

The 5 PM maturity principles are

- **Balanced skill sets** where 10 equal spoke lengths represent the 10 DPM3 components (skill sets) in a wheel that is round to provides a smoother ride. Project managers in mature organizations tasked with leading the project are expected to be "*rounded individuals*" specialized in PM but otherwise a generalist in all the other disciplines. This horizontal part of the "T" skills relates to the need for wide experience and exposure working across multi disciplines and industries that enable individual to be more rounded to better understand, communicate, coordinate, plan and control team of various technical disciplines and experience. Lack of such balance skill set impede the project manager ability to cope, adapt and be flexible to manage the project (Gan & Chin, 2019), just like how *science work because of the balance it struck between open and close mindedness i.e. science should be stable but should never stand still* (Kuhn, 1962).
- **Balanced capabilities** of project manager and the project organization to facilitate coordination and synchronization of resources, ef-

forts, and utilization. Their relative maturity may be unequal, but it should not be so significantly different to make it difficult to manage just like the Penny-farthing bicycle, which was quickly phased out.

- **Maturity increases capabilities.** As maturity increases, so will the radius of the wheel. The larger the wheel radius, the greater distance with it travels per wheel rotation (depicting the capability to accomplish more with the same effort or resource).
- **Adaptable leadership** to steer the project, adapting and maintaining direction and focusing on the project's purpose and strategic intent to be able to cope with the environmental dynamics of the 5th industrial revolution.
- **Automation** depicts dependence on automation, digitization, and adaptability to the disruptive environmental dynamics of the 5th industrial revolution. This principle was added to the Gan & Chin model proposed in 2018.

COMPONENTS OF DPM3 MATURITY

Project managers need to understand the purpose or reason for the project and ensure the initiation process is well planned to meet the purpose at the start. To accomplish this, they are to ensure the project purpose is fully understood, expectations are set and agreed, the project plan is realistic and achievable, and the client fully understands their commitments made and the implications on their routine work commitments.

The client project team members must juggle their time constraints and agree about their time commitments or else they may need to be assisted to justify their management on some level of delegation of their routine functions. Then ensure the project contract has been signed off and notice given to start.

Mature project managers plan their project (except for project rescue when the project needs to be rebase-lined) based on facts available, realistic assumptions and achievable targets. They document their risk management plan for facts required but unknown with realistic assumptions and rationale stated of their risk management strategy taken and appropriate contingency reserves estimated and later summarized and in total, added to the project estimation to arrive at the project total baseline.

Smooth execution of projects also requires careful initiation and realistic planning throughout the project life cycle while keeping a close watch of significant project details focused on the project purpose or goal. It is often said, "*if we do not learn from our mistakes, we are bound to repeat them*". It is the ability to gain insights and leverage on these lessons learned that will go a long way to enhancing the project manager's PM maturity.

All PM functions must in essence be carried out in unison with the PM control function and coordinated to ensure harmonious progress in project activities. Action to address, correct, change, or even delay specific activities must be as prompt and coordinated to ensure the integrated whole is not compromised. The wisdom to change what can be changed, accept what cannot and the wisdom to know the difference aptly apply. The components of PM maturity generically described to allow multi-industry experts to apply and communicate as detailed in Table 4.1

Project Manager's Hard-Skills Components

The project manager is a "*knowledge worker and as such, should know more about their job than their boss does, more than anybody else in the organization*" (Drucker, 1999). Being an expert in one's own field, the project manager must thus be a hard skill specialist in the PM process, life cycle and details in each of the PM domain knowledge (initiation, planning, execution, control and closeout) in order to apply them in any way or form, a general standard laid out in ISO 21500 (Zandhuis, 2012).

This research work classifies these skills as hard skills, learned in formal PM education classes but sub-groups into PM domain knowledge, PM 10 knowledge areas, business acumen (some of it can arguably be inborne traits), general exposure to technical work knowledge or disciplines learned in universities like engineering, quantity surveying, architecture, management (particularly PM), law and accountancy etc.

However, it must be noted that good project performance cannot be predicted by the number of degrees the project manager holds nor the amount of formal management education they had but dependent upon the experience, knowledge and skills they personally acquired at work that involve *leading, changing, developing or working with people* that are vital in their management career progression (Livingston, 1971). He reiterated that "*tasks that are the most important in getting results were usually left to be learned on the job, where few managers ever master them simply because no one teaches them how*".

Based on author's own personal work experience in Malaysia and overseas, those with the experience were too well paid to bother about teaching and those in teaching were too afraid to venture into industry for want of experience, less they be shown to be out of touch with real work life and all these unfortunately continues to perpetuate a vicious cycle of ignorance.

As Livingston puts it, "*respondent behavior is learning how to solve a given problem that required analytical ability in class and that is the easy part. The challenge is in identifying the problem and exploiting the opportunities at the workplace that require decision making based on facts gathered by someone else. Operant behavior (can only be developed by doing what needs to be done) is quite different and something not taught or shared in the classroom*". In consequence, the new inexperience project manager is often faced with analysis paralysis.

Fear of making a wrong decision in the face of incomplete information freezes their logical mind to the point of indecision, which is worse, inevitably causing project delays and cost overrun. A decision in the face of incomplete information could be right and even if it is wrong, once discovered, enable corrections to be made to move forward rather indecision that causes inevitable delay. Such is the case with management of projects where data and information are never ever complete and hence the need for educated assumptions to be made. It is then strategized on how best to deal with those uncertainties and make specific reserves or provisions to address them should they be wrong. This as a result the change initiative to move forward. These PM domain skills or knowledge are described below.

H1(a) PM Domain Knowledge in the Planned Approach (PM Process Understanding)

Initiation Domain

When initiating a project, the following are the imperatives to enhance the chances of PM success:

- A clear distinction should be made as to who is responsible for the design-for-purpose (e.g. Sydney Opera house as an iconic structure) and who is responsible for the construction thereof (a separate party). Alternatively, is it a Design-and-Built project? Where the project is a Design-Built-Operate contract, was it negotiated as 3 separate stages? Each stage requires a separate sign-off thus allowing a clean handover from Design to construction and from Construction to commissioning for operation team to takeover, a practice that is recommended to reduce project risk exposure.
- Expectations of both performing organization and the client are set, realistic and achievable.
- The client fully understood their roles and responsibilities as well as their implications
- Ensuring client team and individuals fully understand their time commitments to the project in the light of their current and expected daily operational routines. This is often overlooked with painful consequences.
- Ensuring the time commitments to the projects are clearly specified in terms of when, how long, all as per calendar dates taking note of public and organization holidays, their time-off, leave planned, non-project training already pre-planned and any other prior time commitments. For example, the use of RACI (Responsibility, Accountability, Consulted and Informed) and RAM (Responsibility Assignment Matric) chart is helpful.
- Project contract has been signed-off and notice to start is given. Else, management approval must be obtained, and implication fully understood and documented before any project resource is mobilized.

Planning Domain

Teamwork involving many parties, multi-discipline, multi-culture, and multi-phase require planning that is formalized, systematic, holistically coordinated and synchronized following internationally recognized recommended good practices. Mature project organizations should plan their projects based on facts available, realistic assumptions and achievable targets. They document their plans and underlying assumptions with rationale behind every decision or approach to be taken and plan for appropriate reserves or project contingencies for these known or anticipated unknowns before arriving at their cost baselines and duly agreed as the basis to manage their project. A mature project manager should be able to articulate their requirements and gain management support or avoid any arguments that create mistrust or misunderstanding of project requirements.

Execution Domain/Construction/Implementation

The smooth execution or running of projects not only requires careful initiation and realistic planning but also requires an eye for details while at the same time an understanding of the big picture requirement and purpose of the project goal. This entails significant knowledge and experience applied throughout every PM life cycle.

This function must in essence be carried out in unison with the PM control function and coordinated to ensure harmonious progress in project activities. Action to address, correct, change, or even delay specific activities must be as prompt and coordinated to ensure its integrated whole is not compromised. The wisdom to change what can be changed, accept what cannot be changed and to know the difference aptly apply.

Phase/Project Close-Out Domain

When all deliverables have been handout over, the delivery should be evidenced by an official signoff. At the end of the project, the task is to ensure ALL deliverables have been signed off, all non-conformance items satisfactorily resolved to client satisfaction and any official project closure meeting stipulated in the contract are carried out as contracted are planned and carried out as stipulated and minutes signed off.

H1(b) PM Domain Knowledge in the Adaptive (AGILE) Approach

Where the project purpose is known but the eventual outcome is uncertain or there are many acceptable outcomes, the planned approach is unsuitable and hence will be better served and managed using the PM adaptive or AGILE approach. These types of projects are likely to use the time and material contract which has the flexibility to accommodate numerous change requests but not too much burn-down by the tightly integrated change request procedure.

In such an environment, the project manager is expected to have the hard skill in AGILE approach to project delivery following the AGILE manifesto. In adopting a mental paradigm that emphasize short but more frequent deliveries over documentation, work spurts in weekly sprints instead of long and large project deliverables, short weekly standup progress review instead of longer project progress reviews.

Leveraging on Project Lessons Learned

It has often been said, *if we do not learn from the mistakes in our history, we are bound to repeat them.* In the same way, the rich history of mistakes made, and opportunities missed in managing the project dynamics, changing priorities, conflicting stakeholder interest and conflicting schedules can enrich all those involved in the project. It is the ability to gain insights and leverage on these lessons learned that will go a long way to enhancing the project manager's PM maturity.

Management of Obligations During Warranty Period

Mature organization expect their team to disband in an organized fashion with a clean handover to the operation team to take over the warranty commitments during the warranty period. This is observed as the practice of large industry players, multi-national companies and large conglomerates that have significant revenues streams from project related work. This is a mature and smarter choice as:

- The operation team can take pride in being experts dealing with lack-of-quality work for all projects in the organization.
- Specialization is more productive when used for bug-fixing, rectification work, rework and missteps in integration.
- Achieve a higher team utility rate.

Keeping a small team for the warranty period is unwise for the following reasons (especially when the organization derives its main revenue from projects):

- The people kept behind for the purpose often feel they are held back.
- The cost in keeping the "*small team*" is often higher than the share of revenue passed over from project to operation.
- Lower productivity
- Team redundancy when all is well during the warranty period.

Project File Archives

When all project formalities have been accomplished, the project files should be systematically organized and archived for completeness and ease of future reference.

Control Domain and Governance

The ability to recognize the early signs of project distress is an expertise honed through experience and formal training. The symptoms that mature project managers look for are:

- The widening gaps in negative schedule variance showing the project losing traction, falling behind in its commitments, frequent missed deadlines and persistent issues of coordination, control, and synchronization of project activities.

- The widening gap in cost variance requiring a more detail analysis to determine if there is a trend of escalating rates being paid higher than anticipated or records of declining efficiency caused by use of lower grades of labor occasioned by a general skill shortage in the project environment.
- It is also possible that the lowering of efficiency could be due to the use of older and less efficient equipment than the equipment type promised and planned for.
- The widening gap in usage variance where more is being used to accomplish the same level of output. Time series graphs of usage variance will usually show a clearer declining trend.
- High frequency of reworks and rejects is often a sign of inexperience workmanship. This however must be viewed in terms of the trade-offs carried out by the project team opting for lower grades of labor available (hence a lower rate of payment) supplemented by greater supervision and acceptance of higher level of rework with the view to prevent project delays that have a high consequential liquidated ascertained damages (LAD) cost.
- Observed team stress as revealed by high team turnover (resignation, higher than expected attrition rate), unusual levels of overtime work/claims, sick leaves and team members seeking transfer elsewhere.

When it is obvious that many adverse factors are due to environmental and or general market trends, a mature project manager can articulate their views and seek management support to recalibrate and re-baseline their schedule and cost to reflect the reality on the ground long before the problems escalate. Mature PM organizations adhere to PMI's ethical conduct in relations to *Responsibility, Respect, Fairness, Honesty* and adherence to the mandatory standards and PMI Aspirational standards (PMBok 6th Ed, 2017 p.3). Unlike all other professional organizations, PMI code of conduct extends not only to its members, PMI certificate holders but also to PMI volunteers.

H2 PM Knowledge

PMBok 6[th]Ed (2017) specified 10 knowledge areas that project managers need to be competent in, namely Integration, Scope, Schedule, Cost, Quality, Risk, Resource, Communication, Procurement and Stakeholders management.

Stakeholder management is closely linked with communication and resource management (with human resource aspect). It is anticipated that these 3 knowledge areas may be combined under one topic for better understanding and appreciation of their interconnectivity. Amongst these details, a few aspects merit special attention. Quality in PM is about meeting the fitness-for-use criteria (originated by Juran) or delivery in conformance to requirements (by Crosby) but more aptly defined by Feigenbaum as *"the grade the client wants and at the price the client is willing to pay"*.

Mature project managers managed resources (e.g. materials, labor, and equipment) effectively through good coordination and synchronization and efficiently through efficient usage of these resources until its disposal. They differentiate and explain the difference between precision, which is a technical specification to be met with absolute certainty whereas accuracy may not be precise but accurate enough within the range of tolerance limit for the given purpose. In project accounting for example, the trial balance must be correct down to the penny, but the financial reports may be rounded (accurately) to the nearest million GBP pounds.

Mature project manager is focused on meeting purpose and scope within the revised project schedule and revised cost baseline, a moving target arising from approved variation order (VO) or because of a *"constructive change"* that they are very familiar with. To be effective, they also recognize when to consider trade-offs as and when opportunities arise. To be effective, they also recognize when to consider trade-offs between varying grades and quantity available as and when opportunities arise or sacrifice cost in exchange for reduced or shorter schedule when penalty for project delay are more significant in value.

H3 Business Acumen

Business acumen is one of 5 hard skills vital to any project manager's success, (Gan & Chin, 2018). These are partly in-born skills, especially those with numerate skills but arguably some of them can be acquired through expert training and business exposure. The important points are:

- The use of breakeven points as a reality check of required business volume just to break even or achieve zero profit
- Cash flow forecasts are just as important as the profit and loss forecast and how profitability trends do not always equate with positive cash flow and can result in severe business consequences.
- Time value of money and cost of capital implications on projects with very differing cash flow streams all of which enable the mature project manager to decide between the relative attractiveness of projects
- How to differentiate relative attractiveness of projects with differing risk profile
- Use of life-cycle-costing to differentiate between capital equipment on offer but each differing acquisition cost, scrap value, maintenance, running cost, capacity, efficiency, life span and general reliability.
- The calculation formulas, while essential are actually based on figures which should be based on assumptions that are realistic and plausible.
- That all assumptions made are risk, and should they be wrong, how they could be addressed using the preplanned strategy and the reserve set aside for the purpose.
- The need for trust for business to work in most cultures and why that is necessary even when the contracts are signed.
- Timeliness in obtaining payments for work accomplished and that risk remains if payment has not been received.
- The impact of inflation and how they impact project cash flow forecast.
- Understand that project-misinformation can be caused by the netting-off effects of variances between rate and efficiency and how seasonal variations can be smoothened using inception-to-date

144

values for earned-value, planned-value and actual-cost instead of period-to-date values.

- Understand the cost behavior of various cost-types, how they behave over time or at varying levels of project activity.
- Understand and explain the concepts of value-for-money.
- Apply constructive change appropriately to good advantage.
- An appropriate understanding of and application of "tipping-points"

PMI's three market focus areas; practitioners, organizations and academics integrate with PMI Talent Triangle of technical kills, leadership skills and strategic skills and business acumen (PMI Today, 2016).

H4 Exposure to Business/Industry/ Application/Environment

Observations at work over the last 20 years by the author have demonstrated there are many arguments generated amongst PM practitioners with two very diametrically opposite views. On the one hand, one group suggested that only technical people could manage technical projects. While this appears logical at face value, realities on the ground paint a very different picture, more different than this group will have liked.

Large and complex projects like infrastructure projects invariably require multi-disciplinary skills set. In such projects, the architect or the civil engineer who undertook the overall design would technically be able to manage the project relating to civil works but unlikely to be able to manage the required geotechnical, civil, structural, mechanical, electrical and electronics specifications. What about the need to manage the procurement, risk and contractual aspects, project estimation, accounting, financing and cash flows and most of all, the management of people that require understanding of human behavior and tendencies?

When one deals with the project details, would the project manager not be locked into the details and overlook the forest for the trees, a big-picture view that the project manager must have throughout the project when changes, decisions and actions need to be taken? Would such an action not be in fact a dereliction of duty and a perfect recipe for disaster like a captain not being at the bridge when his ship is facing critical moments!

On the other hand, the opposing group believes project managers should be a generalist overseeing and integrating people into a holistic team of various discipline, supervising, and facilitating the work, removing project impediments, negotiating, motivating and leading the team. This seems to be PMI official stand where the PMI Talent Triangle (2015) pits technical skills as being *"knowledge, skills and behaviors related to specific domain of project, program and portfolio management"*. In this definition, the PMBok (2017) shows domain as the 5 PM domains in the PM life cycle of initiation, planning, execution, control and closeout, all part of PM technical skills which are certainly generic in principle and practice, but nothing related to technical engineering as many would like to believe.

The confusion in the first group is likely due to their experience in smaller projects where the project managers are not full time but usually doubling up to also deal with the technical requirements and wonders how non-technical project managers could understand and manage them and make sense of discussions involving engineering matters at project meetings. For example, IT/ICT teams talk of files and fields, data structures, file normalization, file storage, logical and physical design, firewalls etc. Those in construction cite discussions of top-down construction that to the uninitiated is wholly illogical, with various stages of handover, merits of fixed price contracts and negotiated contracts, constructive change, incoterms, value for money (VFM) concepts etc.

These jargons are not that difficult to understand and frankly not everybody in the know really knows it all. With hindsight and on balance, it could be argued that a few months of prior exposure to the business, industry, the software application being implemented or the new environment to be encountered would have suffice, supplemented by the project manager's keenest to learn quickly and be involved. It is widely known that it is more difficult to move forward in projects with little business knowledge than it is with lack of technical knowledge.

So, while it is true that PM is a generic application, it is for the sake of being able to follow the communication and discussion at project meeting that project managers should have the appropriate exposure to know in general of what is being discussed and the arguments being put forth.

This study holds the view that, the project manager assigned should at least be exposed to the relevant industry, business, systems (data bases, computer languages), and computer applications (ERP, MRP, HRM, logistics, banking & finance, airline reservation, baggage handling etc.) being managed.

In the era of disruptive technology where the technological life cycle not only got shorter after each decade since the 80s but lately, new waves of change could be experienced every few months. So, the mature PM will do well to be exposed to the impending technological trends. The questions they would need to ask about the trends moving forward is how they might impact the way their projects could be run or if any of them may render their project outcome obsolete. Would the change affect their current operational processes or their client's system and anticipate the challenges to cope with them as they appear on the horizon? Examples of such unrelenting advances from a digitized AI to an autonomous AI world would include:

1. The way commerce is carried out with the dramatic move to a cashless society e.g. Street vendor in China would only accept WeChat transfer as a payment.
2. The exponential growth in application of autonomous artificial intelligence (AI)
3. Autonomous robotic capability
4. Miniaturization of health science and medical equipment
5. Facial recognition technology
6. Big data and cloud computing
7. Internet-every-things etc.

While it is true, no one could possibly keep up with so many and such rapid advances in technology, the mature PM will keep abreast of new technology and be well read and informed of the impending changes to anticipate since such details are nowadays freely available anytime and anywhere so long as Wi-Fi and internet access is available.

As needed, the relevant subject matter could be brought up with the team for briefing, discussion, consideration, threats addressed and if advantages could accrue from any opportunities they present. Such availability includes YouTube where world class leaders and experts present, deliberate, and discuss with learned peers and audiences in world renowned institutions of higher learning and public forums. So, the wider the exposure, the richer will be the project manager's fluency and capability to value-add while in project meeting and discussions of possibilities.

H5 Technical Work Knowledge

It is the responsibility of the project team to select the suitable PM processes, tools, and techniques to apply at the level of rigor appropriate to the project situation. The project manager, however, remains accountable for the results of the choices made (PMBok 6th Ed, 2017). As situation or circumstances change, the mature project manager should adapt accordingly and make best use of each, and every situation deemed appropriate. In a project environment, all projects are *dealt a different set of cards and it is the PM who must make the best of what is given and adapt as the circumstances dictates*. There are two aspects to technical work knowledge in this matter:

1. **The PM performance domain knowledge.**

These are the basic but fundamental PM domain or process knowledge that the project manager needs to have as foundation to begin in the management of projects and advancing knowledge that are needed as PM mature and advance into managing larger and more complex projects. As maturity is gained through experience and exposure, more understanding will be gained of PM concepts of time, time value of money. These would include VFM concept, life cycle management, and techniques for defining project purpose (definition or project brief), logical framework analysis (LFA or LogFrame), earned value management (EVM), interpretation of the project S curve, requirements management, data gathering techniques and advanced aspects of the PM knowledge areas.

2. **The discipline knowledge** is those relating to engineering, geotechnics, petrochem, accounting or industry knowledge like manufacturing techniques, construction methods or banking etc. While it is common that such knowledge is useful for the project manager, they are not critical to their performance as project managers handling larger and more complex projects have teams with multidisciplinary skills to rely on.

It is therefore impossible for any project manager to have all the required multidisciplinary skills that may be needed in projects requiring civil engineering, mechanical and engineering, structural, materials engineering and computer engineering etc. What is needed of the project manager is to be able to understand and be engage in discussion, integration and coordination of these skills sets as and when required but not be involved in the details and get suck-in and lose sight of managing the project's big picture requirements.

PROJECT MANAGER'S SOFT-SKILLS COMPONENTS OF PM MATURITY

There is a strong correlation between the "*soft*" stuff and shareholder returns (McKinsey Quarterly, 2014). In the realms of managing people, "*everything we do is aimed at application, helping people do the work they need to do*" according to Senge et al. (1999). Amongst so many factors that have been written in business literature, soft components that are in essence, is an encapsulation of what really matters in managing a temporary team set up for the purpose.

Prag (2010) said "*the social scientist wanted us to remember that the people are always part of the results*". We can imply that people's skills are the driving force that led and motivate the workforce to perform and produce the results we want.

The importance of the human side of management and more particularly PM is best explained as "We are in the business of forming teams of people to do things for companies that create value for them. *Without our people, we have no business*", Mort Meyerson, former chairman and CEO of Perot Systems and former vice chairman of Eds Fast Company magazine, Apr/May (1996). He emphasized that "*if we only deal on the level of a fair exchange of work for money, we are missing the whole essence of what is happening in the workplace.*" He was convinced it would be better to be able to tap into the experiences, the creativity, and the power of everyone in the organization by approaching the team to "*Let us create value for our customer. Let us create an environment which is good for our people.*" If businesses do work on issues of the community, the environment, family life, and the broader aspect of who and what their employee is, then we will lose the ability to produce a better whole life for the individual because people do not just do for their pay cheque.

The proposed DPM3 model identified the 5 soft skills, the skills to *communicate, lead, negotiate, resolve conflict* and a thinking mindset that is flexible to *adapt* as circumstances dictate, the skills that are imperative to project performance and ultimately the organizational success. There is a strong correlation between the "*soft*" stuff and shareholder returns (McKinsey Quarterly, Sep 2014).

In the realms of managing people "*everything we do is aimed at application, helping people do the work they need to do*" (Senge et al, 1999). To sum up just 5 key components amongst so many that have been written in business literature, soft components are in essence an encapsulation of what really matters in managing a temporary team set up for the purpose. These critical soft skills that mature and successful project managers are:

S1 Communication Skills

More than 90% of the project manager's time is spent on communication (PMBok, 2017) and Mulcahy (2015, p. 381). It is therefore inconceivable for anyone poor in their communication skills to succeed in the management of projects. These includes collecting and analyzing data, formulating, and making effective presentation, good listening skills when answering calls or addressing client complaints or even compliments, managing resources and work conflicts, negotiation, meeting the team, clients and subcontractors, documentation routines, coaching and mentoring, motivating team and individuals, correspondences etc. Failure in these areas is not an option but the ability to articulate and persuade project stakeholders holds the key to success. The ability to articulate an idea being pursued, present project reports that keep their audience attention focused on the main theme are hallmarks of successful people and particularly mature project managers.

Mature project managers provide project status reporting succinctly. They use reports that tend to be short, objective and to the point using appropriate pictures, diagrams, assisted by colors and illustrations, backed up by facts and figures to prove their point convincingly. Their careful choice of words helps the audience to keep focus on the main theme and lead them to the desired conclusion or in a state that enables them to form their own logical conclusion.

Mature project managers are well prepared before meetings; ensuring minutes have been circulated with notice of meetings together with agenda duly circulated in sufficient time for target attendees to act on all action items stipulated in the minutes. They are good timekeepers, ensuring all agenda discussed had been concluded with action assigned with names of assignees and date/s to complete. They manage their meetings professionally and diplomatically ensuring there is minimum time hogging and simultaneously able to draw out attendees who are reticent holding their thoughts.

The ability to gain consensus by emphasizing on commonalities and narrowing out of differences are skills that can only be learned through experience working with people, a skill that Livingston (1971) termed as *operant behavior*, a skill that can only be learned by doing. PMI's Practice Guide Managing Change in Organizations (2013) puts it as "*communication being the key factor in change management, and it is one of the most challenging and demanding aspects in managing change*".

To ensure their message and instructions are heard correctly, understood and related in the right context, mature communicators like successful project managers are mindful that communication barriers can often lead to conflict (PMBok 6th Ed, 2017, p.372) and so mature project managers understood the implications will actively seek to:

1. Ensure they have a prior understanding of the personality profile (e.g. dominance, influence, steadiness, compliance (DISC) profile) of the listener to be familiar with their needs and their communication preferences vis a vis their own and adapt their communication style accordingly.
2. Be sensitive to the multi-culture environment they often face, understand how bias can distort reality that create friction between individuals, emotional states that is not conducive to meeting intended for conflict resolution, background and personality issues that can impact communication effectiveness (PMBok 6th Ed, 2017, p.373)
3. Be aware and understand the pitfalls when native English speakers use English to communicate in a group where English is not the group's native language resulting listeners resentment and suspicion (Thierry, 2018)
4. Be conscious of the pitfalls of native English speakers that failed to be understood in English and lose out in global business (Hazel, 2016).

As much of the project managers work requirement are in writing, written reports and presentation, mature project managers are competent in writing and presentation skills and tend to perform very well in written examinations, a competency that objective test is unable to assess.

S2 Dynamic Leadership Skills

Drucker defined leaders as people who have followers, but researchers need to ask what do leaders do that make people want to follow them? It is not about people with positional leadership roles but leaders who despite their lack of leadership roles who understand human behavior and motivate their team, make people tick and enthused to move forward with their projects, willingly and with a good sense of personal commitment and satisfaction, a view from author presented at the PMI Indonesia International Symposium and Exhibition (April 2019).

When leading change, which is what PM is about? Peters (2014) suggested *"leaders should be recruiting allies and working each other up to have the nerve to try the next experiment, find allies, bringing in one person at a time and face to face"* (even in the face of an increasingly virtual world). Additionally, PMI Talent Triangle (2015), listed leadership skills as one of the three key talents in the management of projects.

In managing performance, the primary role is to lead people, and the goal is to increase productivity of specific strengths and knowledge of everyone (Drucker,1999). Project managers success is dependent on their competence particularly their leadership style (Mu¨ller & Turner, 2007a), They later also found *"different leadership styles have different effectiveness depending on the type of projects"*, (Mu¨ller & Turner, 2007b, 2009).

To lead effectively, leaders should be dynamic in order to better understand changing human behavior and advancing level of maturity at different stages of a project, how people develop as a team as they work and jive together thus requiring a different leadership role as well as the ability to anticipate people's behavioral tendencies, how and when motivational stimulus will work, when motivational stimulus can be inhibited making it ineffective and how different people under different circumstances and situation actually respond to change initiatives.

Dynamic leaders also need to know what makes people tick and when motivators work or when they do not work. Work hygiene factors identified by Herzberg et.al (2011) were factors that must be present for motivators to work to remain relevant and appropriate. Its mere presence, however, would not motivate but its absence creates dissatisfaction.

McGregor (2006) classified people into 2 groups, theory X and theory Y. In broad terms, it appears his observations of theory X people remain relevant as many people could be seen as inherently laidback, working only because they had to put food on the table. Once paid there was the tendency to lay back and enjoy the fruits of their labor and look for work only when their cash ran out. For this group, the leaders need to know how they could help them by spreading labor rewards and help these groups to save by way of deduction as a savings for their retirement. For the theory Y people, work was like play that is essential for their wellbeing and so the leader needs to identify the challenges with rewards that would motivate these people to work hard, work smart and to thrive under those designed challenging circumstances.

People grow and advance in life progressively and so the needs expand as they move up in their maturity scale. According to Maslow (1965), it is a *"set up social conditions so that the goals of the individual merge with the goals of the organization"*. In other words, providing the relevant working conditions and benefits according to their level of maturity that enable people to meet their own needs and, in the process, meeting the company's needs as the author presented at the PMI Indonesia International Symposium and Exhibition (2019).

McClelland's theory of needs suggest delegation of challenging work with recognition needs for those whose primary needs were for feeling of *Achievement*, for those who needed feelings of *Affiliation*, he suggested they be given opportunities to work with others and gain team approvals while those who has primary needs for *Power* be given opportunities to lead, organize and influence others.

In all matters of the living world that is always in a continuous state of change, managers do their best to anticipate, evaluate, respond, and adapt to the environment of disruptive technologies, new inventions, innovation, and new materials just to remain relevant. Others will run out of ideas, regurgitate, and repackage old ideas and styles that then further complicate our world.

In projects, the challenges are even more profound when the project manager must manage a temporary team often with inadequate resources, changing priorities and schedules. As most project managers are likely to have gone through these experiences many times before, it is not uncommon to see them being lull into a *"routine conditioning"* syndrome that will tempt them to provide all the answers to all problems and issues brought up. Sadly, many will really try but fail for lack of appropriate leadership.

Dynamic leaders on the other hand, understand the impediments to project performance and proactively work to understand and mitigate their impact and they are also aware of their limitations and recognize they don't know everything. They understand team dynamics, how different leadership styles have different effects on communication, comprehension, and feedback. They are also aware of their own personality profile and able to adjust to accommodate the different personality profile of individuals in their team. So, they capitalize on their team strength, knowledge, experience, skills, team cohesion and facilitate *"TeamThink"* to tap synergies by engaging with people as a group or team, enquiring, probing, reasoning, discussing possibilities, about what can be and the needs to advance forward. And more effectively leadership skills are one of 5 key soft skills vital to any project manager's success (Gan & Chin, 2018).

To illustrate the need for leadership flexibility to adapt and cope with this new world, Klaus Schwab, founder & executive Chairman of the World Economic Forum address his audience in 2018 saying *"In the new world, it is not the big fish which eats the small fish, it's the fast fish which eats the slow fish"*. The message emphasized the need for the project manager as a leader to be flexible, agile, lean, and adaptable to the dynamic environment especially in the 5th industrial revolution. Dynamic leaders thus encourage independent critical thinking and empower the team to be more flexible and better adapt to their dynamic environment and as the situation demands, mentor and coach the team to a higher level of PM maturity.

Figure 1. Dynamic leadership

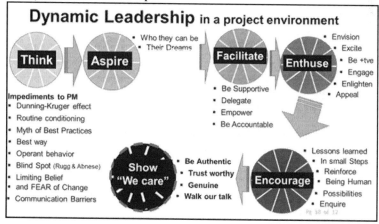

Presented at the PMI Indonesia international symposium, Bali (2019)

Gan & Chin (2019) maintain that in the managing of projects and change initiatives, a form of dynamic leadership (Figure 1) is required, where leaders must adapt their leadership style to accommodate the changing team maturity level. As a leader in a dynamic environment, the project manager has to think ahead of the impediments to PM and how their impact could be mitigated, lead the team to aspire to who they each can be, then act to facilitate and smoothen the process flow, enthuse and encourage the team as they move along the project remembering always and in all action to show they care about the well-being of their team.

The Tuckman ladder (Table 1) described the project team as being a temporary team that go through different stages of team development, from *Forming* stage when the temporary team first come together, are unfamiliar with one another, with members from differing cultures, disciplines, and skill sets. Over time, the team mature to *Storming, Norming* and eventually the *Performing* stage and during the tail end of the project they experience the *Transitioning* stage when the team disperses near the end or at completion stage of the project. To be more effective, Tuckman recommended the leader play the respective recommended role as below:

Table 1. The Tuckman ladder

Tuckman	Stage of Team development				
Ladder	Forming	Storming	Norming	Performing	Transitioning
Effective role to play	Leader role	Facilitate or Referee	Coach or Consult	Collaborator Cheer leader	Reviewer Energizer

Leadership skills are one of the three key talents in the management of projects. PMI's talent diagram (reproduced in Figure 2) seems to suggest it encompasses all soft skills as illustrated in the content page of PMI talent triangle, a departure from past versions of PMBok which listed leadership as being a part of soft skills. This study supports the latter as soft skills are people skills that encompass every aspect relating to people, behavior and their tendencies under all the varying circumstances.

Hence, not everyone with soft skills are leaders and neither do leaders have all the soft skills, just those soft skills that inspire people to be who they can be, having emotional intelligence of themselves, understand and empathize with those they lead and ability to motivate and enthuse people to do their bidding.

From literature review, PM seminar participants' feedback and actual work observation, the following impediments to project success should be addressed constructively and with sufficient diplomacy and tackled.

- **Mental barriers** that blind our team from being who they can be broken or at least mitigated.
- **Managing blind spots** resulting from routine conditioning should be noted with care to minimize their occurrence.
- **Fixation with best practices** that stifle thinking, and innovation should be avoided. Instead use *recommended good practices* and explain the general principles, rules and guidelines but leave the rest to those who work the details.
- **Management myths** should be debunked, status quo that may have prevailed for too long should periodically be examined for its continued relevance through environmental changes and passage of time.
- **Pompous slogans** should be avoided, taking note the devil is often in the details
- **Conflict at work** should be viewed positively as they often create a healthy atmosphere for critical thinking and teamwork. When well-managed, it encourages reasoning and healthy debate
- **Fear of trying** should be removed if it has been thought out and considered worth exploring. Hence allow mistakes but emphasize learning from mistakes and the greater wisdom of learning from the mistakes of others.

Figure 2. PMI talent triangle (2015)

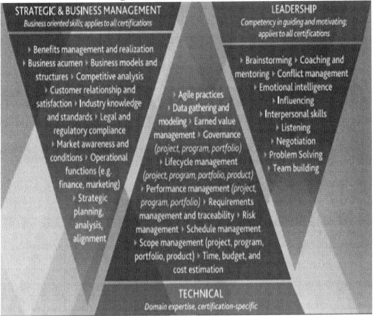

Efforts should be made to:

- **Understand human behavior** by understanding oneself first before reviewing the team members individual personality profile so that the appropriate communication approach and style is applied with optimal effectiveness.
- **Imbue flexibility in the thinking and planning** design that are better able to minimize the impact of disruptive technologies, vagaries of management priorities and ever disruptive schedules changes.
- **Understand barriers-to-change**, how they impact project progress and how they can influence the team and those around them and how their impact can be mitigated.
- **Use Lewin's *forcefield analysis*** to identify and differentiate the relative significance of each force field thereby enabled to take maximum advantage of driving-forces and minimize the impact of restraining-forces.

- **Inculcate team's sense of urgency**, a challenging task that dynamic leaders must constantly apply and be watchful about or suffer the consequences.
- **Facilitate and empower** the team instead of micromanaging.
- **Be a Leader in action** by understanding the role of a dynamic leader, enable and facilitate timely action, the personal attributes that attract success in what they do.

S3 Negotiation Skills

Like all people skills, negotiation skills are learnt throughout our lives. As a child, we learn ways to get our parents' attention. We "*negotiated*" our way to get what we want verbally or through our body language. We grow up learning and often the hard way, realizing that the work environment is somehow quite different, wider in scope, poses more challenges, subtle and often unforgiving. This is best illustrated by Borg (2019) who said, "*good negotiation is the often the final stage in the journey of persuasion*".

Communication skills are a foundational skill at work and for managing people, but it is the negotiation skill that many find great difficulty applying and a big hurdle to overcome while others make it seem so very easy. The hard skills in negotiation, however, can be learned from strategic thinking, forethought and honed through constant practice as becoming an art with much improved outcome, through use of the ROGAN Synergistic Exchange Index (Gan, 2003) and application of Cialdini's first principle of persuasion, the principle of reciprocation which all help enhance the negotiation success (2006).

Figure 3. ROGAN synergistic exchange index

Presented at the PMI Philippines International Symposium (2003)

Leaders know good negotiation skills at the workplace play a significant role in making the work environment conducive, friendly and promotes cooperation that results in synergy which are often overlooked. Such synergies translate into profitable outcomes through lower cost of procurement and higher margins from marketing and sales.

Negotiation is more effective when we are persuasive, well prepared and long before we set out to engage a third party. It requires forethought, good background work and proper understanding of human behavior so that our approach can be strategic and decisive at appropriate moments. Success in negotiation entails clear negotiation objectives, identifying the challenges to expect and the negotiation stance to adopt in the given context and situation. So appropriate preparation and observing the rules of negotiation will help mature project managers to always stay one-step ahead. A win-win outcome from negotiation requires careful thinking. It requires the right techniques, careful preparation, common sense, and careful observation to succeed at the negotiating table.

PMI Talent Triangle (2015) included negotiation skills and conflict management as part of leadership skills. Experience on the ground and feedback from each successive workshop on Conflict Management and Negotiation skills – in a project environment conducted over the last 15 years has convinced the author of its importance and significance to merit its own headline. In his introduction to his book *Persuasion – The art of influencing people*, Borg (2019) said *"The power of persuasion is maybe the ultimate source of advantage in life and work, a critical separation factor between the successful and the rest"*.

This importance is illustrated by Negotiation skill as a specific task 8 under the people skill domain (42%) in the new PMP examination syllabus (2019).

S4 Conflict Management Skills

Conflict is inevitable in a project environment (PMBok, 2017). Sources of conflict include conflicting stakeholders demands, contention for scarce resources, changing scheduling priorities, different working styles, disagreement about team ground rules and differing group norms. Conflicts such as these could be reduced via solid PM practices in good communication planning and role definition. Despite its importance, PMI chose to include conflict management only as a subset of leadership skills (PMI Talent Triangle, 2015).

While conflict is good at work if they are well managed, it can also lead to team dysfunction when it is allowed to fester and left unresolved for too long. Successful resolution in differences of opinion however are known to increase creativity, better decision making, higher productivity and enhanced working relationship (PMBok, 2013).

While PMBok (2013) specified 5 general techniques for resolving conflicts at work, each having its own merits, it did not show how conflicts can be resolved. This was the area where almost all participants at the PMP boot camps and postgraduate students agreed. The participants require not only conflict management skills but also negotiation skills between the conflicting parties. More importantly, the majority responded these skill sets would have given them much greater leverage had it been taught earlier in their post graduate program.

This importance is illustrated by conflict management skill as a specific task 1 under the people skill domain (42%) in the new PMP examination syllabus (2019).

S5 Adaptability/Flexibility Skills

The principles of scientific management that Frederick Winslow Taylor presented in 1911 had worked very well even to this day. It was designed for general and operation management where the organization structure could be made permanent and every process structured, simplified to its lowest level and then standardized or through mechanization and done repetitively but they were designed for a mass production environment. It is questionable if Taylor's scientific management could work in a project environment where projects are unique endeavors almost always with a temporary team, organized for the purpose of producing an outcome often never been done before. It often has varying configuration requirements, in a new environment never previously experienced and to work with contractors of varying cultures, changing priorities and schedules disrupted by factors beyond the team's control. This study note Taylors scientific management could be applied but limited to prefabrication works done elsewhere conveniently located for transport to its large mega construction projects for example the China's modern-day high-speed rail, magnetic levitation (maglev rail) and viaduct construction.

Thus, the need for adaptability and flexibility is obvious in a project environment and identified as one of 5 key soft skills needed by project managers (Gan & Chin, 2019). The flexibility in thinking and to be resourceful about what, where, when, why and how daily operational decisions are made require the project manager to adapt as the circumstances dictate. In addition, the flexibility to adapt their leadership style to accommodate the various types of teams and individual behavior (actions and decisions) and manage the varying degree of expected and unexpected resistance to change (PMI, 2013). Lewin (n.d) argued that successful businesses tend to be constantly adapting to their environment and changing, rather than being inflexible.

Adaptability and flexibility had been identified as one of 5 key soft skills vital to any project manager's success (Gan & Chin, 2018). Successful planning for management of change needs built-in flexibility to accommodate the human aspect in terms of the varying degree of expected and unexpected resistance to change (PMI, 2013).

In the PMI Talent Triangle (2015) sponsored research, it pointed out that adaptive process was known from past research that high-performing organizations were more likely to apply standardized PM practices. Their current findings show that organizations with highly developed cultures of agility were twice as likely to use these practices. These organizations are also more likely to adapt their PM approaches (95% vs 72% of organizations with under-developed cultures) and create hybrid management models that fit their unique organizational cultures.

The senior leadership of Valerus, a world leader in integrated oil and gas handling equipment and services, is committed to hiring and training leaders with agility to change the company and build sustainable success. Between 2011 and 2013, Valerus embraced a talent management framework to help define and drive its transformation in a turbulent business climate. Their model comprised of 5 critical drivers of organizational and strategic agility:

1. The abilities to anticipate change
2. Generate confidence
3. Initiate action
4. Liberate thinking and
5. Evaluate results.

Leaders were coached and trained to apply the model to their day-to-day work. A talent assessment and management process identified high-potential leaders who worked on project teams to solve key business issues facing the company. Human resource-built agility into its talent review process by integrating scenario planning with the process so that it could adjust and adapt its talent portfolio to the demands of a turbulent marketplace. Valerus business resulted 46% revenue growth, year after year, combined with similar earnings before interest, taxes, depreciation, and amortization (EBITDA) growth of 21%, lends credibility to the business impact of this focused alignment between talent management and organizational agility.

Adaptability and flexibility require flexible thinking, thinking of continuous improvement and innovation when managing change. The common basics were to encourage innovation by creating a diverse team, encouraging dissent, and accepting mistakes. By themselves, these will not keep **ExpertThink** and **Groupthink** at bay because adaptability and flexibility needed are often stifled by people who are experienced or too close to the subject being discussed due to their loss in objectivity which Rabe (2006) described as *"paradox of experience"* in her book *"The Innovation Killer: How What We Know Limits What We Can Imagine Talent management and Organizational Agility"*.

Rabe (2006) showed how leaders could overcome **GroupThink**, a tendency that establishes and then vigorously defend what had been established against any threat to its status quo and **ExpertThink** another tendency that rely on the expert who's *"expert power"* had the tendency to stifle innovative thinking. Her proposal to use **Zero-gravity-thinkers**, the impartial observer with a new pair of eyes to recognize possibilities and potential challenges when non-appear to exist to those too close to the problem cannot seem to see. Livingston (1971) pointed out that it was *"the personal experience acquired through their own experience the knowledge and skills that are vital to their effectiveness"* that enable effective leaders to adapt as the circumstances dictate.

It is often quoted in management circles that *the wise change what can be changed, accept what cannot be changed and the wisdom to know the difference*. This aptly applies in the management of projects when many environmental factors are given (subject to some level of influence in some cases) and routinely dynamic in nature, changes that the project manager need to adapt to and make best use of the situation, a wisdom alluded to by the Chinese proverb that *"the wise adapt themselves to circumstances as water molds itself to the pitcher"*.

THE ORGANIZATIONAL ENVIRONMENTAL COMPONENTS

E1 Organizational Structure/Culture

- **Organizational structure**

Mature PM organizations are familiar with the various PM organization structures and choose what they consider appropriate to their type of business or organization, project complexity and geographical layout. In Drucker's Management Challenges for the 21st Century (1999), he pointed out that *"there is no such thing as the one right organization structure that fits everyone and, in every situation,"*. This is particularly true in the 21st century where the fast pace of change will as quickly derail every optimization model that may have worked well in the past. Therefore, the choice of which organization structure must thus be decided by the project organization and team based on their rationale and detailed knowledge of their own capabilities and scope of their project requirements.

Table 2. Type of organization structures

PMBOK® Guide 6th Ed pg 45, 47

Role depends on Types of organizational structures

Organizational Structure	Organic Or Simple	Functional (Centralized)	Multi-dimensional May replicate across Div, decentralized	Weak Matrix	Balanced Matrix
Project Characteristics					
Work group Arrangement	Flexible, people side-by-side	Job being done eg Eng. ICT	Product level, Prod process, Portfolio, Programme, Region Cust type	Job Function	Job Function
PM's authority level	Little/None	Little/None	Little/None	Low	Low to Moderate
Project Manager's role	Part-time, no designated role	Part-time. May or may not have a designed role Coordinator	Part time, May or may not have a designated Job role Coordinator	Part-time, Done as part of another job Coordinator	Part time Embedded Skill/SME Coordinator
Resource availability	Little/None	Little/None	Little/None	Low	Low to Moderate
Budget Management	Owner or Operator	Functional Manager	Functional manager	Functional Manager	Mixed
PM Adm Staff assignment	Little or none	Part-time	Part-time	Part-time	Part-time

Role depends on Types of organizational structures

PMBOK® Guide 6th Ed pg 45, 47

Organizational Structure	Strong Matrix	Project-oriented Composite, hybrid	Virtual	Hybrid	PMO
Project Characteristics					
Work group Arrangement	Job Function PM Function	Project	Network structure with Nodes at point of contact with others	Mix of other types	Mix of other types
PM's authority level	Moderate To high	High to almost total	Little to moderate	Mixed	High to Almost total
Project Manager's role	Full-time Designed Job role	Fulltime Designed Job role	Part time or full-time	Mixed	Full-time Designated Job role
Resource availability	Moderate To high	Project Manager	Low to moderate	Mixed	High to Almost Total
Budget Management	Project Manager	Project Manager	Mixed	Mixed	Project manager
PM Adm Staff assignment	Full-time	Full-time	Part-time or Full-time	Mixed	Full-time

Project managers operate under varying organization structures and the way an organization is structured directly affects the availability of resources and influenced the way projects are conducted (PMBok, 2017).

From Table 2, PMI only recognized project managers who work full time. While project managers operating in a functional organization structure (except those that have special project teams set up for each project initiative) are only recognized as Project Expediters while those operating under a weak matric structure are just Project Coordinators. One can therefore appreciate why it is difficult to compare performance between project managers who operate under different organization structures.

Projectized organization may have various hybrid organization structure where line managers support departments of specific discipline, have their SMEs or expert team on standby until they are called upon to join specific project team and returned only on project completion. While in the project, the team members are dedicated to the project, assigned to and made accountable to their respective project manager (Table 2)

The basic assumption of the one-right organization (in the context of organization structure) is no longer tenable (Drucker, 1999). He reiterated that it should have become clear that there is no such thing as one right organization. Organization is not absolute; it is a tool for making people productive in working together. So, a given organization structure fits certain tasks in certain conditions and at certain times (Drucker, 1999, p.11). One will have to study and to use the "*mixed*" structure rather than "*one-right-organization*" which organization theorist today doggedly practice (Drucker, 1999, p.14).

It should be noted that PM practitioners have already practiced the fluid organization structure and the matrix organization structure as far back as the mid-1990s. The balanced matrix, strong matrix and the projectized organization structure had already been formalized upon the introduction of PMBok 3rd Ed (2004). Drucker (1999) did not mean to do away with organization hierarchy but that should be there to maintain the line of command especially in areas of final authority and in crisis management.

- **Organization culture**

Each organization has their own culture built over time. It then forms the way to do things, think, behave, and accord respect to authorities, superiors, peers and subordinates, general attitude in terms of respect for the individual, risk and social norms. In Western culture, children are taught to be individualistic, independent, direct but respectful and to answer questions even to those that teach them and even elders.

In a project team, members from such Western environment tends to be seen as outspoken, abrasive and often thought of being disrespectful in an Eastern culture where children are taught to be collective in their reasoning, respectful of elders even if they are less educated. When one works in a new and different or multi culture environment, we soon see the challenges.

Candido (2015) concluded that amongst other things, culture also impacts change initiatives. Peters (in McKinsey Quarterly, Sep 2014) contrasted "*managers from Japanese culture where lines of initiatives are blurred* whilst managers in *western culture take responsibilities and initiatives within defined borders*" which he meant "they haven't gotten the corporate-culture message yet". To emphasize his point, he quoted Lou Gerstner having said "*When I came to IBM, I was a guy who believed in strategy and analysis. What I learned was that corporate culture is not part of the game. It is the game*".

E2 Leadership Support

The importance of leadership and their active support for the project team can be seen as pivotal in the performance of project as deduced from PMI latest research that categorized leadership as one of three sides of the PMI Talent Triangle (2015) Continuing Certification Requirement Handbook for PMPs.

Peters (2014) lamented the lack of leadership support where people who work for big businesses tend to come up afterward and say, "*It's the best speech I've ever heard in my life, but I can't do anything—my boss won't let me.*" Unlike small-businesses, people say, "*It was the lousiest speech I've ever heard in my life, but I'm going to take one thing and do it tomorrow morning*" that is given the leeway, they are able to take an *idea to action* with a supportive leadership.

It is also common to hear that management do not walk their talk. "*There is clear sign there is growing disparity between rhetoric and practice*" (Drucker, 1999, p.16).

How are managers who proclaim they practice open door policy when they are seldom available when their team needs them? Advocating the need for appropriate risk taking when mistakes made are repeatedly highlighted and often many years after the event? That all decisions must be cost effective yet make capital investments based on the most sophisticated software application available but often also complicated with many functional areas that are clearly irrelevant or don't need?

Routine conditioning is another human tendency that is often not understood by management. Senge et.al (1999) describes it as "*our personal history in institutions starting with school, has conditioned most of us to see a mechanical world – a world of measure (largely meaning KPIs and OVIs), plans and programs, a world of people "in control" and leaders who "drive" change. This leads us to be blind to critical features of the living world that shape whether we ever have any success in actually sustaining it*".

It was also pointed out extrapolation is a fool's occupation in a non-linear world where even "*perfect knowledge*" leads to highly imperfect predictions. It was also emphasized that effective leaders know intuitively that it was tempting to say "*this is how we did it over there and it worked. So, we should follow the same rules here*" but it was pointed out "*here and now*" are never identical and even small differences can alter the outcome of so call "*tried and true*" (Senge, et.al, 1999).

E3 Management Attitude to Risk

At the turn of the century, the disproportional increase in the number of knowledge workers had increased the proportion of workers who owned their own "*means of production*" and thus possessed much greater job mobility, Drucker (1999) warned that when these workers leave, they leave with their knowledge. So, he opined that management thus had to manage them more like "*volunteers*" even though they were paid employees.

Could management remain complacent and continue to manage by numbers on the "DASHBOARD" while driving the project? Could management continue to push for performance figures and targets, screaming "*if you all cannot, we can find others who can*" without providing adequate support or understanding the long-term implications on the team at large? Additionally, it is seen as a common practice that management continue to take on projects without the team expertise hoping they can procure them soon enough but only after the contract has already been in hand!

The last three decades have seen a notable increase in short management tenures (2 years or less) with clearly defined performance goals. This is seen being played out at work within and amongst the competitors. Such short tenures inevitably mean short term goals and all measure taken are likely geared to achieve short term results that take no heed of organizational long-term implications. Although these are laid out plainly for everyone to see, it merits research into why the risky trend continues unabated despite its shortcomings.

Mature project organization maintained their own core team of professionals supplemented with sub-contractors and PM professional on a project basis. Such engagements have clearly defined role, scope of work with the agreed baseline of time and rates of charge that enable the organization to only hire executives with short term tenure for contract related scope of work without compromising their strategic goals.

E4 Rewards Alignment

One talk incessantly about "*teams*" and every study concluded about top management job does indeed require a team (Drucker, 1999, p.16). Management (including PM) is about getting things done through other people and teamwork but the growing disparity between rhetoric and practice is prevalent when management continues to give incentives that are more personal than for teamwork.

The past 15 years of observations of feedback reveal project salesperson continue to be rewarded for sales effort without penalties for over commitment or for promises they could not keep or not providing for PM services which they conveniently beat down as unnecessary or excuses to exclude project contingencies as merely statistics. Even when such cost was provided, the work scope was often beaten down to bare bones creating unrealistic demands on post-sales team without any management-taking note of it.

At the organization level, project profit is only realized after delivery whereas personnel performance is measured at two points in time, when sales is made (and sales commission paid) and when the project is implemented and delivered to client expectation. The hidden issue is often about the under provision of project cost baseline allowing inflated sales margin and inadequate funds for the delivery of the project with the sales team unfairly benefiting at the expense of the project team. This had been explained and inquired during the boot camp through the following questions:

1. How many of you have experienced this at work? The results were around 10 to 20% showed their hands in agreement to this question.
2. How many continue to experience this issue? The results were the same.

When the reward system is not designed to motivate teamwork and or consciously targeted to align behavior to corporate strategy, the team will become dysfunctional, as we have seen at work and individuals work in silos void of corporate strategic intent and inadvertent conflicts. On the other hand, mature organization tend to maintain a team-reward-pool to encourage teamwork and retain part of the sales commission until the project is delivered to reduce risky-sales-behavior of salespeople's relating to over commitments to clients they know they cannot keep.

E5 Organizational Capacity

Projects are often hard to come by and when opportunities arise, it is not common to see concerted efforts made to secure the deal even though it may be obvious the organization in no way had the capacity to deliver what the sales proposal entails. Once the contract is in hand, only then do they make a frantic search for talents resulting in having to pay a premium to engage the required project resources. In such a rush, some work maybe sub-contracted needing greater and unplanned work coordination; experience a higher learning curve, higher levels of rework errors all of which reduce profits. Such risky behavior is prevalent in the local IT as well as the construction industry, but many remain oblivious to such history and therefore prone to repeat the folly.

Commitments with contractual obligations are onerous and over commitments without the necessary resources to cope with it is most unwise. The author's 20 years in corporate PM and 12 years facilitating PMP Boot camps found attendees' feedback as, "*management is somehow convinced that as long as there is the money (from the contract just won), resources of any kind can be gotten and soon enough*".

The reality is the difficulty getting the right skill set (either full-time staff or subcontractors) in the time schedule required, available in the grade and quantity required and higher cost of urgent recruitment. The challenge is also getting new members of the team to be able hit the road and run to be first familiar with the organization culture, tool set, systems in use, industry being worked on, computer application being implemented and the way their team jive at work. Mature organizations pre-negotiate with their sub-contractors available during the anticipated project schedule and duration to fill the resource gap thus reducing the organization capacity risk.

THE ORGANIZATIONAL FACILITATING COMPONENTS

F1 Standardization

This is key to any complex organization, especially that of a project organization where there are many project dynamics. In a borderless world of PM, standardization maintain a unified glossary, consistency in process, procedures, use of and application of common tools, templates, filing system all with the view to maintain good, effective and efficient communication within the project team and all its stakeholders.

In a keynote address at the PMI Malaysia Chapter's International Symposium in Oct 2016, Dato Dr. Syed Naguib Syed Abu Bakar, a well know specialist in project planning & management highlighted the wisdom of using time tested PMI's PMBok (Zandhuis, 2013) when applying their hands-on experience to projects and adapt accordingly. The amount of effort and funding by PMI and other PM institutes and associations to continuously improve the recommended good practices or standards is a testament to the need for standardization. PMI's every 5 years review of the PMBok or guide to PM practices suggest continuously refining the recommended good practices to adapt and remain relevant to the dynamic and borderless world made chaotic by disruptive technologies.

The importance of standards is clearly demonstrated by PMI Talent Triangle (2015) which stipulates it under strategic and business management skills where there is a need for project manager in understanding standards. Standardization had been identified as one of 5 key organization components of PM maturity. In a borderless world of PM, standardization maintain a unified glossary, consistency in process, procedures, use and application of common tools, templates, filing system all with the view to maintaining good governance, effectiveness and efficient communication within the project team and its stakeholders. This has been implied since 2003 when PMI initiated and continue to sponsor research in PM performance and their PMBok 5-yearly update cycle designed for continuous improvement and standardization of PM practices at the global scale.

The amount of effort and money invested by PMI and other PM institutes and associations to continuously improve their recommended good practices or standards is a testament to the need for standardization. PMI's every 5 yearly review cycles of the PMBok also suggested the need to continuously refine recommended good practices in order to adapt and remain relevant to the dynamic and borderless world made chaotic by disruptive technologies.

The importance of standards is also clearly demonstrated by PMI Talent Triangle (2015) under strategic and business management skills for project managers in understanding standards application. For standards to be effective, mature organizations maintain an enforcement and compliance unit to ensure the globally recognized recommended good practice they adopted are indeed practiced and in compliance with PMI code of ethics.

F2 PM Operating Procedures

This should clearly spell every PM process, PM tools and every project document uniquely coded with a title and a sample. Sample contents are given to facilitate team cross reference and education. Prioritization procedures like the Power-Interest-Grid should be used as a guiding process as what should be prioritized when there are conflicting demands for team attention.

In any complex organization, having the rules and operating procedures to run it is not enough unless they are adequate, sufficiently rigorous and fit for purpose. Completeness and consistency of PM procedures (now renamed as PM Operating procedures) was identified as one of 5 key organization components of PM maturity.

However, it must be emphasized that in a borderless world of PM, standardized operating procedures should be complete to address all the project needs and that they are applied in a consistent manner where form and content must jive, coordinated, and synchronized for effective teamwork and cost effectiveness. The specifications in PMBok's Inputs, Tools, Techniques and Outputs (ITTO) diagrams are a critical example of the need for PM operating procedures that is complete and self-contained showing what inputs to look for, the tools and techniques relevant and the output to be expected from that given PM process.

F3 PMIS Sufficiency (PM Information System)

For PM organizations to be mature, their PM information system (PMIS) should adequately report project performance by project and by phase showing details at the level of rigor the team expects. This should include Period-to-date (PTD) and Inception-to-date (ITD) figures for the S-curve trend showing cumulative progress made relative to planned-value and earned-value. When needed, the system should allow drill-down to isolate variances caused by poor usage, lack of efficiency and unfavorable rate differences.

It should also be sufficient to enable individual projects to be codified and controlled by project by phase and by varying levels of cost types relating to materials, labor, equipment, subcontract and overheads. Items of significant value or a required importance of the material mix (like concrete grades of various cement mix and aggregates), the PMIS should enable each item to capture the quantity, unit of measure and amount.

SMART fields (fields that when defined can automatically move forward or backward depending on the systems current date of reporting) should be available to populate columns or rows and able to recognize dynamic dates to auto advance as daily period advance or using pre-set period cut-offs dates or period between two dates.

It is also in the interest of the organization to have an Enterprise Resource Planning (ERP) system that is fully integrated with its financial system and project accounting. This enables data captured at source, do away with data entry routines that contribute to possible data entry errors and save the system interface time that causes project reporting delays.

The PMIS should enable commitment accounting whereby purchase orders (PO) for projects are tracked to prevent over orders and when goods are received into projects, they are tracked by its relevant PO as well as the invoices that follows. The organization and project managers should be keenly aware that this ERP approach help introduce segregation of duties, an organization Internal-Control system that prevent or reduce project "*leakage*" and losses due to internal collusion.

The system should enable user-defined reports, extract their required data; place them in identified column or row and calculate at column or row levels. It too should allow data capture for not only quantity and amounts for actuals but also its relative value for cost baseline, variation orders and other user defined column for earned value entries that enable EVM reporting.

Finally, all project data should be capable of full integration with the accounting system to avoid the need for monthly account reconciliation that impedes prompt project period reporting. In this way, the mature performing organization will have application software that enable timely project status reporting of progress by work packages or phase of work and at desired level of detail that is not available in standard financial accounting system.

PMI Talent Triangle (2015) under strategic and business management skills list the requirements for project managers to have business-oriented skills and business acumen thus implying the need for PM information that is sufficient for the purpose. The need for such an information system was emphasized over the author's years in PM practice. Many project managers are sorely handicapped by the lack of proper and timely project information because:

- The organization was not familiar with project accounting and control
- No idea where the information should and could connect effectively
- Confused by IT providers who themselves don't know what they don't know
- ERP software was not designed for project control
- Clients who do not know how to ask nor enquire about their information needs

Only earned value (value of work accomplished) reporting could adequately report project performance in progress where the required variables are:

- EV: Earned value (physical inspection at site & value estimated)
- PV: Planned value (value of work that should have been accomplished)
- AC: Actual cost (actual cost incurred to accomplish the value of work accomplished)

Actual cost is the most tedious to obtained in any project accounting including EVM practice and the only practical solution is in the use of an ERP software system that is designed for project accounting and general ledger reporting. They allow user to defined set-up to suit the project manager's project control requirement where the set up could be by):

- Project phase (work package or project deliverables)
- Within the project phase, by cost type for materials, equipment, sub-contract work, labor and overheads.
- Set up by cost type to the project detail control needs defined e.g. budget by materials /concrete /grade
- Set up by cost type at summary level with no lower-level details e.g. budget at summary level for mobilization cost or preliminaries
- Capture project data at source.

Without such an information support system, the project accounting department must toil needlessly for weeks after the event, to collect the transaction records manually or extract from reports elsewhere, making it cumbersome, slow and prone to error. This results in outdated information futile for project control. For sake of confidentiality, no names are mentioned that might in any way promote or inadvertently advertise any software nor disparage any others. Few writers and research venture into this area due to the technical nature of the user requirements with the lack of such exposure and experience in the workplace. The author has more than 20 such projects implemented in the ASEAN region, Singapore, Malaysia, Taiwan, and Hong Kong.

F4 PM Information System (PMIS) Availability

With a suitable PMIS in place, its availability is crucial for management of projects. When the application systems integration is not self-controlled, transactions not captured at source, or the systems suffer high downtime due to power outages or due to systems instability. This will create undue complications and significantly affect project control causing cost and schedule overruns. These are also one of many well-known causes of project failures.

Systems uptime must be contracted for so that the system's vendor is able and prepared to guarantee a service level agreement for any downtime to be no longer than 24 or 48 hours and a guaranteed uptime of agreed n days per calendar year. This is to ensure minimal disruption to data entry at source and project status reporting.

F5 Sufficiency of PM Tools and Techniques

Mature PM organizations are familiar with these but as a responsible and mature PM organization, they should have a pre-selected set of tools, duly coded and organized for easy retrieval and reference. Each tool selected should state its reason for use with how-to-instructions and rules to be followed with a full work example to facilitate education.

There are many PM tools, techniques and templates in the market all purporting to serve the PM community. While some are indeed useful, there are also just as many that are cumbersome, complicated, tedious to apply and hence unused. Project managers being practical and result oriented use the test of validity by asking *"will the project fail or suffer in any way if these tools are not used?"*

PMBok (2017) has a long list of recommended tools and techniques but it does not show how they look like in many cases nor specify how they should be used leaving the market to select what they think they need and how best to use them. Without coaching support from those who have formal PM training, it is not uncommon to see use of the wrong tools and wrong use of the tools. While they may seem common sense on how to use the tools, common sense did not seem so common when errors were frequent in practice.

To better understand the PM role, and how their PM maturity level matches with their PM capability across multi-industry, commerce, banking, NGOs and government initiatives, it can be viewed in the context of the PM seniority level. The DPM3 model proposed a 5 level of PM maturity representing the 5 levels of PM seniority. All descriptions are designed to be in simple layman, where each maturity state describes the stages of maturity and illustrate how it relates to the lower and next higher level of maturity. The level of seniority should invariably align to the level or PM maturity and hence influence their pay scale.

CHARACTERISTIC OF DPM3 MATURITY

DPM3 PM Environmental Maturity Characteristics

The general common observable and verifiable characteristics of PM maturity are grouped to minimize the number of headings to enable a broad understanding of PM maturity. They progressively become more sophisticated as each project manager matures in their PM practice, from *Accidental* level to eventually becoming an *Authority* about PM.

It is possible for an organization to leap-frog to some higher level of maturity by using outside consulting assistance or use of learned mentors and coaches to lead the overall DPM3 maturity improvement initiative. Maturity is achieved only when a PM process is applied, consistently and predictably and the PM artifacts produced can all be observed and verified at any time.

DPM3 maturity at a higher level is attained gradually with the ability to accomplish whatever has been done at all the other lower levels and only after every short coming at the lower levels have been satisfactorily overcome (Table 3 to Table 6).

Table 3. DPM3 characteristics of project environment maturity

DPM3: Project Management Environmental Maturity Characteristics					
Characteristics	**Accidental**	**Enlightened**	**Competent**	**Expert**	**Authority**
Summary	Project manager appointed based on technical expertise. Unconventional use of PM	Use PM on a trial & error basis. Begin to realize lack of PM knowledge & ideas of good practices	Appointed based on PM expertise. Use PM effectively to accomplish project purposes. Appropriate use of EVM/ EV/PV/ AC	Use Portfolio/ Progr & PM to Coordinate, synchronize & control to align PM to corp obj. Judicious use of constructive change	Use PPP to corp & strategic advantage. Leverage use of VFM, constructive change, articulate capability. Act as expert witness
Clarity of purpose	Requirement spec focused	Deliverables focused. No value mgmt.	Deliverables focused. Fit of use. Understand value Use Value Mgmt. & Value Engineering	Purposeful, Biz- value-focused. Emphasis on value linked to deliverables	Purposeful Biz/Vision focused & value linked to corp strategies & VFM
Availability of facilitators	Unfamiliar, ad hoc, limited use of PM tools & techniques	Use of tools learned from seminars & on a discovery basis	Use known tools/Tech, Practice PM Facilitators	Comprehensive use of facilitators. Some level of integration to enhance PM capabilities	Comprehensive documentation Practiced, Organized, well integrated &/or interfaced
Appropriate Org structure	Functional, Weak matrix per org history	Functional or weak matrix, vague idea,	Balanced, Strong Matrix	Strong matrix or projectized	Fluid, Projectized, or Hybrid Structure as appropriate
Sufficiency of PMIS & application support	Unfamiliar use of IT facilities, ad hoc application	Basic idea of IT usage, Limited s/w application	Main appl in place using Gantt chart CPA, Spread sheet, CAD/ CAM	Appropriate use of projectized ERP Sys, integrated or interfaced to Apps	Integrated Project ERP & APPs in Realtime/ online data at source
Documentation completeness control	ad hoc, Unfamiliar Personalized	Limited documentation & organization	Formalized documentation but unenforced	Documentation standards with audit trails	Standardized comprehensive Drill-down ability compliance audit

DPM3 Characteristics of Enablers

Table 4. DPM3 characteristics of project enablers

DPM3: Project Management Facilitators (Enablers) Maturity Characteristics					
Characteristics	**Accidental**	**Enlightened**	**Competent**	**Expert**	**Authority**
PM Terminology PM Tools/Tech	Unfamiliar	Informal	Formalized but not well standardized	Formalized to local standards & some global std	Formalized to global standards Use Consistently
Coaching & Mentoring	Unfamiliar	Understand C&M value, no idea how to start	Limited application of C&M	Practiced C&M	Institutionalized Practiced with performance feedback
Training & Exposure	Ad Hoc Unplanned	Limited training & knowhow	A national practice & exposure	Regional practice & exposure	Global practice & exposure
Corporate Commitment to PM career path	Cursory Stated only at hiring stage	Unclear & limited detail of responsibilities	Clear definition per RAM/RACI chart & org chart	Clear 3P career path, Training, assessment, Dev opportunities	3P career path, career opportunities Formal records of Career development
Portfolio Programme and PM competency	No idea, learn from seminars & workshops	Ad Hoc training records as per seminars & Workshops	Formal training Limited 1/3 team with global certification	Formal training Limited 2/3 team with global certification	All subjected to formal training, Proven global delivery / Consultation
KPI design	Unfamiliar Generally, to achieve profit motive	Limited KPI learned from seminars	Sophistication in KPI designed only to motivate proj Performance	KPIs designed to 3Ps to motivate personal perf in KPAs aligned to corp strategies	KPIs designed to aligned personal perf & behavior for impact optimization on corp strategies & vision

DPM3 PM Process Maturity Characteristics

Table 5. DPM3 characteristics of PM process maturity

DPM3: Project Management Process Maturity Characteristics					
Characteristics	**Accidental**	**Enlightened**	**Competent**	**Expert**	**Authority**
1.Initiation Precontract	Sales "gung-ho" on an all-can-do basis, Proj based on client budget No PM involvement	Vague contract terms. Contract on a best effort basis for scope, schedule, cost Unfamiliar with risk provisions	Assist in drafting the proj Estimate & budget with defined roles & responsibilities.	Assist precontract review & provide input for realistic cost estimates Assist negotiation to ensure solution completeness	Assist presales effort, discussion, contract terms & negotiate Risk contingencies. Value add thru solution proposal & an integrated whole
Post Contract	PM expected to deliver project as per contract without question	Accepts proj as contracted Risk managed on a trial & error basis thus impacting cost	Summarize project brief with high level baselines of scope, sch, cost	Manage client expectations, identify main stakeholders & project risk, Coord & control project Scope, Sch, cost	Help draft proj charter Set & manage client expectations at PSW, identify stakeholders & detail risk, Coord, synchronize, optimize use of processes, people & resources
2.Planning	No Standards applied, each team have their own way, week documentation	Basic planning tools in use but mainly for larger & more complex projects	Standardized at organizational level attempted but limited to senior PMs	PM Leads & direct planning based on good practices & Templates that have proven to be effective	PM use centralized tools & Tech but may tailor level of rigor as appropriate. Use of lessons learned

Table 6. DPM3 characteristics of PM process maturity (cont)

DPM3: Project Management Process Maturity Characteristics					
Characteristics	**Accidental**	**Enlightened**	**Competent**	**Expert**	**Authority**
3.Execution	PM is involved making it difficult for them to make independent review of progress & Performance	PM partly involved making subsequent independent review less transparent	PM only involved with PM specific task	PM Direct, perform QA, Acquire/Develop & Motivate team	PM Perform integration activities and optimize allocate resources
4.Control			PM Main function to coordinate, review, control with some level of compromise	PM Monitor/ control by exception. Manage VOS/ COS and Project scope, risk, cost & schedule	PM accountable for resource utilization effectiveness, risk exposure, Stakeholder satisfaction
5.Close out **- Phase** **- Contracts** **- Project**	Difficulty closing a phase/ project due to perpetual uncontrolled change request	Tedious closeout, frequent client disruption left uncontrolled. Frequent sign-off issues	Deliverables sign-off but dissatisfaction often experienced	Deliverables sign-off against baseline and cross ref to project purpose and stakeholder expectations	Continuous documentation against contract terms & review of lessons learned with stakeholder satisfaction.

DPM3 PM Knowledge Maturity Characteristics

Table 7. DPM3 characteristics of PM knowledge areas

DPM3: Typical Project Management Knowledge Maturity Characteristics					
Characteristics	**Accidental**	**Enlightened**	**Competent**	**Expert**	**Authority**
1.Integration	Unfamiliar with integration. Work on a trial & error basis	Vague understanding. Limited idea of requirements or purpose	Capability to coordinate & Control but with limited project plan	Practical use of multi-disciplinary team to Coord & Control per proj charter	Multidisciplinary team interface &/or integrate Coord & Control per short proj charter
2.Scope	Rely on contract, SOW & WBS, No focus on fitness-for-use, prone to scope creep & "gold plating"	No formal PM training/Unexposed to PM methods, tools & Tech, lengthy sentences, imprecise & suffers scope creep	Rely on SOW, contract or deliverables per WBS. Scope control with lower scope creep & gold plating	Documentation consistency. Enforced VO/ CO control with Biz justification & assessment of impact on Sch, cost, risk, resources & fit-for-purpose	Clarity of purpose, scope, value-add, VE, VM, formalized VO from CO and Internal Change request control Impacting Client Impacting cost Impacting mgnt cost
3.Schedule	Simple common sense approach & often experience coordination issues	Schedule using Spread sheets and experiment with MS Project	Scheduling with Spread sheets, MS Project, Prima Vera. No ERP with Proj control facilities	Use CPM, PDM, PERT & see value in Scheduling soft wares and interface to ERP with project control facilities	Expert use of CPM tools and interface with Projectized ERP applications. Use & articulate EVM concept of project progress reporting of SPI/ SV

continued on following page

Table 7. Continued

Characteristics	Accidental	Enlightened	Competent	Expert	Authority
DPM3: Typical Project Management Knowledge Maturity Characteristics					
4.Cost	Simplistic estimation. Unfamiliar with cost estimation & cost control	Use simple PC based accounting s/w or spread sheet. Time consuming effort in proj cost reporting & often too late to be of mgnt use	Rely on traditional accounting s/w for actual cost Vs BAC. Late proj progress reporting	Estimation tools are interfaced with Proj based ERP with EVM Evaluate relative attractiveness of projects using IRR/ NPV/PBP	Expert use of Proj-based ERP for EVM reporting & trend review. Articulate use of time value of money concept & Risk adjusted IRR
5.Quality	Unclear problem statement. Unfamiliar with project quality definitions	Hazy idea of proj quality. Difficulty differentiating Deliverables from purpose fulfilment	Effort made to differentiate Purpose from Deliverables	Standardized Purpose driven. Per Grade required at price the client is prepared to pay. Note TQM, LCC	Formalized & Contextualised. Biz purpose driven. MBE, Strategic use of Statistical process control. Use TQM, LCC

Table 8. DPM3 characteristics of PM knowledge areas (cont)

DPM3: Typical Project Management Knowledge Maturity Characteristics					
Characteristics	**Accidental**	**Enlightened**	**Competent**	**Expert**	**Authority**
6.Resources	Unclear role of HRM & its effectiveness in PM	Basic appreciation of HR as a capital. Seek information from seminars	Appreciate HR capital & potential development	Effective use of Material, Labour, Equipment &Motivators	Effective use of coaching/ mentoring, Change Mgmt. & Force field analysis
7.Communication	Unfamiliar with exponential impact of team size increase	Do not recognize the effect of the unique project Environment impacting communication	Understand impact of barriers to communication Attempts to understand human behavior	Appreciate the significance of good people skills needed to communicate effectively	Capitalize on soft skills, articulate & address target audience effectively using power of perception convincingly thru careful choice of words
8.Risk	Unfamiliar with purpose of risk mgmt. Do first Think later attitude	Vague about purpose of risk mgmt. No idea of where to begin	Understand value of risk mgmt & its systematic identification. Unfamiliar with its strategic mgmt	Formalized risk mgmt practice. Use of checklist & templates Categorized by SME, reserves provided as per risk register	Sophisticated use of risk mgmt, review alternatives per risk reward assessment. Prioritize risk for mgmt using risk bubble chart. Exploit opportunities

continued on following page

Table 8. Continued

DPM3: Typical Project Management Knowledge Maturity Characteristics					
Characteristics	**Accidental**	**Enlightened**	**Competent**	**Expert**	**Authority**
9. Procurement	Tendency to be self-centered in approach to procurement negotiation using aa win-lose mentality	Competitive & combative in approach with a zero-sum mentality Unfamiliar with procurement strategies, contract terms / terminology	Discrete use of contractors using specific contract terms. Tendency to opt for lowest bid	Familiar use of contract terms. Comparative & competitive bids bulk purchases & negotiate with win-win attitude.	Negotiation strategy with a collaborative and supportive relationship with the view of long-term repeat biz. See contractors as partners in Biz
10. Stakeholders	Trial & error mgnt. Little attention to those impacted nor identified planned strategies to manage target groups.	Lack systematic identification of SH, or grouping to facilitate common strategies to manage each group. Often stressed by conflicting SH demands	Systematic identification of SH & grouped by specific interest. Managed expectations by applying understanding of soft-skills	Use PSW to ensure SH expectations are set and commitments made are realistic and then managed throughout project life cycle. Use soft skills to good advantage	Earned SH respect, confidence & admiration from start to completion on expectations. Ensured client understanding of commitments made. Impact of task & approval delays are explained and see clients as partners in proj succes

LEVELS OF DPM3 MATURITY

The 5 levels of maturity level range from *Accidental* project manager to an *Authority* about PM using simple description that is intuitive for the layman to understand and appreciate how one stage is more mature than the one below it.

Accidental Project Manager

At this fundamental level, the project manager (including the author) often starts their career accidentally being there by chance/accident rather than by choice. They are chosen to lead the project without prior PM knowledge and prerequisite skills needed to manage a project. This phenomenon happens more often in a functional organization or weak matrix organization structure (PMBok 5th Ed, 2013). Project quality is often compromised, higher level of rework, unsatisfactory stakeholders' satisfaction, unduly high exposure to project risk, missed deadlines, cost overruns and missed opportunities.

Enlighten Project Manager

The enlightened project manager commonly works under extreme stress for long hours. With their common sense, they learn through trial and error, mistakes and look for knowledge and experience. As a result, they get enlightened by their experience and exposure.

Competent Project Manager

Through years of practice and often with a formal PM education, some project managers can hire themselves out for a fee. Their ability to get repeat business is a testament of their ability to deliver projects to client satisfaction. They are likely to be in small and medium size projects that have few team members, involving few or no foreigners and are generally localized. Some may settle at this level of comfort and be content to seek no further in advancing their career to take on bigger and more complex projects.

Expert Project Manager

They possess many years of knowledge, skills and experience recognized as industry experts to be entrusted with larger and more complex projects with possible cross-national boundaries. They understand the exponential impact of increasing project team members and the enormous challenges that multi-cultural teams pose. As a result, they understand the need for strict use of internationally recognized terminology and good practices, the appropriate level of rigor to apply and proactively adapt to the changing environment and changing priorities throughout the project life cycle. Expert project manager makes appropriate use of PM tools and techniques like EVM to track and report project progress, life cycle costing

(LCC) and concepts of time value of money (NPV/IRR/Pay-back-period) to differentiate the relative attractiveness of projects.

They use constructive change to good advantage and the importance of strategic alignment to ensure all projects in their portfolio are appropriately controlled and in alignment with organizational direction and goals. In consequence, they recognize project in distress early. As a result, they are often hired to do repeat business and achieve a reasonable level of client satisfaction.

Authority Level Project Manager

Recognized by virtue of the organization or people pre-eminence in PM. They are often called upon for expert advice at national and international level, able to articulate a problem or issue affecting the profession and getting their case heard by the relevant authorities to garner support for action.

They are called upon as *Expert Witness* in arbitration and or legal proceedings involving disputes about quality and appropriateness of PM practices, highly sophisticated, principled and advocates of proper organizational procedures and international standards of recommended good practices. The fundamental characteristics of DPM3 maturity level relative between each level are described in Table 7.3 to Table 7.6.

In Chapter 2, Figure 2.4, the lower levels with a score below 40% are project managers who are literally engaged as "*Expediters* and *Coordinators*" rather than as project managers (PMBok, 2013). They are mainly engaged in their technical domain of engineering, construction, IT/ICT or government policies and procedure implementation but double up as a part-time project manager. In some cases, they only expedite and coordinate the project activities but also double up as part time project managers, a by-the-way responsibility instead of being the project driver. They are classified as *Accidental* and *Enlighten* project managers (Gan & Chin, 2018).

Project managers are supposed to be engaged full-time in the PM function (PMBok, 2017). They are selected based on their competence and with PM formal education. *Competent* project managers (Gan & Chin,

2018) are thus engaged in project delivery which focus on PM main processes of initiating, planning, execution, control, and closure as well as appropriate application of the 10-knowledge area of integration, scope, schedule, cost, quality, risk, communication, resources, procurement and stakeholder management.

Competent project managers could move up their maturity scale to become an **Expert** in the field through more refined and higher level of training and experience. Expert PMs are therefore engaged in some decision processes that are more tactical than those with strategic impact, but all bring value to the PM process to deliver the project value with project purpose being in alignment with organizational vison and strategies.

For the few who excel and called upon for advice, invited as guest speakers to share their knowledge and experience, consulted for expertise, engaged as expert witness and able to make representation as NGOs are considered an **Authority** on the subject of PM (Gan & Chin, 2018).

ROAD MAP TO DPM3 MATURITY

DPM3 roadmap provides the reader a continuous improvement pathway, a bridge to narrow the readers PM maturity gaps and do so in their personal preferred order. The idea is to:

1. Get a fundamental/contextual understanding of what PM maturity means.
2. How project environmental dynamics causes constant challenges?
3. How a project life cycle can in fact be a series of different mini projects?
4. Each of these mini projects can have its their significant impact and are managed by very different people with differing skills sets and accountable for different results. (Figure 2.5 in Chapter 2)

E.g. A Developer has some ideas of making his fortunes. The Developer:

a. Initiates a high-level plan on what can be (Purpose)
b. Formulate ideas of what they would like to have (Deliverables)

c. Expand on their idea and push the boundaries of possibilities
d. Commence a feasibility study (Conduct feasibility study as a project).
e. If the project is found feasible, the Developer may call for a project proposal while making their own internal estimates to counter check the proposals received.
f. Select the preferred proposer.
g. Grant their letter of award to the "Construction or implementation" organization to implement or build according to the Developer's project plan and scope of work.
h. Construction/Implementation organization begins and completes the work including any approved variation orders and hand over to the Developer.
i. Developer accepts the project handover and uses it for the Developer's intended purpose.

If the purpose is fulfilled, the Developer got the right idea and benefited from the initiative begun at stage (a). If the purpose could not be fulfilled, the idea is considered failed or the Developer's failed project.

The above could be considered as one project with 9 simple steps but each step requiring a lot of professional effort at enormous cost. In effect, there are 9 projects each with a different person in charge with skill sets relevant to the respective stage like action (a), (b), (c), (d), (e), (f) and (g) which are normally entrusted to and carried out by the "C" suite managers or the select committee in Board of directors.

Stage (a) could be called a business initiative when the success is judged on whether the project as constructed or implemented had accomplished the purpose for which it was initiated at stage (a) but this can only be known at stage (i) which could be years down the road.

At Stage (d) the project feasibility study may find the project as not feasible and hence a failed idea. If feasible, the business idea will move to the next stage (e) to seek a proposal and select the "best proposal" to implement or build as designed.

The construction/Implementation Stage (h) would likely be made up of several phases. Success at this stage will be judged based on the project manager's PM skills in terms of capability to deliver the project per scope defined and within the agreed baseline of schedule, cost, and risk exposure management, effective resourceful management (materials, people, and equipment) and at the acceptable level of stakeholder satisfaction based on client feedback.

A project could fail at any stage from (a) to (g) and not move forward. If it had succeeded and moved forward to construction, it could also still fail even after project construction/implementation (h) and (i) has completed successfully (having met the hexagonal constraints) using PM planned approach delivered according to the deliverables specified in the project charter or project brief and aligned to the project purpose stipulated in the project charter/brief but the purpose defined did not fulfill the organizational vision, mission, imperatives or it had not addressed the organizational problem for which the project was initiated. Such failures are project failures not project management failures.

On the other hand, a project could be a resounding success even though the way the PM was carried out had failed due to gross schedule and cost overrun like the Sydney Opera house project. The project schedule was overrun by 4.5 half times and cost overran by 14 times causing the New South Wales state government to be replaced. The opera house project was initiated so that Sydney could have an iconic structure. Not only had the opera house recoup its cost within 2 years of its opening, but it had also achieved its purpose by quickly becoming an iconic structure representing Sydney, Australia.

CONCLUSION

The DPM3 model and its components developed in this study is illustrated using the analogy of a motorcycle with both wheels rotate to accomplish work and grow as the skill-components grow and mature with a need to always paddle and steer to keep in balance and adapt to the dynamic project environment. The front wheel represents the project manager while the back wheel represents the organization. Each wheel is supported by 10 equal spoke lengths, and each spoke represents a maturity component. The DPM3 model is based on 5 operating principles and 5 levels of maturity. It assesses the organization and the project manager using naturally occurring observable verifiable indicators along the PM life cycle processes and PM knowledge group assessment outcomes to gauge the conduciveness of the project environment (constraints), adequacy of facilitators (enablers) and the general capability of the project manager assigned. While the maturity scores are placed under 4 component groups of PM maturity namely Environmental factors and Facilitators (Enablers), Hard-skills and Soft-skills. There is operating procedure in the use of DPM3, which the organization should investigate:

1. Respond to the question and or statements made in this DPM3 PM model. The total number of *yes* responses is expressed as a percentage of the total number of "relevant" DPM3 questions or statements.
2. Keep scores separately for the organization under Environmental sub-heading and Facilitator subheading and those of the project manager under Hard skill and Soft skill headings.
3. Measure up the score against DPM3 score to determine where the maturity level is.
4. Be realistic and point to the next higher level you desire. Note the score gap and narrow it at Step 3.
5. Work through all the DPM3 questions or statement where you have a negative response and work to improve them till you can say you have got it *and apply it in practice.*
6. Focus on a rough but gradual improvement in all components such that they all gradually move together in tandem. A balanced skill set out-performs those with imbalanced skills sets.

Not all organizations want to move to the highest level of DPM3 maturity because of its high-cost implications and insignificant return if they have no opportunity to benefit from the economies of scale. You as the reader are the master of your own destiny. If you do not wish or cannot hope to reach the star, aim high enough and still be in the clouds.

REFERENCES

Borg, J. (2019). *Persuasion: the art of influencing people* (2nd ed.). Pearson Business.

Candido, C.J. F. & Santos, S. P., (2015). Strategy implementation: What is the failure rate. *Journal of Management and Organisation, Vol 21* Issue 2. Cambridge University Press and Australian and New Zealand Academy of Management https://doi.org/DOI: 10.1017/jmo.2014.77

Drucker, P. F. (1999). *Management Challenges for the 21st Century*. Harper Collins.

Gan, R. C. C., & Chin, C. M. M. (2018). Components of project management maturity impacting project, programme, portfolio and organisational success. In Karayaz, G., & Silvius, G. (Eds.), *Developing Organizational Maturity for Effective Project Management* (pp. 128–152). IGI Global., DOI: 10.4018/978-1-5225-3197-5.ch007

Gan, R. C. C., & Chin, C. M. M. (2019). Project management guide and project management maturity models as generic tools capable for diverse applications. In Katuu, S. (Ed.), *Diverse Applications and Transferability of Maturity Models* (pp. 269–315). IGI Global., DOI: 10.4018/978-1-5225-7080-6.ch011

Hazel, S. (2016, February 10). Why native English speakers fail to be understood in English – and lose out in global business. *The Conversation*. https://theconversation.com/why-native-english-speakers-fail-to-be-understood-in-english-and-lose-out-in-global-business-54436

Herzberg, F., Mausner, B., & Snyderman, B. B. (2011). *The motivation to work*. Transaction Publishers.

Kuhn, T. (1962). *The structure of scientific revolution*. University of Chicago Press.

Livingston, J. S. (1971, January). Myth of the well-educated Manager, *Harvard Business Review*. https://hbr.org/1971/01/myth-of-the-well-educated-manager\

Maslow, A.H., (1965). *Eupsychian management: a journal.* Irwin, R.D.

McGregor, D. (2006). *The human side of enterprise, annotated edition.* McGraw Hill McKinsey Quarterly, (2014, September 1). Tom Peters on leading the 21st-century organization. McKinsey & Company. https://www.mckinsey.com/capabilities/people-and-organizational-performance/our-insights/tom-peters-on-leading-the-21st-century-organization

Mulcahy, R. (2015). *PMP Exam Prep Book* (8th ed.). RMC Publications Inc.

Müller, R. & Turner, R.(2007a). The influence of project managers on project success criteria and project success by type of project. *European Management Journal* Vol (25), No. 4, 298–309. https://doi:DOI: 10.1016/j.emj.2007.06.003

Müller, R., & Turner, R. (2007b). Matching the project manager's leadership style to project type. *International Journal of Project Management,* 25(1), 21–32. DOI: 10.1016/j.ijproman.2006.04.003

Müller, R., & Turner, R. (2009). Leadership competency profiles of successful project managers *International Journal of Project Management* Vol (28), 437-448. https://doi.org/DOI: 10.1016/j.ijproman.2009.09.003

PMI Pulse of the Profession. (2015). Navigating Complexity. Project Management Institute. https://www.pmi.org/-/media/pmi/documents/public/pdf/learning/thought-leadership/pulse/navigating-complexity.pdf

PMI Pulse of the Profession. (2016). The high cost of low performance. Project Management Institute. www.pmi.org/-/media/pmi/documents/public/pdf/learning/thought-leadership/pulse/improve-business-results-infographic.pdf?la=en

Prag, J. (2010). The Humanist Economist. In Pearce, C. L., Maciariello, J. A., & Yamawaki, H. (Eds.), *The Drucker difference: what the world's greatest management thinker means* (p. 207). McGraw Hill.

Project Management Institute. (2015). *The PMI Talent Triangle.* Project Management Institute.

Project Management Institute (PMI). (2013). *A guide to project management body of knowledge* (PMBOK Guide) (5th ed). Project Management Institute.

Project Management Institute (PMI). (2017). *A guide to project management body of knowledge* (PMBOK Guide) (6th ed). Project Management Institute.

Rabe, C. B. (2006). *The innovation killer*. AMACOM.

Senge, P., Kleiner, A., Roberts, C., Ross, R., Roth, G., & Smith, B. (1999). *The Dance of Change: the challenges to sustaining momentum in a learning organization*. Crown Currency.

Zandhuis, A. (2013). *ISO 21500 in Practice - a Management Guide*. Van Haren Publishing.

ADDITIONAL READING

Crawford, J. K. (2021). *Project Management Maturity Model: Providing a Proven Path to Project Management Excellence* (4th ed.). Auerbach Publications. DOI: 10.1201/9781003129523

Gan, R. C., & Chin, C. M. (2018). Components of Project Management Maturity Impacting Project, Program, Portfolio, and Organizational Success. In Silvius, G., & Karayaz, G. (Eds.), *Developing Organizational Maturity for Effective Project Management* (pp. 128–152). IGI Global Scientific Publishing., DOI: 10.4018/978-1-5225-3197-5.ch007

Wallace, M. (2019). *Motorcycle Metaphor: Leadership Lessons for the Progressive Organization*. Black Card Books.

KEY TERMS AND DEFINITIONS

Agile: Is a flexible, iterative approach to project management to deliver value incrementally through adaptability. For example, adopting a mental paradigm that emphasizes short but more frequent deliveries over documentation, work spurts in weekly sprints instead of long and large project deliverables, short weekly standup progress review instead of longer project progress reviews. Some common AGILE frameworks are SCRUM, Kanban, and LEAN.

Automation: The use of technology, software or machinery to perform tasks with minimal or no human intervention. It aims to improve efficiency, reduce errors and enhance productivity.

Domain Knowledge: It refers to a deep understanding of and expertise in a specific field of study. It includes terminology, processes, and best practices such as PMBOK guidelines.

Dynamic Leadership: This refers to where leaders must adapt their leadership style to accommodate the changing team maturity level. As a leader in a dynamic environment, the project manager has to think ahead of the impediments to PM and how their impact could be mitigated, lead the team to aspire to who they each can be, then act to facilitate and smoothen the process flow, enthuse and encourage the team as they move along the project remembering always and in all action to show they care about the well-being of their team.

Hard Skills: It refers to specific, measurable abilities that are acquired through education, training etc. Examples are technical skills, language skills, software or machinery skills.

Roadmap: This is a strategic plan that outlines the steps, direction with milestones and deliverables over the project life cycle. This gives project manager and stakeholders a continuous improvement pathway.

Rounded Individual: This refers to a team member who possesses a balanced combination of technical expertise, soft skills and adaptability. With the lack of such balance skill sets, it can impede the project manager's ability to cope, adapt and be flexible to manage the project.

Soft Skills: This refers to personal abilities or attributes that enable individuals to interact with others. Examples are communication skills, leadership skills, problem-solving skills or time management skills.

Value of Money (VFM): This refers to the optimal balance of cost, quality, and benefits of the project lifespan. This concept helps project managers and stakeholders to ensure resources are efficiently maximized and waste are minimized.

Section 6

DPM3 Key to Organizational Performance

Chapter 8
Conclusion and Contributions

ABSTRACT

A foundational work carried out and documented under Chapter 1 and 2 providing the broad understanding of the research background and how the PM profession had evolved over the last five decades. The impediments to PM were highlighted as they cause project performance to falter while reported short comings of current prominent PM3 models and factors that inhibit PM3 adoption were included to serve as lessons learned. Chapter 4 detailed the approach that was undertaken to mitigate the impact of those impediments and what could and should be done when designing the new PM3 to avoid the pitfalls already experienced. While Chapter 5 to 7 describe the proposed DPM3 model that can be used to measure organizational performances in the industry. Hence, Chapter 8 concludes the research investigation conducted throughout the years and discusses its contribution, implications to theory and practices and the further development of work that can be carried out.

CONTRIBUTION TO THE BODY OF KNOWLEDGE

This study originally initiated with 9 objectives and was narrowed down to 4 research objectives to focus attention on the aim of improving organization performance through enhancing organization PM maturity. It was also to better understand the reasons for the persistent high proj-

DOI: 10.4018/979-8-3693-1439-5.ch008

ect failure rate reported by Candido (2015) in their study of 35 years of research papers and what lessons could be learnt from them. It has often been quoted *"if we don't learn from the history of our mistakes, we are bound to repeat them"*.

This research thus addresses the 4 research objectives with its respective research outcome and contribution to knowledge summarised below:

1. **What are the components of PM maturity?**

Literature review regarding components of PM maturity and study of the more prominent PM3s in the market did not yield sufficient result to form a structured and more holistic view of what PM3 components should be. The prominent PM3 models reviewed almost entirely focus on the PM policies, processes, and procedures but little by way of human capacity and capabilities that drives the project forward. The model by PwC had included the strategic imperatives but did not identify the components of PM3 maturity.

PMI's PMBok provided some of the information but their various subsequent versions reveal there were indecisions from PMBok drafters when the versions had PM3 maturity attributes like PM3 components being grouped and later regroup in subsequent releases while others were later seen as inverted views.

As a result, this study had to rely on the 20 years of actual PM implementation experience and survey during 19 years of teaching and coaching project managers to clearly see *that there were really two parties that drive projects* forward. This realization is encapsulated in DPM3 under chapter 5 to 7 using a simple motorbike as a *pictorial diagram to clearly illustrate the 5 DPM3 operating principles*, the *5 levels of PM maturity*, the *10 components of PM maturity* of both the performing organization and that of the project manager. Each component is explained with their respective identifiable characteristics.

This research concludes with the pathway to DPM3 maturity, the background thinking needed before deciding on the level of DPM3 maturity (base on the benefit/cost ratio) relevant to management vision of where they want to be and the strategy they wish to employ to be ahead of their competition.

2. The levels of PM maturity

DPM3 associates the key PM responsibilities by reference to the project manager's organization given role and seniority where each advancing level moves the project manager up the PM maturity scale. The model allows users to benchmark their present level of maturity, the level they aspire to be (not everyone can or are necessarily keen to be at the top of the maturity scale due to its relative disproportional cost/benefit ratio) and the gap in maturity to work on. In this way, they can move up the maturity ladder more effectively thereby contributing to organizational performance.

3. The characteristics of DPM3 maturity level

DPM3 detail the specific characteristics that best describe each PM maturity attribute so that users can focus on the more significant aspect of what improves PM maturity, the characteristics they already possess but could be improved and those desirable characteristics they lack so they could progressively work on them all of which will contribute to their organizational performance.

4. The road map to DPM3 maturity

DPM3 uniqueness also explains the alternatives in bridging users' PM maturity gap and how users could work on them to move up the maturity ladder thereby enhancing their personal and organizational capability and overall performance.

The general picture painted by researchers of alarming project failures should be viewed with caution. Research data and their summaries that do not differentiate crucial information about which leader leads which stage lack the contextual framework needed to relate accountability to the assigned responsibility and hence cannot be relied on as a basis to isolate root cause of a project or PM problem. Failing to identify the various leaders (e.g. CEO, CFO, COO, CIO or C suite managers) that are accountable for the respective stage of a project from those that are appointed to take charge of the construction or implementation stage as project managers creates a fuzzy understanding and misleading half-truths.

This study differentiates the many prior stages that projects normally go through from *idea to action*, each stage with the respective assignee responsible for its outcome until the stage when construction or implementation takes place using PM approach or PM methodology. The stages vary and are industry specific requiring industry expertise to draft for each type of project. The respective leadership roles should always be clearly segregated for each stage that they are entrusted.

Another unique feature that DPM3 provides is the 5 operating principles of PM maturity that uses the analogy of a motorbike to encapsulate pictorially the 5 salient features required of a PM maturity model. DPM3 allows self-test to gauge the organization and their project manager's level of maturity with a view to assessing what they know and what they do not, in order that they can identify what they lack and which aspects they wish to give priority. All these specified in simple English and using familiar PM terminology enable project managers to intuitively understand and apply.

Like all economic enterprises and not-for profit organizations, the objective is to be cost effective and hence seek maturity enhancement to the level they aspire and in line with their organization strategy but to aim high enough to remain competitive and always one step ahead of the competition. Should the organization wish to assess how they fare in comparison with their peers, they should then engage an independent assessor familiar with multiple industry, with the relevant experience and familiarity with the type of business and project environment being assessed.

The proposed DPM3 model is a preliminary version but already addresses the more significant attributes required of a PM3 and summarized from literature review and validated by user feedback. The robustness is expected to be worked on, improved or refined over time but always kept as simple and relevant to organizational performance enhancement to gain the market acceptance needed for it to thrive.

IMPLICATIONS TO THE THEORY AND PRACTICE OF PM3

The evolving nature of the PM profession over the last 3 decades has been particularly significant, greatly improved and the practices of PM made more refined. The last 2 decades have seen significant changes in the way PM is viewed by management as an effective vehicle to bring management strategic plans into fruition. On one hand, the organized nature of PM practices allows role delineation and better accountability for putting management strategic plans into action. In contrast, it also enables responsibilities to be isolated for root cause of deficiencies which may not be to the liking of non-performing managers.

This study output highlights the need for project failure statistics to be differentiated by stage of project failure to isolate the key result area responsible. This then enables determination of cause and effect, afford a better understanding of the various levels of players involved and the lessons that could be learned to improve future PM endeavors.

The lack of a global consensus on the standardization of PM terminology to facilitate communication between project personnel, project managers and non-project stakeholders, DPM3 rely on PMI for leadership, it being the largest and fastest growing PM body in the world with 1.4 million PMPs certificate holders and 700,000 members (PMI, 2024). In addition, PMI was also the chosen PM body to be the ISO secretariat, and its PM lexicon used as the initial base in the drafting of the ISO 21500 (2017), all a testament of PMI's pre-eminence and influence in the world of PM and with the widest level of PM user acceptance. The theory, principles and coverage remain unchanged but the way in which the theory is applied is made fluid to enable it to be adaptable as the circumstance dictate. To ensure sufficient width of knowledge and depth of expertise, DPM3 is designed with 2-dimensional assessment:

- **Width of coverage**, (knowing and implementing the PM maturity attribute)
- **Depth of expertise** to ensure optimal use of the PM maturity attribute (maturity level)

The width of coverage is a binary response featured in this research model. Until the model has gained sufficient market acceptance, DPM3 will be expanded in the future to also assess the 5 levels or degree of understanding of each attribute and its contextual use. This is the preferred design approach to gain market acceptance in 2 stages to achieve optimal organizational performance. The aim is to draw attention to the benefits of PM maturity and gain market acceptance through ease of use and flexible application. The organizational performance improvement should first be accomplished with a lower overall total cost of implementation before embarking on the continuous improvement culture that maintains organizational competitive advantage.

Research Limitations

This research has been designed to ensure a sufficiently wide coverage of experienced PM practitioners from a sufficiently wide number of industrial sectors, commerce, banking, energy, government, and enforcement agencies. However, projects and change initiatives are all pervasive and therefore unlikely that all would be covered. Suffice it to say, PM and PM3 are for generic application, and it is hope, the principles and practices can be applied and adapted, failing which the parties involved should make the effort to seek additional PM professional support.

There is around 80% of the research sample are from MNCs, large local conglomerates and GLCs. As a result, the 10% SME/SMIs and 10% of others in the sample maybe on the low side as these smaller enterprises were definitively more in terms of pure numbers. The mitigating factor however is, they have smaller and less complicated projects, less organised and less sophisticated management and hence unlikely to offer significant PM expertise. As a result, it is hope, this will not in any way invalidate this research findings.

Although this research has identified the human factor as being the key contributor of project performance, the time limit, and resources available in this research will be wholly unrealistic to cover the wide spectrum of human behavior and what motivates the individuals and harness its capability and capacity to bring value to future PM3 endeavors. This research highlighted the value of human enterprise, resourcefulness and human ingenuity to perform, adapt and make best use of given resources. Future researchers could take advantage of this finding and make more efforts to identify what really makes the project team tick and perform under all the trying circumstances and still relish its challenges.

The dynamic environmental factors surrounding projects and complexity of human behavior are often also interdependent making the idiosyncratic response difficult to definitively understand and measure for cause and effect. Nevertheless, it provides future research with the challenge to think and fine ways to better understand and elucidate. Due to the limited field testing using a survey of a dozen senior project managers, future research could be undertaken to validate the robustness and reliability of the model.

RECOMMENDATION FOR FUTURE RESEARCH

The use of interviews with open-ended questions was used in the initial survey to gain a big picture of the scope of this research project. Theory and experience showed it required a lot more time not only to get the appointment, conduct the interviews, recording the responses, deciphering the responses, and collating the knowledge was indeed tedious and difficult to map for commonality as each respondent had different ways in responding to each survey question and some responses could be open to different interpretation. Despite the limitations, it did give a broad picture of the likely scope and magnitude of work to be expected and an indication of how the research structure should look like.

To gain a wider survey sample for better data reliability, the knowledge gained from the interviews provided the basis for a survey questionnaire requiring binary feedback to yield results that could be quantitatively assessed, and trends observed. This could easily be tabulated for a more objective result, but it will lack the richness and depth of knowledge that might otherwise be obtained from responses obtained from open ended interview questionnaire. Enormous potential can be derived from the PM approach to managing change or management of projects to enhance organizational performance. In particular, the following may interest future researchers:

- Analyzing factors such as digital transformation, agile methodoogies or globalization may impact the relevance and applicability of DPM3
- Inclusion of practical tools, assessment templates, worksheets or checklist to visualize the operationalization of DPM3
- To explore how the DPM3 evolution in response to changing business environments, technological advancements and shift in PM practices
- Importance of the human factor in PM and PM3
- Enhancing good soft skills as the key to promote project success
- Identifying and agreeing to a set of common project performance matrix
- PM is about managing change but how do change management help PM
- Negotiation skills is central to working with people

CONCLUSION

It is hope that this research has isolated the many impediments that plague project managers and their team will enable reader to see how PM and PM3 tools, techniques and conceptual understanding should be read in context so that they can and are applied appropriately. In the management of change, there are many environmental factors that are not only dynamic but also often interdependent and beyond the control of the project manager and their team. DPM3 have identified these factors and kept them simple and in terminology that PMs are familiar with to forewarn the readers of such impediments, how they could be addressed, or their impact mitigated. This research also provides the means for PM practitioners to advance their PM maturity as well as providing a cost-effective pathway to enhance their level of PM maturity thereby improving their chances of PM success consistently and more predictably.

REFERENCES

Candido, C.J. F. & Santos, S. P., (2015). Strategy implementation: What is the failure rate. *Journal of Management and Organisation, Vol 21* Issue 2. Cambridge University Press and Australian and New Zealand Academy of Management DOI: 10.1017/jmo.2014.77

Gan, R. C. C., & Chin, C. M. M. (2018). Components of project management maturity impacting project, programme, portfolio and organisational success. In Karayaz, G., & Silvius, G. (Eds.), *Developing Organizational Maturity for Effective Project Management* (pp. 128–152). IGI Global., DOI: 10.4018/978-1-5225-3197-5.ch007

Gan, R. C. C., & Chin, C. M. M. (2019). Project management guide and project management maturity models as generic tools capable for diverse applications. In Katuu, S. (Ed.), *Diverse Applications and Transferability of Maturity Models* (pp. 269–315). IGI Global., DOI: 10.4018/978-1-5225-7080-6.ch011

Project Management Institute (PMI). (2024). Project Management Professional (PMP). *PMI* https://www.pmi.org/certifications/project-management -pmp

ADDITIONAL READING

Kerzner, H. (2015). *Project Management 2.0: Leveraging Tools, Distributed Collaboration, and Metrics for Project Success.* Wiley. DOI: 10.1002/9781119020042

Martinelli, S. R., Waddell, M. J., & Rahschulte, J. T. (2017). *Projects Without Boundaries: Successfully Leading Teams and Managing Projects in a Virtual World.* Wiley.

Siebel, M. T. (2019). *Digital Transformation: Survive and Thrive in an Era of Mass Extinction*. Rodin Books. Highsmith, J. (2009). *Agile Project Management: Creating Innovative Products (Agile Software Development)*. (2nd ed). Addison-Wesley Professional.

KEY TERMS AND DEFINITIONS

DPM3: It is a model based on 5 operating principles and 5 levels of maturity by Gan & Chin, (2018, 2019). It assesses the organization and the project manager using naturally occurring observable verifiable indicators along the PM life cycle processes and PM knowledge group assessment outcomes to gauge the conduciveness of the project environment (constraints), adequacy of facilitators (enablers) and the general capability of the project manager assigned. The maturity scores are placed under 4 component groups of PM maturity namely Environmental factors and Facilitators (Enablers), Hard-skills and Soft-skills.

Implication: It refers to how the research findings contribute to both theory and practice.

Research Limitations: it refers to the constraints that may impact the scope of research, validity of study. For example, constraint in sample size, analytical techniques, researcher's perspective. Identifying these limitations enable researchers to address it in future studies.

Glossary

Accountability: Being answerable for the overall quality of the result or outcome expected from the given role or initiative/s.

Actionable Environmental Constraints: Are within the control of the project organization, factors that can be improved or changed either in the short or long term

Non-Actionable Environmental Constraints: On the other hand like the client's national legal framework, industry standards, and inclement weather conditions are beyond the control of the project organization and the team. These factors limit the options available and, to a varying degree, may negatively impact the project progress. As a result, it is the responsibility of the project team to assess each constraint and proactively manage them in their risk management mitigation plan and provide the cost contingency provision in the overall project budget.

Capability: The ability to demonstrate one's capability to carry out given responsibilities in each environment, with the given resources in the required time frame to achieve the required outcome.

Capacity: Volume of business an organization can undertake without compromising its standard of delivery and capabilities.

Continuous Improvement: The state of being in a continuous and dynamic environment that necessitates constant check and balance so that all capabilities and competencies are always in full and constant readiness to address all that is needed to accomplish organizational objectives effectively, efficiently and holistically.

Competency: The ability to demonstrate one's expertise and capability and articulate the reasons for a given decision made and convincing presentation of their business case and demonstrated ability to do what had been described.

Constraints: Known factors in the internal project environment (environmental constraints) or conditions imposed by management (management constraints) all of which can and do limit the project, programme or portfolio manager's decision, strategy and operating options. Constraints with negative influence and can become so restrictive as to be an issue requiring management intervention. Constraints are controllable and are actionable in the long term.

Internal Project Environmental Factors: Are within the control of the organization like organization structure/s, IT/ICT infrastructure and support, availability of project artifacts, lessons learned etc.

External Project Environmental Factors: Are constraints beyond organization control e.g. Legislated standards, industry standards, inclement weather conditions, economic and market situations, geographical contours, lack of local resources, restrictive local cultures etc.,

Culture: The way people do things as an identifiable group. The group, organization or people's general view of things observed, expects from and interacts with one another and the way they do things as part of their normal daily routines or habits.

Enablers: Also meaning facilitators that include PM tools, techniques, procedures, policies, templates and PM information system that together as a whole enable or facilitate the effective performance of project, programme, portfolio which in total would enhance organizational performance.

Good Practices: These are often referred to as Recommended Good Practices. Good practice is a way of practicing knowledge and skills in the project environment and there is a consensus that its correct application will enhance the probability of project success, in most projects, programmes, portfolio and situations. Good practices imply there are possibilities of it being improved as circumstances dictate if the team can justify the change, stating why and how improvement could be accomplished because of that documented change. Best-practice on the other hand implies it is best for all seasons and being best, connotes nothing can better it thus stifling team creativity (Gan and Chin, 2018).

Grade: A category assigned to products or services having the same functional use but having a different technical characteristic (PMBok® Guide, 2013 p.228). The quality characteristics of a specified product or outcome.

Hard Skills: Skills, techniques, rules and theories that can be learned in the classroom or written work or text books. Some hard skills are tacit knowledge like artisan work and tradesman can only be learned with hands-on practice like handicraft, pottery work, artwork, accountancy, engineering etc.

Hawthorne Effect: The general tendency for people to work harder than they otherwise would, had they not been informed that they were participants in a research experiment.

Key Performance Area: KPA are identified aspects of and areas relevant to measurement of performance. They define the area or scope within which a set of KPIs will be developed and used to measure the key performances of that KPA.

Key Performance Indicator: KPI are specific measures of performance within its specific KPAs that measure how well performance has been achieved against the given agreed target or expectation.

Knowledge: Knowledge is better explained after classification under three types.

o   **Explicit** knowledge is knowledge that can be explained in words, illustrated or written. Often referred to as book-knowledge. It tends to be more effective if the communication is well explained and articulated.

o   **Implicit** knowledge is knowledge gain through experience and ex-posure to an organization, culture, work environment or project en-vironment etc. Implicit knowledge is difficult to explain in words but can be shared between people with similar knowledge and experience.

o   **Tacit** knowledge is knowledge that can only be acquired through personal hands-on experience, experiential learning by actual doing and practice. In limited cases it can also be acquired through personal experiment and iteration with or without prior learning, mentoring or coaching. Tacit knowledge examples include professional practice experience in engineering, accountancy, advocacy, surgery, people management, negotiation, conflict management, stakeholder expectation management, plastering, welding, pottery work, cycling, programming and the practice of systems design etc.,

Knowledge Management:

o **Data:** Raw observation of the numbers at work. By itself, it has no meaning as it needs context or reference to be useful or meaningful.
o **Information:** Relevant data obtained that can be contextualized against expectations or performance benchmarks or in a series that shows trends or pattern of behavior e.g., actual inception-to-date cost incurred against the value earned.
o **Knowledge:** Information that has context, understood, related and can allow or provide reflection and application.
o **Wisdom:** Convergence of contextualized knowledge and information that can be gainfully applied in various form, situation and the possibility to profit from it.

Leaders: Someone who has followers (Drucker, n.a). One who is capable of persuading others by their words or actions, to believe in their cause and enthused to act purposefully and willingly towards that cause and sometimes even at high or extreme personal cost/sacrifice.

Maturity: The state of being fully developed with all faculties on its own or, is capable of functioning at its optimal level of capability. With these two principles in hand, project management like all management principles are about getting work done through other people, (Drucker, 1999).

Maturity Pillars: Like the wheel, they are significant controllable factors of PM Maturity. There are many aspects or factors in the project organization which are controllable/actionable and have a direct impact of either enabling or restraining the project and/or programme management work. Being actionable, it is within the means of the organization to effect the change thereby enhancing organizational performance. These factors are internal, and they are initiated, planned or structured and controlled by management. These pillars are groups by their common characteristics of:

o **E Environmental Factors:** Constraints that may limit the project manager's options
o **F Facilitators or Enablers:** Enablers that facilitate the project manager's work. The lack of it can hinder or frustrate the project manager's performance.

Organization: The performing organization that performs or carries out the project or group of people organized under a specific legal entity or purpose.

Outcome: The result arising from a given course of action, initiative or project.

PM3 (Project Management Maturity Model): Generic PM maturity assessment tools designed to measure the approximate level of balanced state of the organization and its team maturity in terms of its overall capability and capacity to manage projects or change initiatives, with the implicit view that more mature organizations are better enabled to manage projects with improved results more consistently as well as more predictably.

Project: A temporary endeavor undertaken to create a unique outcome, product, service or result (PMBok, 2017).

Project Complexity: The level of difficulty to be expected in a project as a result of existence of any or combination of some of the project complexity variables.

Project Complexity Variables: Variables in a project whose existence create complexity in the management of such projects. Such variables includes stakeholders with multi-cultures and languages, number of people involved, impacted and or affected by the project process or its outcome, complexity of design, high level of performance expectations, team inexperience in the project industry, insufficient PM and related knowledge, disparate applications, applications designed and developed using different computer languages, disparate systems to be integrated, unfamiliar tools and techniques, environmental factors of extreme weather conditions, inadequate infrastructure, compliance requirements relating to regulations, bylaws, industry standards, procedures and guidelines, lack of a suitable PM information system like project ERP system to facilitate procurement, coordination and control of orders committed, goods received on site, supplier and contractor invoicing and lack of timely capture of project transactions as and when they occur.

Project Failure: Project outcome that is unable to fulfill the project purpose for which it was designed, purposes that include strategic imperatives defined by the C-suite management, Portfolio or programme managers to fulfill the organization's vision, mission, strategies or management imperative/s. A partial fulfilment of purpose would be deem a partial project purpose failure.

Project Management Failure: The project manager and the team's inability to complete a given project within any one or more permitted range (deviation tolerance level) of the constraints of scope, schedule, cost, adequate management of project risk exposure, effective or balanced management of given resources and satisfactory fulfilment of key stakeholder's expectations.

Project Management (PM): The application of knowledge, skills, tools & techniques to project activities to meet project requirements (PMBok® Guide, 6th Ed, 2017).

PM Guide: PM guides are statement of good practices in management of projects. They state what should be done, the rationale behind the requirement, the input needed, tools that could be used and the expected output but no instructions on how to do it.

PM Methodology: A documented step by step approach to a PM process to arrive at an expected project outcome. Unlike a guide which broadly states what needs to be done, a methodology addresses the full scope of work required sometimes in the form of a roadmap and how each process within the roadmap is to be carried out, step by step including artifacts, samples and templates, from start to conclusion.

PM Maturity: The state at which an organization can provide the environment, organization structure/s, policies, procedures, tools/techniques and resources (people, equipment, materials) that is conducive for a competent PM team to engage any or all projects within its scope and capacity. When applied to project managers, it is the balanced state of competency and capability at which the project manager can lead a project to accomplish the project outcome within the given project constraints of scope, schedule, cost, risk, resources and stakeholders' expectations.

Programme: a group of projects each having their own required outcome but together they are designed to accomplish the common programme purpose, goal or outcome. A programme may have an indicative (or changed as circumstances dictate) target date or dates of delivery or target state or level of accomplishment over a given time.

Programme Management: The process of effectively managing a programme using generally recognized recommended good practices, tools, techniques, policies, procedures, templates and any facilitators to apply organizational resources of people, equipment, materials and services to coordinate and control all projects within its programme. The role includes ensuring that projects under its control when completed will together accomplish the given programme benefits statement/s, objective/s or purpose. While some programmes have performance target by target dates, e.g. Poverty eradication of the urban poor in XYZ City so all families have their own accommodation, basic infra structure with a minimum income exceeding $n per head, others maybe an ongoing endeavor like the Malaysia Vision 2020, i.e. a measurable goal to reach developed-nation-status by the year 2020.

Portfolio: Any grouping of projects and or programmes or any combination thereof for the purpose of identification and assignment of responsibilities to manage the portfolio effectively.

Portfolio Manager: May be given different sets of performance indicators for different sub-portfolio, one or several for each group of projects or programme in their given portfolio.

Portfolio Management: The process of effectively managing the given portfolio of investment, projects or programmes using generally recognized recommended good practices, tools, techniques, policies, procedures, templates and any facilitators to apply organizational resources of people and equipment, materials and services effectively to coordinate, synchronize and control all projects and or programmes under its purview so as to ensure when they are all completed within their defined target dates, they will collectively or in subgroups accomplish the respective portfolio objective for each group, purpose or performance goal.

Quality: The outcome that meets the "fitness for use" criteria (Juran, n.a).

Meeting the Project or Programme Purpose: Fitness for use and meeting specifications or grade specified and at the price the client is prepared to pay (Feigenbaum, n.a).

Responsibility: The role to do or carry out the activities and tasks defined in the responsibility assignment matrix or RAM chart.

Roadmap: A structured or organized approach, designed to lead the reader or user from one point commonly referred to as the *as-is status* or state to another desired state or *to-be status,* using knowledge, experience, tools, techniques, policies, procedures, templates and facilitators to apply organizational resources of people, equipment, materials and services to plan, coordinate and control all programmes and or projects under their purview within their environment so as to ensure when they are all completed, they will together accomplish the given portfolio, programme or project objective or purpose.

Soft Skills: Human relations skills that are learned and hone at the workplace, social network or interaction with people.

Strategy: Action plan designed to accomplish decisive competitive advantage. It is planned with the big picture in mind, holistic and contextual in application and actionable with specific purpose/goal and sequence of action. Strategies are generally designed to achieve long term decisive competitive advantage. It may also be designed to create opportunities for other strategies to work more effectively and thus gain optimum impact.

ADDITIONAL READING

Backlund, F., Chronéer, D., & Sundqvist, E. (2014). Project Management Maturity Models – A Critical Review: A Case Study within Swedish Engineering and Construction Organizations. *Procedia: Social and Behavioral Sciences*, *119*, 837–846. DOI: 10.1016/j.sbspro.2014.03.094

Demir, C., & Kocabas, I. (2010). Project Management Maturity Model (PMMM) in educational organizations. *Procedia: Social and Behavioral Sciences*, *9*, 1641–1645. DOI: 10.1016/j.sbspro.2010.12.379

Domingues, L., & Ribeiro, P. (2023). Project Management Maturity Models: Proposal of a Framework for Models Comparison. *Procedia Computer Science*, *219*, 2011–2018. DOI: 10.1016/j.procs.2023.01.502

Eshtehardian, E., & Saeedi, F. (2016). Developing Improvement Planning Phase in Project Management Maturity Models. *Modern Applied Science*, *10*(1), 1. Advance online publication. DOI: 10.5539/mas.v10n9p1

Fabbro, E. and Tonchia, S., (2021). *Project management maturity models: Literature review and new developments*. The Journal of Modern Project Management, Vol.8(3).

Lu, X., Shu, L., & Li, J. (2008). *Correlation analysis between maturity factors and performance indexes in software project. IEEE International Conference on Industrial Engineering and Engineering Management*, pp.1793-1797. DOI: 10.1109/IEEM.2008.4738181

Machado, F., Duarte, N., & Amaral, A. (2023). Project Management Maturity in Renovation and Remodelling Construction Firms. *Buildings (Basel, Switzerland)*, *13*(2), 557. DOI: 10.3390/buildings13020557

Moreno-Monsalve, N., & Delgado-Ortiz, S. (2021). *Knowledge Management and Its Relationship With Organizational Maturity Processes*. The Handbook of Research on International Business and Models for Global Purpose-Driven Companies. pp.276-288 DOI: 10.4018/978-1-7998-4909-4.ch015

Reis, T., Mathias, M., & Oliveira, O. (2016). Maturity models: Identifying the state-of-the-art and the scientific gaps from a bibliometric study. *Scientometrics*, *110*(2), 643–672. DOI: 10.1007/s11192-016-2182-0

Röglinger, M., Pöppelbuß, J., & Becker, J. (2012). Maturity models in business process management. *Business Process Management Journal*, *18*(2), 328–346. DOI: 10.1108/14637151211225225

Tahri, H., & Drissi-Kaitouni, O. (2015). New Design for Calculating Project Management Maturity (PMM). *Procedia: Social and Behavioral Sciences*, *181*, 171–177. DOI: 10.1016/j.sbspro.2015.04.878

Viana, J., & Mota, C. (2016). *Enhancing Organizational Project Management Maturity: a framework based on the value focused thinking model*. Production Journal, Vol. 26(2), pp.313-329. DOI: 10.1590/0103-6513.169913

Compilation of References

Association of Project Management. (2019). *APM Body of knowledge* (7th ed.). Association of Project Management.

Black, J. S., & Gregersen, H. B. (2002). *Leading Strategic Change: Breaking Through the Brain Barrier*. Pearson.

Borg, J. (2019). *Persuasion: the art of influencing people* (2nd ed.). Pearson Business.

Candido, C.J. F. & Santos, S. P., (2015). Strategy implementation: What is the failure rate. *Journal of Management and Organisation,* Vol (21) Issue 2. Cambridge University Press and Australian and New Zealand Academy of Management https://doi.org/DOI: 10.1017/jmo.2014.77

Crawford, J. K. (2007), Project Management Maturity Model (2nd Ed). Auerback Publications, Drucker, P.F, (1999), *Management Challenges for the 21st Century*. Harper Collins.

Crawford, J. K. (2007), Project Management Maturity Model *2nd Ed*, Auerback Publications, Drucker, P.F, (1999), *Management Challenges for the 21st Century*. Harper Collins.

Creswell, J. W. (2003). Research Design: Qualitative, Quantitative, and Mixed Methods Approaches. *Sage (Atlanta, Ga.)*.

Drucker, P. F. (1999). *Management Challenges for the 21st Century*. Harper Collins.

Gan, R. C. C., & Chin, C. M. M. (2018). Components of project management maturity impacting project, programme, portfolio and organisational success. In Karayaz, G., & Silvius, G. (Eds.), *Developing Organizational Maturity for Effective Project Management* (pp. 128–152). IGI Global., DOI: 10.4018/978-1-5225-3197-5.ch007

Gan, R. C. C., & Chin, C. M. M. (2019). Project management guide and project management maturity models as generic tools capable for diverse applications. In Katuu, S. (Ed.), *Diverse Applications and Transferability of Maturity Models* (pp. 269–315). IGI Global., DOI: 10.4018/978-1-5225-7080-6.ch011

Gefen, D., Zviran, M., & Elman, N. (2006), What can be learned from CMMI failures? Communications of the Association for Information Systems. 17. (pp. 36). https://doi.org/DOI: 10.17705/1CAIS.01736

Greatbatch, D., & Clark, T. (2005). *Management Speak: Why We Listen to What Management Guru Tell Us*. Routledge. DOI: 10.4324/9780203087718

Halvorson, H. G., & Higgins, E. T. (2013). *Focus, use different ways of seeing the world for success and influence*. Penguin Group.

Hazel, S. (2016, February 10). Why native English speakers fail to be understood in English – and lose out in global business. *The Conversation*. https://theconversation.com/why-native-english-speakers-fail-to-be-understood-in-english-and-lose-out-in-global-business-54436

Herzberg, F., Mausner, B., & Snyderman, B. B. (2011). *The motivation to work*. Transaction Publishers.

International Standard Publication 21500 (2021), *Project, programme and portfolio management: Context and concepts*, (2nd Ed). International Standard Publication

Jung, D. (2006), Reviewed work: Management Speak: Why we listen to what Management Gurus tell us by David Greatbach, Timothy Clark. *Administrative Science Quarterly,* Vol (51), 4, pp.669-671. https://www.jstor.org/stable/20109897

Kasse, T. (2004). *Practical Insights into CMMi*. Artech House Computing Library.

Kruger, J., & Dunning, D. (1999). Unskilled and unaware of it: How difficulties in recognizing one's own incompetence lead to inflated self-assessments. *Journal of Personality and Social Psychology, 77*(6), 1121–1134. DOI: 10.1037/0022-3514.77.6.1121 PMID: 10626367

Kuhn, T. (1962). *The structure of scientific revolution*. University of Chicago Press.

Legerman, A., Zandhuis, A., Silvius, G., Rober, R., & Stellingwerft, R. (2013). *ISO 21500 in Practice A Management Guide*. Van Haren.

Livingston, J. S. (1971, January). Myth of the well-educated Manager, *Harvard Business Review*. https://hbr.org/1971/01/myth-of-the-well-educated-manager\

Maslow, A.H., (1965). *Eupsychian management: a journal*. Irwin, R.D.

McGregor, D. (2006). *The human side of enterprise, annotated edition*. McGraw Hill McKinsey Quarterly, (2014, September 1). Tom Peters on leading the 21st-century organization. McKinsey & Company. https://www.mckinsey.com/capabilities/people-and-organizational-performance/our-insights/tom-peters-on-leading-the-21st-century-organization

McKinsey, Q. (2014, September 1). Tom Peters on leading the 21st-century organization. McKinsey & Company. https://www.mckinsey.com/capabilities/people-and-organizational-performance/our-insights/tom-peters-on-leading-the-21st-century-organization

Montero, G., Onieva, L., & Palacin, R. (2015), Selection and Implementation of a Set of Key Performance Indicators for Project Management. *International Journal of Applied Engineering Research*. Vol (10), 18, pp.39473-39484. https://www.ripublication.com/Volume/ijaerv10n18.htm

Mu¨ller, R. & Turner, R.(2007a). The influence of project managers on project success criteria and project success by type of project. *European Management Journal* Vol (25), No. 4, 298–309. https://doi:DOI: 10.1016/j.emj.2007.06.003

Mu¨ller, R., & Turner, R. (2009). Leadership competency profiles of successful project managers *International Journal of Project Management* Vol (28), 437-448. https://doi.org/DOI: 10.1016/j.ijproman.2009.09.003

Mu¨ller, R., & Turner, R. (2007b). Matching the project manager's leadership style to project type. *International Journal of Project Management*, 25(1), 21–32. DOI: 10.1016/j.ijproman.2006.04.003

Mulcahy, R. (2015). PMP Exam Prep Book (8th Ed). RMC Publications Inc. International Standard Publication 21500 (2021), *Project, programme and portfolio management: Context and concepts*, (2nd Ed). International Standard Publication

Mulcahy, R. (2015). *PMP Exam Prep Book* (8th ed.). RMC Publications Inc.

Nieto-Rodriguez, A. (2019b, October 3). The Project Manifesto. *Project Manifesto*.https://www.linkedin.com/pulse/project-manifesto-antonio -nieto-rodriguez/

Nieto-Rodriguez, A., & Evrard, D. (2004). *Boosting Business Performance through Programme & Project Management*, PricewaterhouseCoopers. https://www.mosaicprojects.com.au/PDF/PwC_PM_Survey_210604.pdf

Nieto-Rodriguez, A., & Sampietro, M. (2017). Why business schools keep neglecting project management competencies. *PM World Journal, Vol. (VI)*, Issue XI. https://pmworldlibrary.net/wp-content/uploads/2017/11/pmwj64-Nov2017-Rodriguez-Sampietro-why-business-schools-neglect -project-management.pdf

Nieto-Rodriguez, A. (2019a). *The project revolution. How to succeed in a project driven world*. LID Publishing.

OGC. (2010), *PRINCE2 Maturity Model (P2MM) Self-Assessment*, Office of Government Commerce.http://miroslawdabrowski.com/downloads/ PRINCE2/Maturity%20models/PRINCE2%20Maturity%20Model%20 P2MM%20v2.1%20-%20Self%20Assessment%20.pdf

Papke-Shields, K. E., Beise, C., & Quan, J. (2009). Do project managers practice what they preach, and does it matter to project success? *International Journal of Project Management*, 28(7), 650–662. DOI: 10.1016/j. ijproman.2009.11.002

Peters, T. (1987). *Thriving on Chaos*. Harper Perennial.

PM Solutions Centre for Business Centre for Business Practices. (2006). *Project management maturity: A benchmark of current best*. Center for Business Practices.

PMI Pulse of the Profession. (2015). Navigating Complexity. Project Management Institute. https://www.pmi.org/-/media/pmi/documents/ public/pdf/learning/thought-leadership/pulse/navigating-complexity.pdf

PMI Pulse of the Profession. (2016). The high cost of low performance. Project Management Institute. www.pmi.org/-/media/pmi/documents/ public/pdf/learning/thought-leadership/pulse/improve-business-results -infographic.pdf?la=en

Prag, J. (2010). The Humanist Economist. In Pearce, C. L., Maciariello, J. A., & Yamawaki, H. (Eds.), *The Drucker difference: what the world's greatest management thinker means* (p. 207). McGraw Hill.

Project Management Institute (PMI). (2004). *A guide to project management body of knowledge* (PMBOK Guide) (3rd ed). Project Management Institute.

Project Management Institute (PMI). (2008). *A guide to project management body of knowledge* (PMBOK Guide) (4th ed). Project Management Institute.

Project Management Institute (PMI). (2008b). *A guide to project management body of knowledge* (PMBOK Guide) (4th ed). Project Management Institute.

Project Management Institute (PMI). (2013). *A guide to project management body of knowledge* (PMBOK Guide) (5th ed). Project Management Institute.

Project Management Institute (PMI). (2017). *A guide to project management body of knowledge* (PMBOK Guide) (6th ed). Project Management Institute.

Project Management Institute (PMI). (2017). *Agile Practice Guide*. Project Management Institute.

Project Management Institute (PMI). (2018, March). Customers- How to be the Central Point of their Success. *PMI Today*

Project Management Institute (PMI). (2024). Project Management Professional (PMP). *PMI* https://www.pmi.org/certifications/project-management-pmp

Project Management Institute Malaysia Chapter (PMIMY). (2024, August). *PMI MY Pulse*. https://pmi.org.my/2024/09/04/pmi-my-pulse-august-2024/ . Project Management Institute Malaysia Chapter.

Project Management Institute. (2015). *The PMI Talent Triangle*. Project Management Institute.

Rabe, C. B. (2006). *The innovation killer*. AMACOM.

Rugg, G., & D'Agnese, J. (2013). *Blind spot*. Harper Collins.

Sarbines-Oxley Act. (2002), Senate and House of Representatives of the United States of America in Congress. chrome-extension://efaidnbmnnnibpcajpcglclefindmkaj/https://www.govinfo.gov/content/pkg/COMPS-1883/pdf/COMPS-1883.pdf

Saunders, M. N. K. Lewis, & P., Thornhill, A., (2000). *Research methods for business students*. Prentice Hall.

Schwab, K. (2018). *The Global Competitiveness Report*, World Economic Forum 2018. https://www3.weforum.org/docs/GCR2018/05FullReport/TheGlobalCompetitivenessReport2018.pdf

Senge, P., Kleiner, A., Roberts, C., Ross, R., Roth, G., & Smith, B. (1999). *The Dance of Change*. Crown Currency.

Senge, P., Kleiner, A., Roberts, C., Ross, R., Roth, G., & Smith, B. (1999). *The Dance of Change: the challenges to sustaining momentum in a learning organization*. Crown Currency.

Sungjin J. H. (2015). When do MNCs fail to learn from prior failure experience? *Canadian Journal of Administrative Sciences*. Vol (33), Issue 1. https://doi.org/DOI: 10.1002/cjas.1324

Sunstein, C. R. (2013). *Simple-The Future of government*. Simon & Schuster.

Wendler, R (2012), The maturity of maturity model research: A systematic mapping study. *Information and Software Technology*. Vol (52), Issue 12, 1317-1339. https://doi.org/DOI: 10.1016/j.infsof.2012.07.007

Williams, G. (2010). *PRINCE2 Maturity Model*. Office of Government Commerce.

Zandhuis, A. (2013). *ISO 21500 in Practice - a Management Guide*. Van Haren Publishing.

Related References

To continue our tradition of advancing information science and technology research, we have compiled a list of recommended IGI Global readings. These references will provide additional information and guidance to further enrich your knowledge and assist you with your own research and future publications.

Abdul Razak, R., & Mansor, N. A. (2021). Instagram Influencers in Social Media-Induced Tourism: Rethinking Tourist Trust Towards Tourism Destination. In M. Dinis, L. Bonixe, S. Lamy, & Z. Breda (Eds.), *Impact of New Media in Tourism* (pp. 135-144). IGI Global. https://doi.org/10.4018/978-1-7998-7095-1.ch009

Abir, T., & Khan, M. Y. (2022). Importance of ICT Advancement and Culture of Adaptation in the Tourism and Hospitality Industry for Developing Countries. In Ramos, C., Quinteiro, S., & Gonçalves, A. (Eds.), *ICT as Innovator Between Tourism and Culture* (pp. 30–41). IGI Global. https://doi.org/10.4018/978-1-7998-8165-0.ch003

Abtahi, M. S., Behboudi, L., & Hasanabad, H. M. (2017). Factors Affecting Internet Advertising Adoption in Ad Agencies. *International Journal of Innovation in the Digital Economy*, 8(4), 18–29. DOI: 10.4018/IJIDE.2017100102

Aburezeq, I. M., & Dweikat, F. F. (2017). Cloud Applications in Language Teaching: Examining Pre-Service Teachers' Expertise, Perceptions and Integration. *International Journal of Distance Education Technologies*, 15(4), 39–60. DOI: 10.4018/IJDET.2017100103

Acharjya, B., & Das, S. (2022). Adoption of E-Learning During the COVID-19 Pandemic: The Moderating Role of Age and Gender. *International Journal of Web-Based Learning and Teaching Technologies, 17*(2), 1–14. https://doi.org/10.4018/IJWLTT.20220301.oa4

Adams, J. L., & Thomas, S. K. (2022). Non-Linear Curriculum Experiences for Student Learning and Work Design: What Is the Maximum Potential of a Chat Bot? In Ramlall, S., Cross, T., & Love, M. (Eds.), *Handbook of Research on Future of Work and Education: Implications for Curriculum Delivery and Work Design* (pp. 299–306). IGI Global. https://doi.org/10.4018/978-1-7998-8275-6.ch018

Adera, B. (2017). Supporting Language and Literacy Development for English Language Learners. In Keengwe, J. (Ed.), *Handbook of Research on Promoting Cross-Cultural Competence and Social Justice in Teacher Education* (pp. 339–354). Hershey, PA: IGI Global. DOI: 10.4018/978-1-5225-0897-7.ch018

Afenyo-Agbe, E., & Mensah, I. (2022). Principles, Benefits, and Barriers to Community-Based Tourism: Implications for Management. In Mensah, I., & Afenyo-Agbe, E. (Eds.), *Prospects and Challenges of Community-Based Tourism and Changing Demographics* (pp. 1–29). IGI Global. DOI: 10.4018/978-1-7998-7335-8.ch001

Agbo, V. M. (2022). Distributive Justice Issues in Community-Based Tourism. In Mensah, I., & Afenyo-Agbe, E. (Eds.), *Prospects and Challenges of Community-Based Tourism and Changing Demographics* (pp. 107–129). IGI Global. https://doi.org/10.4018/978-1-7998-7335-8.ch005

Agrawal, S. (2017). The Impact of Emerging Technologies and Social Media on Different Business(es): Marketing and Management. In Rishi, O., & Sharma, A. (Eds.), *Maximizing Business Performance and Efficiency Through Intelligent Systems* (pp. 37–49). Hershey, PA: IGI Global. DOI: 10.4018/978-1-5225-2234-8.ch002

Ahamer, G. (2017). Quality Assurance for a Developmental "Global Studies" (GS) Curriculum. In I. Management Association (Ed.), *Educational Leadership and Administration: Concepts, Methodologies, Tools, and Applications* (pp. 438-477). Hershey, PA: IGI Global. https://doi.org/ DOI: 10.4018/978-1-5225-1624-8.ch023

Ahmad, A., & Johari, S. (2022). Georgetown as a Gastronomy Tourism Destination: Visitor Awareness Towards Revisit Intention of Nasi Kandar Restaurant. In Valeri, M. (Ed.), *New Governance and Management in Touristic Destinations* (pp. 71–83). IGI Global. https://doi.org/10.4018/ 978-1-6684-3889-3.ch005

Akayoğlu, S., & Seferoğlu, G. (2019). An Analysis of Negotiation of Meaning Functions of Advanced EFL Learners in Second Life: Negotiation of Meaning in Second Life. In Kruk, M. (Ed.), *Assessing the Effectiveness of Virtual Technologies in Foreign and Second Language Instruction* (pp. 61–85). IGI Global. https://doi.org/10.4018/978-1-5225-7286-2.ch003

Akella, N. R. (2022). Unravelling the Web of Qualitative Dissertation Writing!: A Student Reflects. In Zimmerman, A. (Ed.), *Methodological Innovations in Research and Academic Writing* (pp. 260–282). IGI Global. https://doi.org/10.4018/978-1-7998-8283-1.ch014

Alegre de la Rosa, O. M., & Angulo, L. M. (2017). Social Inclusion and Intercultural Values in a School of Education. In Mukerji, S., & Tripathi, P. (Eds.), *Handbook of Research on Administration, Policy, and Leadership in Higher Education* (pp. 518–531). Hershey, PA: IGI Global. DOI: 10.4018/978-1-5225-0672-0.ch020

Alexander, C. (2019). Using Gamification Strategies to Cultivate and Measure Professional Educator Dispositions. *International Journal of Game-Based Learning*, 9(1), 15–29. https://doi.org/10.4018/IJGBL.2019010102

Alkhatib, G., & Bayouq, S. T. (2021). A TAM-Based Model of Technological Factors Affecting Use of E-Tourism. *International Journal of Tourism and Hospitality Management in the Digital Age*, 5(2), 50–67. https://doi.org/10.4018/IJTHMDA.20210701.oa1

Altinay Ozdemir, M. (2021). Virtual Reality (VR) and Augmented Reality (AR) Technologies for Accessibility and Marketing in the Tourism Industry. In C. Eusébio, L. Teixeira, & M. Carneiro (Eds.), *ICT Tools and Applications for Accessible Tourism* (pp. 277-301). IGI Global. https://doi.org/10.4018/978-1-7998-6428-8.ch013

Anantharaman, R. N., Rajeswari, K. S., Angusamy, A., & Kuppusamy, J. (2017). Role of Self-Efficacy and Collective Efficacy as Moderators of Occupational Stress Among Software Development Professionals. *International Journal of Human Capital and Information Technology Professionals*, 8(2), 45–58. DOI: 10.4018/IJHCITP.2017040103

Anderson, K. M. (2017). Preparing Teachers in the Age of Equity and Inclusion. In I. Management Association (Ed.), *Medical Education and Ethics: Concepts, Methodologies, Tools, and Applications* (pp. 1532-1554). Hershey, PA: IGI Global. DOI: 10.4018/978-1-5225-0978-3.ch069

Aninze, F., El-Gohary, H., & Hussain, J. (2018). The Role of Microfinance to Empower Women: The Case of Developing Countries. *International Journal of Customer Relationship Marketing and Management*, 9(1), 54–78. DOI: 10.4018/IJCRMM.2018010104

Antosova, G., Sabogal-Salamanca, M., & Krizova, E. (2021). Human Capital in Tourism: A Practical Model of Endogenous and Exogenous Territorial Tourism Planning in Bahía Solano, Colombia. In Costa, V., Moura, A., & Mira, M. (Eds.), *Handbook of Research on Human Capital and People Management in the Tourism Industry* (pp. 282–302). IGI Global. https://doi.org/10.4018/978-1-7998-4318-4.ch014

Arsenijević, O. M., Orčić, D., & Kastratović, E. (2017). Development of an Optimization Tool for Intangibles in SMEs: A Case Study from Serbia with a Pilot Research in the Prestige by Milka Company. In Vemić, M. (Ed.), *Optimal Management Strategies in Small and Medium Enterprises* (pp. 320–347). Hershey, PA: IGI Global. DOI: 10.4018/978-1-5225-1949-2.ch015

Aryanto, V. D., Wismantoro, Y., & Widyatmoko, K. (2018). Implementing Eco-Innovation by Utilizing the Internet to Enhance Firm's Marketing Performance: Study of Green Batik Small and Medium Enterprises in Indonesia. *International Journal of E-Business Research*, *14*(1), 21–36. DOI: 10.4018/IJEBR.2018010102

Asero, V., & Billi, S. (2022). New Perspective of Networking in the DMO Model. In Valeri, M. (Ed.), *New Governance and Management in Touristic Destinations* (pp. 105–118). IGI Global. https://doi.org/10.4018/978-1-6684-3889-3.ch007

Atiku, S. O., & Fields, Z. (2017). Multicultural Orientations for 21st Century Global Leadership. In Baporikar, N. (Ed.), *Management Education for Global Leadership* (pp. 28–51). Hershey, PA: IGI Global. DOI: 10.4018/978-1-5225-1013-0.ch002

Atiku, S. O., & Fields, Z. (2018). Organisational Learning Dimensions and Talent Retention Strategies for the Service Industries. In Baporikar, N. (Ed.), *Global Practices in Knowledge Management for Societal and Organizational Development* (pp. 358–381). Hershey, PA: IGI Global. DOI: 10.4018/978-1-5225-3009-1.ch017

Atsa'am, D. D., & Kuset Bodur, E. (2021). Pattern Mining on How Organizational Tenure Affects the Psychological Capital of Employees Within the Hospitality and Tourism Industry: Linking Employees' Organizational Tenure With PsyCap. *International Journal of Tourism and Hospitality Management in the Digital Age*, *5*(2), 17–28. https://doi.org/10.4018/IJTHMDA.2021070102

Ávila, L., & Teixeira, L. (2018). The Main Concepts Behind the Dematerialization of Business Processes. In M. Khosrow-Pour, D.B.A. (Ed.), *Encyclopedia of Information Science and Technology, Fourth Edition* (pp. 888-898). Hershey, PA: IGI Global. https://doi.org/DOI: 10.4018/978-1-5225-2255-3.ch076

Awdziej, M. (2017). Case Study as a Teaching Method in Marketing. In Latusek, D. (Ed.), *Case Studies as a Teaching Tool in Management Education* (pp. 244–263). Hershey, PA: IGI Global. DOI: 10.4018/978-1-5225-0770-3.ch013

Ayorekire, J., Mugizi, F., Obua, J., & Ampaire, G. (2022). Community-Based Tourism and Local People's Perceptions Towards Conservation: The Case of Queen Elizabeth Conservation Area, Uganda. In Mensah, I., & Afenyo-Agbe, E. (Eds.), *Prospects and Challenges of Community-Based Tourism and Changing Demographics* (pp. 56–82). IGI Global. https://doi.org/10.4018/978-1-7998-7335-8.ch003

Bakos, J. (2019). Sociolinguistic Factors Influencing English Language Learning. In Erdogan, N., & Wei, M. (Eds.), *Applied Linguistics for Teachers of Culturally and Linguistically Diverse Learners* (pp. 403–424). IGI Global. https://doi.org/10.4018/978-1-5225-8467-4.ch017

Baleiro, R. (2022). Tourist Literature and the Architecture of Travel in Olga Tokarczuk and Patti Smith. In R. Baleiro & R. Pereira (Eds.), *Global Perspectives on Literary Tourism and Film-Induced Tourism* (pp. 202-216). IGI Global. https://doi.org/10.4018/978-1-7998-8262-6.ch011

Banas, J. R., & York, C. S. (2017). Pre-Service Teachers' Motivation to Use Technology and the Impact of Authentic Learning Exercises. In Tomei, L. (Ed.), *Exploring the New Era of Technology-Infused Education* (pp. 121–140). Hershey, PA: IGI Global. DOI: 10.4018/978-1-5225-1709-2.ch008

Barat, S. (2021). Looking at the Future of Medical Tourism in Asia. *International Journal of Tourism and Hospitality Management in the Digital Age*, 5(1), 19–33. https://doi.org/10.4018/IJTHMDA.2021010102

Barbosa, C. A., Magalhães, M., & Nunes, M. R. (2021). Travel Instagramability: A Way of Choosing a Destination? In M. Dinis, L. Bonixe, S. Lamy, & Z. Breda (Eds.), *Impact of New Media in Tourism* (pp. 173-190). IGI Global. https://doi.org/10.4018/978-1-7998-7095-1.ch011

Bari, M. W., & Khan, Q. (2021). Pakistan as a Destination of Religious Tourism. In E. Alaverdov & M. Bari (Eds.), *Global Development of Religious Tourism* (pp. 1-10). IGI Global. https://doi.org/10.4018/978-1-7998-5792-1.ch001

Bartens, Y., Chunpir, H. I., Schulte, F., & Voß, S. (2017). Business/IT Alignment in Two-Sided Markets: A COBIT 5 Analysis for Media Streaming Business Models. In De Haes, S., & Van Grembergen, W. (Eds.), *Strategic IT Governance and Alignment in Business Settings* (pp. 82–111). Hershey, PA: IGI Global. DOI: 10.4018/978-1-5225-0861-8.ch004

Barton, T. P. (2021). Empowering Educator Allyship by Exploring Racial Trauma and the Disengagement of Black Students. In Reneau, C., & Villarreal, M. (Eds.), *Handbook of Research on Leading Higher Education Transformation With Social Justice, Equity, and Inclusion* (pp. 186–197). IGI Global. https://doi.org/10.4018/978-1-7998-7152-1.ch013

Bashayreh, A. M. (2018). Organizational Culture and Organizational Performance. In Lee, W., & Sabetzadeh, F. (Eds.), *Contemporary Knowledge and Systems Science* (pp. 50–69). Hershey, PA: IGI Global. DOI: 10.4018/978-1-5225-5655-8.ch003

Bechthold, L., Lude, M., & Prügl, R. (2021). Crisis Favors the Prepared Firm: How Organizational Ambidexterity Relates to Perceptions of Organizational Resilience. In Zehrer, A., Glowka, G., Schwaiger, K., & Ranacher-Lackner, V. (Eds.), *Resiliency Models and Addressing Future Risks for Family Firms in the Tourism Industry* (pp. 178–205). IGI Global. https://doi.org/10.4018/978-1-7998-7352-5.ch008

Bedford, D. A. (2018). Sustainable Knowledge Management Strategies: Aligning Business Capabilities and Knowledge Management Goals. In Baporikar, N. (Ed.), *Global Practices in Knowledge Management for Societal and Organizational Development* (pp. 46–73). Hershey, PA: IGI Global. DOI: 10.4018/978-1-5225-3009-1.ch003

Bekjanov, D., & Matyusupov, B. (2021). Influence of Innovative Processes in the Competitiveness of Tourist Destination. In Soares, J. (Ed.), *Innovation and Entrepreneurial Opportunities in Community Tourism* (pp. 243–263). IGI Global. https://doi.org/10.4018/978-1-7998-4855-4.ch014

Benhima, M. (2021). Moroccan English Department Student Attitudes Towards the Use of Distance Education During COVID-19: Moulay Ismail University as a Case Study. *International Journal of Information and Communication Technology Education*, *17*(3), 105–122. https://doi .org/10.4018/IJICTE.20210701.oa7

Beycioglu, K., & Wildy, H. (2017). Principal Preparation: The Case of Novice Principals in Turkey. In I. Management Association (Ed.), *Educational Leadership and Administration: Concepts, Methodologies, Tools, and Applications* (pp. 1152-1169). Hershey, PA: IGI Global. https://doi .org/DOI: 10.4018/978-1-5225-1624-8.ch054

Bharwani, S., & Musunuri, D. (2018). Reflection as a Process From Theory to Practice. In M. Khosrow-Pour, D.B.A. (Ed.), *Encyclopedia of Information Science and Technology, Fourth Edition* (pp. 1529-1539). Hershey, PA: IGI Global. DOI: 10.4018/978-1-5225-2255-3.ch132

Bharwani, S., & Musunuri, D. (2018). Reflection as a Process From Theory to Practice. In M. Khosrow-Pour, D.B.A. (Ed.), *Encyclopedia of Information Science and Technology, Fourth Edition* (pp. 1529-1539). Hershey, PA: IGI Global. DOI: 10.4018/978-1-5225-2255-3.ch132

Bhatt, G. D., Wang, Z., & Rodger, J. A. (2017). Information Systems Capabilities and Their Effects on Competitive Advantages: A Study of Chinese Companies. *Information Resources Management Journal*, *30*(3), 41–57. DOI: 10.4018/IRMJ.2017070103

Bhushan, A., Garza, K. B., Perumal, O., Das, S. K., Feola, D. J., Farrell, D., & Birnbaum, A. (2022). Lessons Learned From the COVID-19 Pandemic and the Implications for Pharmaceutical Graduate Education and Research. In Ford, C., & Garza, K. (Eds.), *Handbook of Research on Updating and Innovating Health Professions Education: Post-Pandemic Perspectives* (pp. 324–345). IGI Global. https://doi.org/10.4018/978-1 -7998-7623-6.ch014

Bhushan, M., & Yadav, A. (2017). Concept of Cloud Computing in ESB. In Bhadoria, R., Chaudhari, N., Tomar, G., & Singh, S. (Eds.), *Exploring Enterprise Service Bus in the Service-Oriented Architecture Paradigm* (pp. 116–127). Hershey, PA: IGI Global. DOI: 10.4018/978-1-5225-2157-0.ch008

Bhushan, S. (2017). System Dynamics Base-Model of Humanitarian Supply Chain (HSCM) in Disaster Prone Eco-Communities of India: A Discussion on Simulation and Scenario Results. *International Journal of System Dynamics Applications*, 6(3), 20–37. DOI: 10.4018/IJSDA.2017070102

Binder, D., & Miller, J. W. (2021). A Generations' Perspective on Employer Branding in Tourism. In Costa, V., Moura, A., & Mira, M. (Eds.), *Handbook of Research on Human Capital and People Management in the Tourism Industry* (pp. 152–174). IGI Global. https://doi.org/10.4018/978-1-7998-4318-4.ch008

Bintz, W., Ciecierski, L. M., & Royan, E. (2021). Using Picture Books With Instructional Strategies to Address New Challenges and Teach Literacy Skills in a Digital World. In Haas, L., & Tussey, J. (Eds.), *Connecting Disciplinary Literacy and Digital Storytelling in K-12 Education* (pp. 38–58). IGI Global. https://doi.org/10.4018/978-1-7998-5770-9.ch003

Birch Freeman, A. A., Mensah, I., & Antwi, K. B. (2022). Smiling vs. Frowning Faces: Community Participation for Sustainable Tourism in Ghanaian Communities. In Mensah, I., & Afenyo-Agbe, E. (Eds.), *Prospects and Challenges of Community-Based Tourism and Changing Demographics* (pp. 83–106). IGI Global. https://doi.org/10.4018/978-1-7998-7335-8.ch004

Biswas, A., & De, A. K. (2017). On Development of a Fuzzy Stochastic Programming Model with Its Application to Business Management. In Trivedi, S., Dey, S., Kumar, A., & Panda, T. (Eds.), *Handbook of Research on Advanced Data Mining Techniques and Applications for Business Intelligence* (pp. 353–378). Hershey, PA: IGI Global. DOI: 10.4018/978-1-5225-2031-3.ch021

Bohjanen, S. L., Cameron-Standerford, A., & Meidl, T. D. (2018). Capacity Building Pedagogy for Diverse Learners. In Keengwe, J. (Ed.), *Handbook of Research on Pedagogical Models for Next-Generation Teaching and Learning* (pp. 195–212). Hershey, PA: IGI Global. DOI: 10.4018/978-1-5225-3873-8.ch011

Boragnio, A., & Faracce Macia, C. (2021). "Taking Care of Yourself at Home": Use of E-Commerce About Food and Care During the COVID-19 Pandemic in the City of Buenos Aires. In Korstanje, M. (Ed.), *Socio-Economic Effects and Recovery Efforts for the Rental Industry: Post-COVID-19 Strategies* (pp. 45–71). IGI Global. https://doi.org/10.4018/978-1-7998-7287-0.ch003

Borges, V. D. (2021). Happiness: The Basis for Public Policy in Tourism. In Perinotto, A., Mayer, V., & Soares, J. (Eds.), *Rebuilding and Restructuring the Tourism Industry: Infusion of Happiness and Quality of Life* (pp. 1–25). IGI Global. https://doi.org/10.4018/978-1-7998-7239-9.ch001

Brewer, J. C. (2018). Measuring Text Readability Using Reading Level. In M. Khosrow-Pour, D.B.A. (Ed.), *Encyclopedia of Information Science and Technology, Fourth Edition* (pp. 1499-1507). Hershey, PA: IGI Global. DOI: 10.4018/978-1-5225-2255-3.ch129

Brookbanks, B. C. (2022). Student Perspectives on Business Education in the USA: Current Attitudes and Necessary Changes in an Age of Disruption. In Zhuplev, A., & Koepp, R. (Eds.), *Global Trends, Dynamics, and Imperatives for Strategic Development in Business Education in an Age of Disruption* (pp. 214–231). IGI Global. DOI: 10.4018/978-1-7998-7548-2.ch011

Brown, L. V., Dari, T., & Spencer, N. (2019). Addressing the Impact of Trauma in High Poverty Elementary Schools: An Ecological Model for School Counseling. In Daniels, K., & Billingsley, K. (Eds.), *Creating Caring and Supportive Educational Environments for Meaningful Learning* (pp. 135–153). IGI Global. https://doi.org/10.4018/978-1-5225-5748-7.ch008

Brown, S. L. (2017). A Case Study of Strategic Leadership and Research in Practice: Principal Preparation Programs that Work – An Educational Administration Perspective of Best Practices for Master's Degree Programs for Principal Preparation. In Wang, V. (Ed.), *Encyclopedia of Strategic Leadership and Management* (pp. 1226–1244). Hershey, PA: IGI Global. DOI: 10.4018/978-1-5225-1049-9.ch086

Brzozowski, M., & Ferster, I. (2017). Educational Management Leadership: High School Principal's Management Style and Parental Involvement in School Management in Israel. In Potocan, V., Üngan, M., & Nedelko, Z. (Eds.), *Handbook of Research on Managerial Solutions in Non-Profit Organizations* (pp. 55–74). Hershey, PA: IGI Global. DOI: 10.4018/978-1-5225-0731-4.ch003

Bücker, J., & Ernste, K. (2018). Use of Brand Heroes in Strategic Reputation Management: The Case of Bacardi, Adidas, and Daimler. In Erdemir, A. (Ed.), *Reputation Management Techniques in Public Relations* (pp. 126–150). Hershey, PA: IGI Global. DOI: 10.4018/978-1-5225-3619-2.ch007

Buluk Eşitti, B. (2021). COVID-19 and Alternative Tourism: New Destinations and New Tourism Products. In Demir, M., Dalgıç, A., & Ergen, F. (Eds.), *Handbook of Research on the Impacts and Implications of COVID-19 on the Tourism Industry* (pp. 786–805). IGI Global. https://doi.org/10.4018/978-1-7998-8231-2.ch038

Bureš, V. (2018). Industry 4.0 From the Systems Engineering Perspective: Alternative Holistic Framework Development. In Brunet-Thornton, R., & Martinez, F. (Eds.), *Analyzing the Impacts of Industry 4.0 in Modern Business Environments* (pp. 199–223). Hershey, PA: IGI Global. DOI: 10.4018/978-1-5225-3468-6.ch011

Buzady, Z. (2017). Resolving the Magic Cube of Effective Case Teaching: Benchmarking Case Teaching Practices in Emerging Markets – Insights from the Central European University Business School, Hungary. In Latusek, D. (Ed.), *Case Studies as a Teaching Tool in Management Education* (pp. 79–103). Hershey, PA: IGI Global. DOI: 10.4018/978-1-5225-0770-3.ch005

Cahapay, M. B. (2020). Delphi Technique in the Development of Emerging Contents in High School Science Curriculum. *International Journal of Curriculum Development and Learning Measurement*, 1(2), 1–9. https://doi.org/10.4018/IJCDLM.2020070101

Camacho, L. F., & Leon Guerrero, A. E. (2022). Indigenous Student Experience in Higher Education: Implementation of Culturally Sensitive Support. In Pangelinan, P., & McVey, T. (Eds.), *Learning and Reconciliation Through Indigenous Education in Oceania* (pp. 254–266). IGI Global. https://doi.org/10.4018/978-1-7998-7736-3.ch016

Camillo, A. (2021). *Legal Matters, Risk Management, and Risk Prevention: From Forming a Business to Legal Representation*. IGI Global. DOI: 10.4018/978-1-7998-4342-9.ch004

Cannaday, J. (2017). The Masking Effect: Hidden Gifts and Disabilities of 2e Students. In Dickenson, P., Keough, P., & Courduff, J. (Eds.), *Preparing Pre-Service Teachers for the Inclusive Classroom* (pp. 220–231). Hershey, PA: IGI Global. DOI: 10.4018/978-1-5225-1753-5.ch011

Căpusneanu, S., & Topor, D. I. (2018). Business Ethics and Cost Management in SMEs: Theories of Business Ethics and Cost Management Ethos. In Oncioiu, I. (Ed.), *Ethics and Decision-Making for Sustainable Business Practices* (pp. 109–127). Hershey, PA: IGI Global. DOI: 10.4018/978-1-5225-3773-1.ch007

Cederquist, S., Fishman, B., & Teasley, S. D. (2022). What's Missing From the College Transcript?: How Employers Make Sense of Student Skills. In Huang, Y. (Ed.), *Handbook of Research on Credential Innovations for Inclusive Pathways to Professions* (pp. 234–253). IGI Global. https://doi.org/10.4018/978-1-7998-3820-3.ch012

Chan, R. L., Mo, P. L., & Moon, K. K. (2018). Strategic and Tactical Measures in Managing Enterprise Risks: A Study of the Textile and Apparel Industry. In Strang, K., Korstanje, M., & Vajjhala, N. (Eds.), *Research, Practices, and Innovations in Global Risk and Contingency Management* (pp. 1–19). Hershey, PA: IGI Global. DOI: 10.4018/978-1-5225-4754-9.ch001

Charlier, S. D., Burke-Smalley, L. A., & Fisher, S. L. (2018). Undergraduate Programs in the U.S: A Contextual and Content-Based Analysis. In Mendy, J. (Ed.), *Teaching Human Resources and Organizational Behavior at the College Level* (pp. 26–57). Hershey, PA: IGI Global. DOI: 10.4018/978-1-5225-2820-3.ch002

Chumillas, J., Güell, M., & Quer, P. (2022). The Use of ICT in Tourist and Educational Literary Routes: The Role of the Guide. In Ramos, C., Quinteiro, S., & Gonçalves, A. (Eds.), *ICT as Innovator Between Tourism and Culture* (pp. 15–29). IGI Global. https://doi.org/10.4018/978-1-7998-8165-0.ch002

Cockrell, P., & Gibson, T. (2019). The Untold Stories of Black and Brown Student Experiences in Historically White Fraternities and Sororities. In Hoffman-Miller, P., James, M., & Hermond, D. (Eds.), *African American Suburbanization and the Consequential Loss of Identity* (pp. 153–171). IGI Global. https://doi.org/10.4018/978-1-5225-7835-2.ch009

Cohen, M. (2022). Leveraging Content Creation to Boost Student Engagement. In Driscoll, T.III, (Ed.), *Designing Effective Distance and Blended Learning Environments in K-12* (pp. 223–239). IGI Global. https://doi.org/10.4018/978-1-7998-6829-3.ch013

Contreras, E. C., & Contreras, I. I. (2018). Development of Communication Skills through Auditory Training Software in Special Education. In M. Khosrow-Pour, D.B.A. (Ed.), *Encyclopedia of Information Science and Technology, Fourth Edition* (pp. 2431-2441). Hershey, PA: IGI Global. DOI: 10.4018/978-1-5225-2255-3.ch212

Cooke, L., Schugar, J., Schugar, H., Penny, C., & Bruning, H. (2020). Can Everyone Code?: Preparing Teachers to Teach Computer Languages as a Literacy. In Mitchell, J., & Vaughn, E. (Eds.), *Participatory Literacy Practices for P-12 Classrooms in the Digital Age* (pp. 163–183). IGI Global. https://doi.org/10.4018/978-1-7998-0000-2.ch009

Cooley, D., & Whitten, E. (2017). Special Education Leadership and the Implementation of Response to Intervention. In Topor, F. (Ed.), *Handbook of Research on Individualism and Identity in the Globalized Digital Age* (pp. 265–286). Hershey, PA: IGI Global. DOI: 10.4018/978-1-5225-0522-8.ch012

Cosner, S., Tozer, S., & Zavitkovsky, P. (2017). Enacting a Cycle of Inquiry Capstone Research Project in Doctoral-Level Leadership Preparation. In I. Management Association (Ed.), *Educational Leadership and Administration: Concepts, Methodologies, Tools, and Applications* (pp. 1460-1481). Hershey, PA: IGI Global. DOI: 10.4018/978-1-5225-1624-8.ch067

Crawford, C. M. (2018). Instructional Real World Community Engagement. In M. Khosrow-Pour, D.B.A. (Ed.), *Encyclopedia of Information Science and Technology, Fourth Edition* (pp. 1474-1486). Hershey, PA: IGI Global. DOI: 10.4018/978-1-5225-2255-3.ch127

Crosby-Cooper, T., & Pacis, D. (2017). Implementing Effective Student Support Teams. In Dickenson, P., Keough, P., & Courduff, J. (Eds.), *Preparing Pre-Service Teachers for the Inclusive Classroom* (pp. 248–262). Hershey, PA: IGI Global. DOI: 10.4018/978-1-5225-1753-5.ch013

Curran, C. M., & Hawbaker, B. W. (2017). Cultivating Communities of Inclusive Practice: Professional Development for Educators – Research and Practice. In Curran, C., & Petersen, A. (Eds.), *Handbook of Research on Classroom Diversity and Inclusive Education Practice* (pp. 120–153). Hershey, PA: IGI Global. DOI: 10.4018/978-1-5225-2520-2.ch006

Dahlberg, T., Kivijärvi, H., & Saarinen, T. (2017). IT Investment Consistency and Other Factors Influencing the Success of IT Performance. In De Haes, S., & Van Grembergen, W. (Eds.), *Strategic IT Governance and Alignment in Business Settings* (pp. 176–208). Hershey, PA: IGI Global. DOI: 10.4018/978-1-5225-0861-8.ch007

Damnjanović, A. M. (2017). Knowledge Management Optimization through IT and E-Business Utilization: A Qualitative Study on Serbian SMEs. In Vemić, M. (Ed.), *Optimal Management Strategies in Small and Medium Enterprises* (pp. 249–267). Hershey, PA: IGI Global. DOI: 10.4018/978-1-5225-1949-2.ch012

Daneshpour, H. (2017). Integrating Sustainable Development into Project Portfolio Management through Application of Open Innovation. In Vemić, M. (Ed.), *Optimal Management Strategies in Small and Medium Enterprises* (pp. 370–387). Hershey, PA: IGI Global. DOI: 10.4018/978-1-5225-1949-2.ch017

Daniel, A. D., & Reis de Castro, V. (2018). Entrepreneurship Education: How to Measure the Impact on Nascent Entrepreneurs. In Carrizo Moreira, A., Guilherme Leitão Dantas, J., & Manuel Valente, F. (Eds.), *Nascent Entrepreneurship and Successful New Venture Creation* (pp. 85–110). Hershey, PA: IGI Global. DOI: 10.4018/978-1-5225-2936-1.ch004

Dass, S., & Dabbagh, N. (2018). Faculty Adoption of 3D Avatar-Based Virtual World Learning Environments: An Exploratory Case Study. In I. Management Association (Ed.), *Technology Adoption and Social Issues: Concepts, Methodologies, Tools, and Applications* (pp. 1000-1033). Hershey, PA: IGI Global. https://doi.org/DOI: 10.4018/978-1-5225-5201-7.ch045

David, R., Swami, B. N., & Tangirala, S. (2018). Ethics Impact on Knowledge Management in Organizational Development: A Case Study. In Baporikar, N. (Ed.), *Global Practices in Knowledge Management for Societal and Organizational Development* (pp. 19–45). Hershey, PA: IGI Global. DOI: 10.4018/978-1-5225-3009-1.ch002

Davison, A. M., & Scholl, K. G. (2017). Inclusive Recreation as Part of the IEP Process. In Curran, C., & Petersen, A. (Eds.), *Handbook of Research on Classroom Diversity and Inclusive Education Practice* (pp. 311–330). Hershey, PA: IGI Global. DOI: 10.4018/978-1-5225-2520-2.ch013

De Uña-Álvarez, E., & Villarino-Pérez, M. (2022). Fostering Ecocultural Resources, Identity, and Tourism in Inland Territories (Galicia, NW Spain). In G. Fernandes (Ed.), *Challenges and New Opportunities for Tourism in Inland Territories: Ecocultural Resources and Sustainable Initiatives* (pp. 1-16). IGI Global. https://doi.org/10.4018/978-1-7998-7339-6.ch001

DeCoito, I. (2018). Addressing Digital Competencies, Curriculum Development, and Instructional Design in Science Teacher Education. In M. Khosrow-Pour, D.B.A. (Ed.), *Encyclopedia of Information Science and Technology, Fourth Edition* (pp. 1420-1431). Hershey, PA: IGI Global. https://doi.org/DOI: 10.4018/978-1-5225-2255-3.ch122

DeCoito, I., & Richardson, T. (2017). Beyond Angry Birds™: Using Web-Based Tools to Engage Learners and Promote Inquiry in STEM Learning. In Levin, I., & Tsybulsky, D. (Eds.), *Digital Tools and Solutions for Inquiry-Based STEM Learning* (pp. 166–196). Hershey, PA: IGI Global. DOI: 10.4018/978-1-5225-2525-7.ch007

Delias, P., & Lakiotaki, K. (2018). Discovering Process Horizontal Boundaries to Facilitate Process Comprehension. *International Journal of Operations Research and Information Systems*, 9(2), 1–31. DOI: 10.4018/IJORIS.2018040101

Delmas, P. M. (2017). Research-Based Leadership for Next-Generation Leaders. In Styron, R.Jr, & Styron, J. (Eds.), *Comprehensive Problem-Solving and Skill Development for Next-Generation Leaders* (pp. 1–39). Hershey, PA: IGI Global. DOI: 10.4018/978-1-5225-1968-3.ch001

Demiray, U., & Ekren, G. (2018). Administrative-Related Evaluation for Distance Education Institutions in Turkey. In Buyuk, K., Kocdar, S., & Bozkurt, A. (Eds.), *Administrative Leadership in Open and Distance Learning Programs* (pp. 263–288). Hershey, PA: IGI Global. DOI: 10.4018/978-1-5225-2645-2.ch011

Denholm, J., & Lee-Davies, L. (2018). Success Factors for Games in Business and Project Management. In *Enhancing Education and Training Initiatives Through Serious Games* (pp. 34–68). Hershey, PA: IGI Global. DOI: 10.4018/978-1-5225-3689-5.ch002

Deshpande, M. (2017). Best Practices in Management Institutions for Global Leadership: Policy Aspects. In Baporikar, N. (Ed.), *Management Education for Global Leadership* (pp. 1–27). Hershey, PA: IGI Global. DOI: 10.4018/978-1-5225-1013-0.ch001

Deshpande, M. (2018). Policy Perspectives for SMEs Knowledge Management. In Baporikar, N. (Ed.), *Knowledge Integration Strategies for Entrepreneurship and Sustainability* (pp. 23–46). Hershey, PA: IGI Global. DOI: 10.4018/978-1-5225-5115-7.ch002

Dezdar, S. (2017). ERP Implementation Projects in Asian Countries: A Comparative Study on Iran and China. *International Journal of Information Technology Project Management*, 8(3), 52–68. DOI: 10.4018/IJITPM.2017070104

Dickenson, P. (2017). What do we Know and Where Can We Grow?: Teachers Preparation for the Inclusive Classroom. In Dickenson, P., Keough, P., & Courduff, J. (Eds.), *Preparing Pre-Service Teachers for the Inclusive Classroom* (pp. 1–22). Hershey, PA: IGI Global. DOI: 10.4018/978-1-5225-1753-5.ch001

Ding, Q., & Zhu, H. (2021). Flipping the Classroom in STEM Education. In Keengwe, J. (Ed.), *Handbook of Research on Innovations in Non-Traditional Educational Practices* (pp. 155–173). IGI Global. https://doi.org/10.4018/978-1-7998-4360-3.ch008

Dixon, T., & Christison, M. (2021). Teaching English Grammar in a Hybrid Academic ESL Course: A Mixed Methods Study. In Kelch, K., Byun, P., Safavi, S., & Cervantes, S. (Eds.), *CALL Theory Applications for Online TESOL Education* (pp. 229–251). IGI Global. https://doi.org/10.4018/978-1-7998-6609-1.ch010

Domingos, D., Respício, A., & Martinho, R. (2017). Reliability of IoT-Aware BPMN Healthcare Processes. In Reis, C., & Maximiano, M. (Eds.), *Internet of Things and Advanced Application in Healthcare* (pp. 214–248). Hershey, PA: IGI Global. DOI: 10.4018/978-1-5225-1820-4.ch008

Donne, V., & Hansen, M. (2017). Teachers' Use of Assistive Technologies in Education. In Tomei, L. (Ed.), *Exploring the New Era of Technology-Infused Education* (pp. 86–101). Hershey, PA: IGI Global. DOI: 10.4018/978-1-5225-1709-2.ch006

Donne, V., & Hansen, M. A. (2018). Business and Technology Educators: Practices for Inclusion. In I. Management Association (Ed.), *Business Education and Ethics: Concepts, Methodologies, Tools, and Applications* (pp. 471-484). Hershey, PA: IGI Global. https://doi.org/DOI: 10.4018/978-1-5225-3153-1.ch026

Dos Santos, L. M. (2022). Completing Student-Teaching Internships Online: Instructional Changes During the COVID-19 Pandemic. In Alaali, M. (Ed.), *Assessing University Governance and Policies in Relation to the COVID-19 Pandemic* (pp. 106–127). IGI Global. https://doi.org/10.4018/978-1-7998-8279-4.ch007

Dosumu, O., Hussain, J., & El-Gohary, H. (2017). An Exploratory Study of the Impact of Government Policies on the Development of Small and Medium Enterprises in Developing Countries: The Case of Nigeria. *International Journal of Customer Relationship Marketing and Management*, 8(4), 51–62. DOI: 10.4018/IJCRMM.2017100104

Dreon, O., Shettel, J., & Bower, K. M. (2017). Preparing Next Generation Elementary Teachers for the Tools of Tomorrow. In Grassetti, M., & Brookby, S. (Eds.), *Advancing Next-Generation Teacher Education through Digital Tools and Applications* (pp. 143–159). Hershey, PA: IGI Global. DOI: 10.4018/978-1-5225-0965-3.ch008

Durak, H. Y., & Güyer, T. (2018). Design and Development of an Instructional Program for Teaching Programming Processes to Gifted Students Using Scratch. In Cannaday, J. (Ed.), *Curriculum Development for Gifted Education Programs* (pp. 61–99). Hershey, PA: IGI Global. DOI: 10.4018/978-1-5225-3041-1.ch004

Durst, S., Bruns, G., & Edvardsson, I. R. (2017). Retaining Knowledge in Smaller Building and Construction Firms. *International Journal of Knowledge and Systems Science*, 8(3), 1–12. DOI: 10.4018/IJKSS.2017070101

Edvardsson, I. R., & Durst, S. (2017). Outsourcing, Knowledge, and Learning: A Critical Review. *International Journal of Knowledge-Based Organizations*, 7(2), 13–26. DOI: 10.4018/IJKBO.2017040102

Edwards, J. S. (2018). Integrating Knowledge Management and Business Processes. In M. Khosrow-Pour, D.B.A. (Ed.), *Encyclopedia of Information Science and Technology, Fourth Edition* (pp. 5046-5055). Hershey, PA: IGI Global. DOI: 10.4018/978-1-5225-2255-3.ch437

Egorkina, E., Ivanov, M., & Valyavskiy, A. Y. (2018). Students' Research Competence Formation of the Quality of Open and Distance Learning. In Mkrttchian, V., & Belyanina, L. (Eds.), *Handbook of Research on Students' Research Competence in Modern Educational Contexts* (pp. 364–384). Hershey, PA: IGI Global. DOI: 10.4018/978-1-5225-3485-3.ch019

Eichelberger, S., & Peters, M. (2021). Family Firm Management in Turbulent Times: Opportunities for Responsible Tourism. In Zehrer, A., Glowka, G., Schwaiger, K., & Ranacher-Lackner, V. (Eds.), *Resiliency Models and Addressing Future Risks for Family Firms in the Tourism Industry* (pp. 103–124). IGI Global. https://doi.org/10.4018/978-1-7998-7352-5.ch005

Eide, D., Hjalager, A., & Hansen, M. (2022). Innovative Certifications in Adventure Tourism: Attributes and Diffusion. In R. Augusto Costa, F. Brandão, Z. Breda, & C. Costa (Eds.), *Planning and Managing the Experience Economy in Tourism* (pp. 161-175). IGI Global. https://doi.org/10.4018/978-1-7998-8775-1.ch009

Ejiogu, A. O. (2018). Economics of Farm Management. In *Agricultural Finance and Opportunities for Investment and Expansion* (pp. 56–72). Hershey, PA: IGI Global. DOI: 10.4018/978-1-5225-3059-6.ch003

Ekanem, I., & Abiade, G. E. (2018). Factors Influencing the Use of E-Commerce by Small Enterprises in Nigeria. *International Journal of ICT Research in Africa and the Middle East*, 7(1), 37–53. DOI: 10.4018/IJICTRAME.2018010103

Ekanem, I., & Alrossais, L. A. (2017). Succession Challenges Facing Family Businesses in Saudi Arabia. In Zgheib, P. (Ed.), *Entrepreneurship and Business Innovation in the Middle East* (pp. 122–146). Hershey, PA: IGI Global. DOI: 10.4018/978-1-5225-2066-5.ch007

Ekren, G., Karataş, S., & Demiray, U. (2017). Understanding of Leadership in Distance Education Management. In I. Management Association (Ed.), *Educational Leadership and Administration: Concepts, Methodologies, Tools, and Applications* (pp. 34-50). Hershey, PA: IGI Global. https://doi.org/DOI: 10.4018/978-1-5225-1624-8.ch003

El Faquih, L., & Fredj, M. (2017). Ontology-Based Framework for Quality in Configurable Process Models. *Journal of Electronic Commerce in Organizations*, *15*(2), 48–60. DOI: 10.4018/JECO.2017040104

Elmore, W. M., Young, J. K., Harris, S., & Mason, D. (2017). The Relationship between Individual Student Attributes and Online Course Completion. In Shelton, K., & Pedersen, K. (Eds.), *Handbook of Research on Building, Growing, and Sustaining Quality E-Learning Programs* (pp. 151–173). Hershey, PA: IGI Global. DOI: 10.4018/978-1-5225-0877-9.ch008

Ercegovac, I. R., Alfirević, N., & Koludrović, M. (2017). School Principals' Communication and Co-Operation Assessment: The Croatian Experience. In I. Management Association (Ed.), *Educational Leadership and Administration: Concepts, Methodologies, Tools, and Applications* (pp. 1568-1589). Hershey, PA: IGI Global. https://doi.org/DOI: 10.4018/978-1-5225-1624-8.ch072

Everhart, D., & Seymour, D. M. (2017). Challenges and Opportunities in the Currency of Higher Education. In Rasmussen, K., Northrup, P., & Colson, R. (Eds.), *Handbook of Research on Competency-Based Education in University Settings* (pp. 41–65). Hershey, PA: IGI Global. DOI: 10.4018/978-1-5225-0932-5.ch003

Faisal, M. N., & Talib, F. (2017). Building Ambidextrous Supply Chains in SMEs: How to Tackle the Barriers? *International Journal of Information Systems and Supply Chain Management*, *10*(4), 80–100. DOI: 10.4018/IJISSCM.2017100105

Farmer, L. S. (2017). Managing Portable Technologies for Special Education. In Wang, V. (Ed.), *Encyclopedia of Strategic Leadership and Management* (pp. 977–987). Hershey, PA: IGI Global. DOI: 10.4018/978-1-5225-1049-9.ch068

Farmer, L. S. (2018). Optimizing OERs for Optimal ICT Literacy in Higher Education. In Keengwe, J. (Ed.), *Handbook of Research on Mobile Technology, Constructivism, and Meaningful Learning* (pp. 366–390). Hershey, PA: IGI Global. DOI: 10.4018/978-1-5225-3949-0.ch020

Ferguson, B. T. (2019). Supporting Affective Development of Children With Disabilities Through Moral Dilemmas. In Ikuta, S. (Ed.), *Handmade Teaching Materials for Students With Disabilities* (pp. 253–275). IGI Global. DOI: 10.4018/978-1-5225-6240-5.ch011

Fernandes, T. M., Gomes, J., & Romão, M. (2017). Investments in E-Government: A Benefit Management Case Study. *International Journal of Electronic Government Research*, *13*(3), 1–17. DOI: 10.4018/IJEGR.2017070101

Figueira, L. M., Honrado, G. R., & Dionísio, M. S. (2021). Human Capital Management in the Tourism Industry in Portugal. In Costa, V., Moura, A., & Mira, M. (Eds.), *Handbook of Research on Human Capital and People Management in the Tourism Industry* (pp. 1–19). IGI Global. DOI: 10.4018/978-1-7998-4318-4.ch001

Fındık, L. Y. (2017). Self-Assessment of Principals Based on Leadership in Complexity. In I. Management Association (Ed.), *Educational Leadership and Administration: Concepts, Methodologies, Tools, and Applications* (pp. 978-991). Hershey, PA: IGI Global. https://doi.org/DOI: 10.4018/978-1-5225-1624-8.ch047

Flor, A. G., & Gonzalez-Flor, B. (2018). Dysfunctional Digital Demeanors: Tales From (and Policy Implications of) eLearning's Dark Side. In I. Management Association (Ed.), The Dark Web: Breakthroughs in Research and Practice (pp. 37-50). Hershey, PA: IGI Global. https://doi.org/DOI: 10.4018/978-1-5225-3163-0.ch003

Floyd, K. K., & Shambaugh, N. (2017). Instructional Design for Simulations in Special Education Virtual Learning Spaces. In Kidd, T., & Morris, L.Jr., (Eds.), *Handbook of Research on Instructional Systems and Educational Technology* (pp. 202–215). Hershey, PA: IGI Global. DOI: 10.4018/978-1-5225-2399-4.ch018

Freeland, S. F. (2020). Community Schools: Improving Academic Achievement Through Meaningful Engagement. In Kronick, R. (Ed.), *Emerging Perspectives on Community Schools and the Engaged University* (pp. 132–144). IGI Global. https://doi.org/10.4018/978-1-7998-0280-8.ch008

Gao, S. S., Oreal, S., & Zhang, J. (2018). Contemporary Financial Risk Management Perceptions and Practices of Small-Sized Chinese Businesses. In I. Management Association (Ed.), *Global Business Expansion: Concepts, Methodologies, Tools, and Applications* (pp. 917-931). Hershey, PA: IGI Global. DOI: 10.4018/978-1-5225-5481-3.ch041

Garg, R., & Berning, S. C. (2017). Indigenous Chinese Management Philosophies: Key Concepts and Relevance for Modern Chinese Firms. In Christiansen, B., & Koc, G. (Eds.), *Transcontinental Strategies for Industrial Development and Economic Growth* (pp. 43–57). Hershey, PA: IGI Global. DOI: 10.4018/978-1-5225-2160-0.ch003

Gencer, Y. G. (2017). Supply Chain Management in Retailing Business. In Akkucuk, U. (Ed.), *Ethics and Sustainability in Global Supply Chain Management* (pp. 197–210). Hershey, PA: IGI Global. DOI: 10.4018/978-1-5225-2036-8.ch011

Gera, R., Arora, S., & Malik, S. (2021). Emotional Labor in the Tourism Industry: Strategies, Antecedents, and Outcomes. In Costa, V., Moura, A., & Mira, M. (Eds.), *Handbook of Research on Human Capital and People Management in the Tourism Industry* (pp. 73–91). IGI Global. https://doi.org/10.4018/978-1-7998-4318-4.ch004

Ghanbarzadeh, R., & Ghapanchi, A. H. (2019). Applied Areas of Three Dimensional Virtual Worlds in Learning and Teaching: A Review of Higher Education. In I. Management Association (Ed.), *Virtual Reality in Education: Breakthroughs in Research and Practice* (pp. 172-192). IGI Global. https://doi.org/10.4018/978-1-5225-8179-6.ch008

Giacosa, E. (2018). The Increasing of the Regional Development Thanks to the Luxury Business Innovation. In Carvalho, L. (Ed.), *Handbook of Research on Entrepreneurial Ecosystems and Social Dynamics in a Globalized World* (pp. 260–273). Hershey, PA: IGI Global. DOI: 10.4018/978-1-5225-3525-6.ch011

Giovannini, J. M. (2017). Technology Integration in Preservice Teacher Education Programs: Research-based Recommendations. In Grassetti, M., & Brookby, S. (Eds.), *Advancing Next-Generation Teacher Education through Digital Tools and Applications* (pp. 82–102). Hershey, PA: IGI Global. DOI: 10.4018/978-1-5225-0965-3.ch005

Glowka, G., Tusch, M., & Zehrer, A. (2021). The Risk Perception of Family Business Owner-Manager in the Tourism Industry: A Qualitative Comparison of the Intra-Firm Senior and Junior Generation. In Zehrer, A., Glowka, G., Schwaiger, K., & Ranacher-Lackner, V. (Eds.), *Resiliency Models and Addressing Future Risks for Family Firms in the Tourism Industry* (pp. 126–153). IGI Global. https://doi.org/10.4018/978-1-7998-7352-5.ch006

Glykas, M., & George, J. (2017). Quality and Process Management Systems in the UAE Maritime Industry. *International Journal of Productivity Management and Assessment Technologies*, 5(1), 20–39. DOI: 10.4018/IJPMAT.2017010102

Glykas, M., Valiris, G., Kokkinaki, A., & Koutsoukou, Z. (2018). Banking Business Process Management Implementation. *International Journal of Productivity Management and Assessment Technologies*, 6(1), 50–69. DOI: 10.4018/IJPMAT.2018010104

Gomes, J., & Romão, M. (2017). The Balanced Scorecard: Keeping Updated and Aligned with Today's Business Trends. *International Journal of Productivity Management and Assessment Technologies*, 5(2), 1–15. DOI: 10.4018/IJPMAT.2017070101

Gomes, J., & Romão, M. (2017). Aligning Information Systems and Technology with Benefit Management and Balanced Scorecard. In De Haes, S., & Van Grembergen, W. (Eds.), *Strategic IT Governance and Alignment in Business Settings* (pp. 112–131). Hershey, PA: IGI Global. DOI: 10.4018/978-1-5225-0861-8.ch005

Good, S., & Clarke, V. B. (2017). An Integral Analysis of One Urban School System's Efforts to Support Student-Centered Teaching. In Keengwe, J., & Onchwari, G. (Eds.), *Handbook of Research on Learner-Centered Pedagogy in Teacher Education and Professional Development* (pp. 45–68). Hershey, PA: IGI Global. DOI: 10.4018/978-1-5225-0892-2.ch003

Goyal, A. (2021). Communicating and Building Destination Brands With New Media. In M. Dinis, L. Bonixe, S. Lamy, & Z. Breda (Eds.), *Impact of New Media in Tourism* (pp. 1-20). IGI Global. https://doi.org/10.4018/978-1-7998-7095-1.ch001

Grefen, P., & Turetken, O. (2017). Advanced Business Process Management in Networked E-Business Scenarios. *International Journal of E-Business Research*, *13*(4), 70–104. DOI: 10.4018/IJEBR.2017100105

Guasca, M., Van Broeck, A. M., & Vanneste, D. (2021). Tourism and the Social Reintegration of Colombian Ex-Combatants. In J. da Silva, Z. Breda, & F. Carbone (Eds.), *Role and Impact of Tourism in Peacebuilding and Conflict Transformation* (pp. 66-86). IGI Global. https://doi.org/10.4018/978-1-7998-5053-3.ch005

Guetzoian, E. (2022). Gamification Strategies for Higher Education Student Worker Training. In Lane, C. (Ed.), *Handbook of Research on Acquiring 21st Century Literacy Skills Through Game-Based Learning* (pp. 164–179). IGI Global. https://doi.org/10.4018/978-1-7998-7271-9.ch009

Haider, A., & Saetang, S. (2017). Strategic IT Alignment in Service Sector. In Rozenes, S., & Cohen, Y. (Eds.), *Handbook of Research on Strategic Alliances and Value Co-Creation in the Service Industry* (pp. 231–258). Hershey, PA: IGI Global. DOI: 10.4018/978-1-5225-2084-9.ch012

Hajilari, A. B., Ghadaksaz, M., & Fasghandis, G. S. (2017). Assessing Organizational Readiness for Implementing ERP System Using Fuzzy Expert System Approach. *International Journal of Enterprise Information Systems*, *13*(1), 67–85. DOI: 10.4018/IJEIS.2017010105

Haldorai, A., Ramu, A., & Murugan, S. (2018). Social Aware Cognitive Radio Networks: Effectiveness of Social Networks as a Strategic Tool for Organizational Business Management. In Bansal, H., Shrivastava, G., Nguyen, G., & Stanciu, L. (Eds.), *Social Network Analytics for Contemporary Business Organizations* (pp. 188–202). Hershey, PA: IGI Global. DOI: 10.4018/978-1-5225-5097-6.ch010

Hall, O. P.Jr. (2017). Social Media Driven Management Education. *International Journal of Knowledge-Based Organizations*, 7(2), 43–59. DOI: 10.4018/IJKBO.2017040104

Hamidi, F., Owuor, P. M., Hynie, M., Baljko, M., & McGrath, S. (2017). Potentials of Digital Assistive Technology and Special Education in Kenya. In Ayo, C., & Mbarika, V. (Eds.), *Sustainable ICT Adoption and Integration for Socio-Economic Development* (pp. 125–151). Hershey, PA: IGI Global. DOI: 10.4018/978-1-5225-2565-3.ch006

Hamim, T., Benabbou, F., & Sael, N. (2022). Student Profile Modeling Using Boosting Algorithms. *International Journal of Web-Based Learning and Teaching Technologies*, 17(5), 1–13. https://doi.org/10.4018/IJWLTT .20220901.oa4

Hanifah, H., Halim, H. A., Ahmad, N. H., & Vafaei-Zadeh, A. (2017). Innovation Culture as a Mediator Between Specific Human Capital and Innovation Performance Among Bumiputera SMEs in Malaysia. In Ahmad, N., Ramayah, T., Halim, H., & Rahman, S. (Eds.), *Handbook of Research on Small and Medium Enterprises in Developing Countries* (pp. 261–279). Hershey, PA: IGI Global. DOI: 10.4018/978-1-5225-2165-5.ch012

Hartlieb, S., & Silvius, G. (2017). Handling Uncertainty in Project Management and Business Development: Similarities and Differences. In Raydugin, Y. (Ed.), *Handbook of Research on Leveraging Risk and Uncertainties for Effective Project Management* (pp. 337–362). Hershey, PA: IGI Global. DOI: 10.4018/978-1-5225-1790-0.ch016

Hass, K. B. (2017). Living on the Edge: Managing Project Complexity. In Raydugin, Y. (Ed.), *Handbook of Research on Leveraging Risk and Uncertainties for Effective Project Management* (pp. 177–201). Hershey, PA: IGI Global. DOI: 10.4018/978-1-5225-1790-0.ch009

Hawking, P., & Carmine Sellitto, C. (2017). Developing an Effective Strategy for Organizational Business Intelligence. In Tavana, M. (Ed.), *Enterprise Information Systems and the Digitalization of Business Functions* (pp. 222–237). Hershey, PA: IGI Global. DOI: 10.4018/978-1-5225-2382-6.ch010

Hawking, P., & Sellitto, C. (2017). A Fast-Moving Consumer Goods Company and Business Intelligence Strategy Development. *International Journal of Enterprise Information Systems*, *13*(2), 22–33. DOI: 10.4018/IJEIS.2017040102

Hawking, P., & Sellitto, C. (2017). Business Intelligence Strategy: Two Case Studies. *International Journal of Business Intelligence Research*, *8*(2), 17–30. DOI: 10.4018/IJBIR.2017070102

Hee, W. J., Jalleh, G., Lai, H., & Lin, C. (2017). E-Commerce and IT Projects: Evaluation and Management Issues in Australian and Taiwanese Hospitals. *International Journal of Public Health Management and Ethics*, *2*(1), 69–90. DOI: 10.4018/IJPHME.2017010104

Henderson, L. K. (2017). Meltdown at Fukushima: Global Catastrophic Events, Visual Literacy, and Art Education. In Shin, R. (Ed.), *Convergence of Contemporary Art, Visual Culture, and Global Civic Engagement* (pp. 80–99). Hershey, PA: IGI Global. DOI: 10.4018/978-1-5225-1665-1.ch005

Hernandez, A. A. (2018). Exploring the Factors to Green IT Adoption of SMEs in the Philippines. *Journal of Cases on Information Technology*, *20*(2), 49–66. DOI: 10.4018/JCIT.2018040104

Hollman, A., Bickford, S., & Hollman, T. (2017). Cyber InSecurity: A Post-Mortem Attempt to Assess Cyber Problems from IT and Business Management Perspectives. *Journal of Cases on Information Technology*, *19*(3), 42–70. DOI: 10.4018/JCIT.2017070104

Hudgins, T., & Holland, J. L. (2018). Digital Badges: Tracking Knowledge Acquisition Within an Innovation Framework. In I. Management Association (Ed.), *Wearable Technologies: Concepts, Methodologies, Tools, and Applications* (pp. 1118-1132). Hershey, PA: IGI Global. https://doi.org/DOI: 10.4018/978-1-5225-5484-4.ch051

Hwang, R., Lin, H., Sun, J. C., & Wu, J. (2019). Improving Learning Achievement in Science Education for Elementary School Students via Blended Learning. *International Journal of Online Pedagogy and Course Design*, 9(2), 44–62. https://doi.org/10.4018/IJOPCD.2019040104

Ibrahim, F., & Zainin, N. M. (2021). Exploring the Technological Impacts: The Case of Museums in Brunei Darussalam. *International Journal of Tourism and Hospitality Management in the Digital Age*, 5(1), 1–18. https://doi.org/10.4018/IJTHMDA.2021010101

Igbinakhase, I. (2017). Responsible and Sustainable Management Practices in Developing and Developed Business Environments. In Fields, Z. (Ed.), *Collective Creativity for Responsible and Sustainable Business Practice* (pp. 180–207). Hershey, PA: IGI Global. DOI: 10.4018/978-1-5225-1823-5.ch010

Iwata, J. J., & Hoskins, R. G. (2017). Managing Indigenous Knowledge in Tanzania: A Business Perspective. In Jain, P., & Mnjama, N. (Eds.), *Managing Knowledge Resources and Records in Modern Organizations* (pp. 198–214). Hershey, PA: IGI Global. DOI: 10.4018/978-1-5225-1965-2.ch012

Jain, P. (2017). Ethical and Legal Issues in Knowledge Management Life-Cycle in Business. In Jain, P., & Mnjama, N. (Eds.), *Managing Knowledge Resources and Records in Modern Organizations* (pp. 82–101). Hershey, PA: IGI Global. DOI: 10.4018/978-1-5225-1965-2.ch006

James, S., & Hauli, E. (2017). Holistic Management Education at Tanzanian Rural Development Planning Institute. In Baporikar, N. (Ed.), *Management Education for Global Leadership* (pp. 112–136). Hershey, PA: IGI Global. DOI: 10.4018/978-1-5225-1013-0.ch006

Jančec, L., & Vodopivec, J. L. (2019). The Implicit Pedagogy and the Hidden Curriculum in Postmodern Education. In Vodopivec, J., Jančec, L., & Štemberger, T. (Eds.), *Implicit Pedagogy for Optimized Learning in Contemporary Education* (pp. 41–59). IGI Global. https://doi.org/10.4018/978-1-5225-5799-9.ch003

Janošková, M., Csikósová, A., & Čulková, K. (2018). Measurement of Company Performance as Part of Its Strategic Management. In Leon, R. (Ed.), *Managerial Strategies for Business Sustainability During Turbulent Times* (pp. 309–335). Hershey, PA: IGI Global. DOI: 10.4018/978-1-5225-2716-9.ch017

Janus, M., & Siddiqua, A. (2018). Challenges for Children With Special Health Needs at the Time of Transition to School. In I. Management Association (Ed.), *Autism Spectrum Disorders: Breakthroughs in Research and Practice* (pp. 339-371). Hershey, PA: IGI Global. DOI: 10.4018/978-1-5225-3827-1.ch018

Jean-Vasile, A., & Alecu, A. (2017). Theoretical and Practical Approaches in Understanding the Influences of Cost-Productivity-Profit Trinomial in Contemporary Enterprises. In Jean Vasile, A., & Nicolò, D. (Eds.), *Sustainable Entrepreneurship and Investments in the Green Economy* (pp. 28–62). Hershey, PA: IGI Global. DOI: 10.4018/978-1-5225-2075-7.ch002

Jesus, R. A. (2018). Screencasts and Learning Styles. In M. Khosrow-Pour, D.B.A. (Ed.), *Encyclopedia of Information Science and Technology, Fourth Edition* (pp. 1548-1558). Hershey, PA: IGI Global. DOI: 10.4018/978-1-5225-2255-3.ch134

John, G., Francis, N., & Santhakumar, A. B. (2022). Student Engagement: Past, Present, and Future. In Ramlall, S., Cross, T., & Love, M. (Eds.), *Handbook of Research on Future of Work and Education: Implications for Curriculum Delivery and Work Design* (pp. 329–341). IGI Global. https://doi.org/10.4018/978-1-7998-8275-6.ch020

Joia, L. A., & Correia, J. C. (2018). CIO Competencies From the IT Professional Perspective: Insights From Brazil. *Journal of Global Information Management*, 26(2), 74–103. DOI: 10.4018/JGIM.2018040104

Juma, A., & Mzera, N. (2017). Knowledge Management and Records Management and Competitive Advantage in Business. In Jain, P., & Mnjama, N. (Eds.), *Managing Knowledge Resources and Records in Modern Organizations* (pp. 15–28). Hershey, PA: IGI Global. DOI: 10.4018/978-1-5225-1965-2.ch002

K., I., & A, V. (2018). Monitoring and Auditing in the Cloud. In K. Munir (Ed.), *Cloud Computing Technologies for Green Enterprises* (pp. 318-350). Hershey, PA: IGI Global. https://doi.org/DOI: 10.4018/978-1-5225-3038-1.ch013

Kabra, G., Ghosh, V., & Ramesh, A. (2018). Enterprise Integrated Business Process Management and Business Intelligence Framework for Business Process Sustainability. In Paul, A., Bhattacharyya, D., & Anand, S. (Eds.), *Green Initiatives for Business Sustainability and Value Creation* (pp. 228–238). Hershey, PA: IGI Global. DOI: 10.4018/978-1-5225-2662-9.ch010

Kaoud, M. (2017). Investigation of Customer Knowledge Management: A Case Study Research. *International Journal of Service Science, Management, Engineering, and Technology*, 8(2), 12–22. DOI: 10.4018/IJSSMET.2017040102

Karpinski, A. C., D'Agostino, J. V., Williams, A. K., Highland, S. A., & Mellott, J. A. (2018). The Relationship Between Online Formative Assessment and State Test Scores Using Multilevel Modeling. In M. Khosrow-Pour, D.B.A. (Ed.), *Encyclopedia of Information Science and Technology, Fourth Edition* (pp. 5183-5192). Hershey, PA: IGI Global. DOI: 10.4018/978-1-5225-2255-3.ch450

Kats, Y. (2017). Educational Leadership and Integrated Support for Students with Autism Spectrum Disorders. In I. Management Association (Ed.), *Educational Leadership and Administration: Concepts, Methodologies, Tools, and Applications* (pp. 101-114). Hershey, PA: IGI Global. https://doi.org/DOI: 10.4018/978-1-5225-1624-8.ch007

Katuu, S. (2018). A Comparative Assessment of Enterprise Content Management Maturity Models. In Gwangwava, N., & Mutingi, M. (Eds.), *E-Manufacturing and E-Service Strategies in Contemporary Organizations* (pp. 93–118). Hershey, PA: IGI Global. DOI: 10.4018/978-1-5225-3628-4.ch005

Kaya, G., & Altun, A. (2018). Educational Ontology Development. In M. Khosrow-Pour, D.B.A. (Ed.), *Encyclopedia of Information Science and Technology, Fourth Edition* (pp. 1441-1450). Hershey, PA: IGI Global. DOI: 10.4018/978-1-5225-2255-3.ch124

Keough, P. D., & Pacis, D. (2017). Best Practices Implementing Special Education Curriculum and Common Core State Standards using UDL. In Dickenson, P., Keough, P., & Courduff, J. (Eds.), *Preparing Pre-Service Teachers for the Inclusive Classroom* (pp. 107–123). Hershey, PA: IGI Global. DOI: 10.4018/978-1-5225-1753-5.ch006

Khan, M. Y., & Abir, T. (2022). The Role of Social Media Marketing in the Tourism and Hospitality Industry: A Conceptual Study on Bangladesh. In Ramos, C., Quinteiro, S., & Gonçalves, A. (Eds.), *ICT as Innovator Between Tourism and Culture* (pp. 213–229). IGI Global. https://doi.org/10.4018/978-1-7998-8165-0.ch013

Kilburn, M., Henckell, M., & Starrett, D. (2018). Factors Contributing to the Effectiveness of Online Students and Instructors. In M. Khosrow-Pour, D.B.A. (Ed.), *Encyclopedia of Information Science and Technology, Fourth Edition* (pp. 1451-1462). Hershey, PA: IGI Global. DOI: 10.4018/978-1-5225-2255-3.ch125

Kinnunen, S., Ylä-Kujala, A., Marttonen-Arola, S., Kärri, T., & Baglee, D. (2018). Internet of Things in Asset Management: Insights from Industrial Professionals and Academia. *International Journal of Service Science, Management, Engineering, and Technology, 9*(2), 104–119. DOI: 10.4018/IJSSMET.2018040105

Klein, A. Z., Sabino de Freitas, A., Machado, L., Freitas, J. C.Jr, Graziola, P. G.Jr, & Schlemmer, E. (2017). Virtual Worlds Applications for Management Education. In Tomei, L. (Ed.), *Exploring the New Era of Technology-Infused Education* (pp. 279–299). Hershey, PA: IGI Global. DOI: 10.4018/978-1-5225-1709-2.ch017

Koban Koç, D. (2021). Gender and Language: A Sociolinguistic Analysis of Second Language Writing. In Hancı-Azizoglu, E., & Kavaklı, N. (Eds.), *Futuristic and Linguistic Perspectives on Teaching Writing to Second Language Students* (pp. 161–177). IGI Global. https://doi.org/10.4018/978-1-7998-6508-7.ch010

Konecny, L. T. (2017). Hybrid, Online, and Flipped Classrooms in Health Science: Enhanced Learning Environments. In I. Management Association (Ed.), *Flipped Instruction: Breakthroughs in Research and Practice* (pp. 355-370). Hershey, PA: IGI Global. https://doi.org/DOI: 10.4018/978-1-5225-1803-7.ch020

Kővári, E., Saleh, M., & Steinbachné Hajmásy, G. (2022). The Impact of Corporate Digital Responsibility (CDR) on Internal Stakeholders' Satisfaction in Hungarian Upscale Hotels. In Valeri, M. (Ed.), *New Governance and Management in Touristic Destinations* (pp. 35–51). IGI Global. https://doi.org/10.4018/978-1-6684-3889-3.ch003

Kożuch, B., & Jabłoński, A. (2017). Adopting the Concept of Business Models in Public Management. In Lewandowski, M., & Kożuch, B. (Eds.), *Public Sector Entrepreneurship and the Integration of Innovative Business Models* (pp. 10–46). Hershey, PA: IGI Global. DOI: 10.4018/978-1-5225-2215-7.ch002

Kumar, J., Adhikary, A., & Jha, A. (2017). Small Active Investors' Perceptions and Preferences Towards Tax Saving Mutual Fund Schemes in Eastern India: An Empirical Note. *International Journal of Asian Business and Information Management, 8*(2), 35–45. DOI: 10.4018/IJABIM.2017040103

Kupietz, K. D. (2021). Gaming and Simulation in Public Education: Teaching Others to Help Themselves and Their Neighbors. In Drumhiller, N., Wilkin, T., & Srba, K. (Eds.), *Simulation and Game-Based Learning in Emergency and Disaster Management* (pp. 41–62). IGI Global. https://doi.org/10.4018/978-1-7998-4087-9.ch003

Kwee, C. T. (2022). Assessing the International Student Enrolment Strategies in Australian Universities: A Case Study During the COVID-19 Pandemic. In Alaali, M. (Ed.), *Assessing University Governance and Policies in Relation to the COVID-19 Pandemic* (pp. 162–188). IGI Global. https://doi.org/10.4018/978-1-7998-8279-4.ch010

Latusi, S., & Fissore, M. (2021). Pilgrimage Routes to Happiness: Comparing the Camino de Santiago and Via Francigena. In Perinotto, A., Mayer, V., & Soares, J. (Eds.), *Rebuilding and Restructuring the Tourism Industry: Infusion of Happiness and Quality of Life* (pp. 157–182). IGI Global. https://doi.org/10.4018/978-1-7998-7239-9.ch008

Lauricella, S., & McArthur, F. A. (2022). Taking a Student-Centred Approach to Alternative Digital Credentials: Multiple Pathways Toward the Acquisition of Microcredentials. In Piedra, D. (Ed.), *Innovations in the Design and Application of Alternative Digital Credentials* (pp. 57–69). IGI Global. https://doi.org/10.4018/978-1-7998-7697-7.ch003

Lavassani, K. M., & Movahedi, B. (2017). Applications Driven Information Systems: Beyond Networks toward Business Ecosystems. *International Journal of Innovation in the Digital Economy, 8*(1), 61–75. DOI: 10.4018/IJIDE.2017010104

Lazzareschi, V. H., & Brito, M. S. (2017). Strategic Information Management: Proposal of Business Project Model. In Jamil, G., Soares, A., & Pessoa, C. (Eds.), *Handbook of Research on Information Management for Effective Logistics and Supply Chains* (pp. 59–88). Hershey, PA: IGI Global. DOI: 10.4018/978-1-5225-0973-8.ch004

Lechuga Sancho, M. P., & Martín Navarro, A. (2022). Evolution of the Literature on Social Responsibility in the Tourism Sector: A Systematic Literature Review. In Fernandes, G. (Ed.), *Challenges and New Opportunities for Tourism in Inland Territories: Ecocultural Resources and Sustainable Initiatives* (pp. 169–186). IGI Global. https://doi.org/10.4018/978-1-7998-7339-6.ch010

Lederer, M., Kurz, M., & Lazarov, P. (2017). Usage and Suitability of Methods for Strategic Business Process Initiatives: A Multi Case Study Research. *International Journal of Productivity Management and Assessment Technologies*, 5(1), 40–51. DOI: 10.4018/IJPMAT.2017010103

Lee, I. (2017). A Social Enterprise Business Model and a Case Study of Pacific Community Ventures (PCV). In Potocan, V., Üngǎn, M., & Nedelko, Z. (Eds.), *Handbook of Research on Managerial Solutions in Non-Profit Organizations* (pp. 182–204). Hershey, PA: IGI Global. DOI: 10.4018/978-1-5225-0731-4.ch009

Leon, L. A., Seal, K. C., Przasnyski, Z. H., & Wiedenman, I. (2017). Skills and Competencies Required for Jobs in Business Analytics: A Content Analysis of Job Advertisements Using Text Mining. *International Journal of Business Intelligence Research*, 8(1), 1–25. DOI: 10.4018/IJBIR.2017010101

Levy, C. L., & Elias, N. I. (2017). SOHO Users' Perceptions of Reliability and Continuity of Cloud-Based Services. In Moore, M. (Ed.), *Cybersecurity Breaches and Issues Surrounding Online Threat Protection* (pp. 248–287). Hershey, PA: IGI Global. DOI: 10.4018/978-1-5225-1941-6.ch011

Levy, M. (2018). Change Management Serving Knowledge Management and Organizational Development: Reflections and Review. In Baporikar, N. (Ed.), *Global Practices in Knowledge Management for Societal and Organizational Development* (pp. 256–270). Hershey, PA: IGI Global. DOI: 10.4018/978-1-5225-3009-1.ch012

Lewandowski, M. (2017). Public Organizations and Business Model Innovation: The Role of Public Service Design. In Lewandowski, M., & Kożuch, B. (Eds.), *Public Sector Entrepreneurship and the Integration of Innovative Business Models* (pp. 47–72). Hershey, PA: IGI Global. DOI: 10.4018/978-1-5225-2215-7.ch003

Lhannaoui, H., Kabbaj, M. I., & Bakkoury, Z. (2017). A Survey of Risk-Aware Business Process Modelling. *International Journal of Risk and Contingency Management*, 6(3), 14–26. DOI: 10.4018/IJRCM.2017070102

Li, J., Sun, W., Jiang, W., Yang, H., & Zhang, L. (2017). How the Nature of Exogenous Shocks and Crises Impact Company Performance?: The Effects of Industry Characteristics. *International Journal of Risk and Contingency Management*, 6(4), 40–55. DOI: 10.4018/IJRCM.2017100103

Llamas, M. F. (2019). Intercultural Awareness in Teaching English for Early Childhood: A Film-Based Approach. In Domínguez Romero, E., Bobkina, J., & Stefanova, S. (Eds.), *Teaching Literature and Language Through Multimodal Texts* (pp. 54–68). IGI Global. https://doi.org/10.4018/978-1-5225-5796-8.ch004

Lokhtina, I., & Kkese, E. T. (2022). Reflecting and Adapting to an Academic Workplace Before and After the Lockdown in Greek-Speaking Cyprus: Opportunities and Challenges. In Zhuplev, A., & Koepp, R. (Eds.), *Global Trends, Dynamics, and Imperatives for Strategic Development in Business Education in an Age of Disruption* (pp. 126–148). IGI Global. https://doi.org/10.4018/978-1-7998-7548-2.ch007

Lopez-Fernandez, M., Perez-Perez, M., Serrano-Bedia, A., & Cobo-Gonzalez, A. (2021). Small and Medium Tourism Enterprise Survival in Times of Crisis: "El Capricho de Gaudí. In Toubes, D., & Araújo-Vila, N. (Eds.), *Risk, Crisis, and Disaster Management in Small and Medium-Sized Tourism Enterprises* (pp. 103–129). IGI Global. DOI: 10.4018/978-1-7998-6996-2.ch005

Lovell, K. L. (2017). Development and Evaluation of Neuroscience Computer-Based Modules for Medical Students: Instructional Design Principles and Effectiveness. In Stefaniak, J. (Ed.), *Advancing Medical Education Through Strategic Instructional Design* (pp. 262–276). Hershey, PA: IGI Global. DOI: 10.4018/978-1-5225-2098-6.ch013

Mahajan, A., Maidullah, S., & Hossain, M. R. (2022). Experience Toward Smart Tour Guide Apps in Travelling: An Analysis of Users' Reviews on Audio Odigos and Trip My Way. In R. Augusto Costa, F. Brandão, Z. Breda, & C. Costa (Eds.), *Planning and Managing the Experience Economy in Tourism* (pp. 255-273). IGI Global. https://doi.org/10.4018/978-1-7998-8775-1.ch014

Maher, D. (2019). The Use of Course Management Systems in Pre-Service Teacher Education. In Keengwe, J. (Ed.), *Handbook of Research on Blended Learning Pedagogies and Professional Development in Higher Education* (pp. 196–213). IGI Global. https://doi.org/10.4018/978-1-5225 -5557-5.ch011

Makewa, L. N. (2019). Teacher Technology Competence Base. In Makewa, L., Ngussa, B., & Kuboja, J. (Eds.), *Technology-Supported Teaching and Research Methods for Educators* (pp. 247–267). IGI Global. https://doi .org/10.4018/978-1-5225-5915-3.ch014

Malega, P. (2017). Small and Medium Enterprises in the Slovak Republic: Status and Competitiveness of SMEs in the Global Markets and Possibilities of Optimization. In Vemić, M. (Ed.), *Optimal Management Strategies in Small and Medium Enterprises* (pp. 102–124). Hershey, PA: IGI Global. DOI: 10.4018/978-1-5225-1949-2.ch006

Malewska, K. M. (2017). Intuition in Decision-Making on the Example of a Non-Profit Organization. In Potocan, V., Ünğan, M., & Nedelko, Z. (Eds.), *Handbook of Research on Managerial Solutions in Non-Profit Organizations* (pp. 378–399). Hershey, PA: IGI Global. DOI: 10.4018/978-1-5225-0731-4.ch018

Mallett, C. A. (2022). School Resource (Police) Officers in Schools: Impact on Campus Safety, Student Discipline, and Learning. In Crews, G. (Ed.), *Impact of School Shootings on Classroom Culture, Curriculum, and Learning* (pp. 53–70). IGI Global. https://doi.org/10.4018/978-1-7998 -5200-1.ch004

Marinho, J. E., Freitas, I. R., Leão, I. B., Pacheco, L. O., Gonçalves, M. P., Castro, M. J., Silva, P. D., & Moreira, R. J. (2022). Project-Based Learning Application in Higher Education: Student Experiences and Perspectives. In Alves, A., & van Hattum-Janssen, N. (Eds.), *Training Engineering Students for Modern Technological Advancement* (pp. 146–164). IGI Global. https://doi.org/10.4018/978-1-7998-8816-1.ch007

Maroofi, F. (2017). Entrepreneurial Orientation and Organizational Learning Ability Analysis for Innovation and Firm Performance. In Baporikar, N. (Ed.), *Innovation and Shifting Perspectives in Management Education* (pp. 144–165). Hershey, PA: IGI Global. DOI: 10.4018/978-1-5225-1019-2.ch007

Marques, M., Moleiro, D., Brito, T. M., & Marques, T. (2021). Customer Relationship Management as an Important Relationship Marketing Tool: The Case of the Hospitality Industry in Estoril Coast. In M. Dinis, L. Bonixe, S. Lamy, & Z. Breda (Eds.), *Impact of New Media in Tourism* (pp. 39-56). IGI Global. https://doi.org/DOI: 10.4018/978-1-7998-7095-1.ch003

Martins, P. V., & Zacarias, M. (2017). A Web-based Tool for Business Process Improvement. *International Journal of Web Portals*, 9(2), 68–84. DOI: 10.4018/IJWP.2017070104

Matthies, B., & Coners, A. (2017). Exploring the Conceptual Nature of e-Business Projects. *Journal of Electronic Commerce in Organizations*, 15(3), 33–63. DOI: 10.4018/JECO.2017070103

Mayer, V. F., Fraga, C. C., & Silva, L. C. (2021). Contributions of Neurosciences to Studies of Well-Being in Tourism. In Perinotto, A., Mayer, V., & Soares, J. (Eds.), *Rebuilding and Restructuring the Tourism Industry: Infusion of Happiness and Quality of Life* (pp. 108–128). IGI Global. https://doi.org/10.4018/978-1-7998-7239-9.ch006

McCleskey, J. A., & Melton, R. M. (2022). Rolling With the Flow: Online Faculty and Student Presence in a Post-COVID-19 World. In Ramlall, S., Cross, T., & Love, M. (Eds.), *Handbook of Research on Future of Work and Education: Implications for Curriculum Delivery and Work Design* (pp. 307–328). IGI Global. https://doi.org/10.4018/978-1-7998-8275-6.ch019

McCormack, V. F., Stauffer, M., Fishley, K., Hohenbrink, J., Mascazine, J. R., & Zigler, T. (2018). Designing a Dual Licensure Path for Middle Childhood and Special Education Teacher Candidates. In Polly, D., Putman, M., Petty, T., & Good, A. (Eds.), *Innovative Practices in Teacher Preparation and Graduate-Level Teacher Education Programs* (pp. 21–36). Hershey, PA: IGI Global. DOI: 10.4018/978-1-5225-3068-8.ch002

McDaniel, R. (2017). Strategic Leadership in Instructional Design: Applying the Principles of Instructional Design through the Lens of Strategic Leadership to Distance Education. In Wang, V. (Ed.), *Encyclopedia of Strategic Leadership and Management* (pp. 1570–1584). Hershey, PA: IGI Global. DOI: 10.4018/978-1-5225-1049-9.ch109

McKee, J. (2018). Architecture as a Tool to Solve Business Planning Problems. In M. Khosrow-Pour, D.B.A. (Ed.), *Encyclopedia of Information Science and Technology, Fourth Edition* (pp. 573-586). Hershey, PA: IGI Global. DOI: 10.4018/978-1-5225-2255-3.ch050

McKinney, R. E., Halli-Tierney, A. D., Gold, A. E., Allen, R. S., & Carroll, D. G. (2022). Interprofessional Education: Using Standardized Cases in Face-to-Face and Remote Learning Settings. In Ford, C., & Garza, K. (Eds.), *Handbook of Research on Updating and Innovating Health Professions Education: Post-Pandemic Perspectives* (pp. 24–42). IGI Global. https://doi.org/10.4018/978-1-7998-7623-6.ch002

McMurray, A. J., Cross, J., & Caponecchia, C. (2018). The Risk Management Profession in Australia: Business Continuity Plan Practices. In Bajgoric, N. (Ed.), *Always-On Enterprise Information Systems for Modern Organizations* (pp. 112–129). Hershey, PA: IGI Global. DOI: 10.4018/978-1-5225-3704-5.ch006

Meddah, I. H., & Belkadi, K. (2018). Mining Patterns Using Business Process Management. In Hamou, R. (Ed.), *Handbook of Research on Biomimicry in Information Retrieval and Knowledge Management* (pp. 78–89). Hershey, PA: IGI Global. DOI: 10.4018/978-1-5225-3004-6.ch005

Meintjes, H. H. (2021). Learner Views of a Facebook Page as a Supportive Digital Pedagogical Tool at a Public South African School in a Grade 12 Business Studies Class. *International Journal of Smart Education and Urban Society*, *12*(2), 32–45. https://doi.org/10.4018/IJSEUS.2021040104

Melero-García, F. (2022). Training Bilingual Interpreters in Healthcare Settings: Student Perceptions of Online Learning. In LeLoup, J., & Swanson, P. (Eds.), *Handbook of Research on Effective Online Language Teaching in a Disruptive Environment* (pp. 288–310). IGI Global. https://doi.org/10.4018/978-1-7998-7720-2.ch015

Meletiadou, E. (2022). The Use of Peer Assessment as an Inclusive Learning Strategy in Higher Education Institutions: Enhancing Student Writing Skills and Motivation. In Meletiadou, E. (Ed.), *Handbook of Research on Policies and Practices for Assessing Inclusive Teaching and Learning* (pp. 1–26). IGI Global. https://doi.org/10.4018/978-1-7998-8579-5.ch001

Melian, A. G., & Camprubí, R. (2021). The Accessibility of Museum Websites: The Case of Barcelona. In Eusébio, C., Teixeira, L., & Carneiro, M. (Eds.), *ICT Tools and Applications for Accessible Tourism* (pp. 234–255). IGI Global. https://doi.org/10.4018/978-1-7998-6428-8.ch011

Memon, R. N., Ahmad, R., & Salim, S. S. (2018). Critical Issues in Requirements Engineering Education. In I. Management Association (Ed.), *Computer Systems and Software Engineering: Concepts, Methodologies, Tools, and Applications* (pp. 1953-1976). Hershey, PA: IGI Global. DOI: 10.4018/978-1-5225-3923-0.ch081

Mendenhall, R. (2017). Western Governors University: CBE Innovator and National Model. In Rasmussen, K., Northrup, P., & Colson, R. (Eds.), *Handbook of Research on Competency-Based Education in University Settings* (pp. 379–400). Hershey, PA: IGI Global. DOI: 10.4018/978-1-5225-0932-5.ch019

Mendes, L. (2017). TQM and Knowledge Management: An Integrated Approach Towards Tacit Knowledge Management. In Jaziri-Bouagina, D., & Jamil, G. (Eds.), *Handbook of Research on Tacit Knowledge Management for Organizational Success* (pp. 236–263). Hershey, PA: IGI Global. DOI: 10.4018/978-1-5225-2394-9.ch009

Menezes, V. D., & Cavagnaro, E. (2021). Communicating Sustainable Initiatives in the Hotel Industry: The Case of the Hotel Jakarta Amsterdam. In F. Brandão, Z. Breda, R. Costa, & C. Costa (Eds.), *Handbook of Research on the Role of Tourism in Achieving Sustainable Development Goals* (pp. 224-234). IGI Global. https://doi.org/10.4018/978-1-7998-5691-7.ch013

Menezes, V. D., & Cavagnaro, E. (2021). Communicating Sustainable Initiatives in the Hotel Industry: The Case of the Hotel Jakarta Amsterdam. In F. Brandão, Z. Breda, R. Costa, & C. Costa (Eds.), *Handbook of Research on the Role of Tourism in Achieving Sustainable Development Goals* (pp. 224-234). IGI Global. https://doi.org/10.4018/978-1-7998-5691-7.ch013

Mense, E. G., Griggs, D. M., & Shanks, J. N. (2018). School Leaders in a Time of Accountability and Data Use: Preparing Our Future School Leaders in Leadership Preparation Programs. In Mense, E., & Crain-Dorough, M. (Eds.), *Data Leadership for K-12 Schools in a Time of Accountability* (pp. 235–259). Hershey, PA: IGI Global. DOI: 10.4018/978-1-5225-3188-3.ch012

Mense, E. G., Griggs, D. M., & Shanks, J. N. (2018). School Leaders in a Time of Accountability and Data Use: Preparing Our Future School Leaders in Leadership Preparation Programs. In Mense, E., & Crain-Dorough, M. (Eds.), *Data Leadership for K-12 Schools in a Time of Accountability* (pp. 235–259). Hershey, PA: IGI Global. DOI: 10.4018/978-1-5225-3188-3.ch012

Mestry, R., & Naicker, S. R. (2017). Exploring Distributive Leadership in South African Public Primary Schools in the Soweto Region. In I. Management Association (Ed.), *Educational Leadership and Administration: Concepts, Methodologies, Tools, and Applications* (pp. 1041-1064). Hershey, PA: IGI Global. DOI: 10.4018/978-1-5225-1624-8.ch050

Mitas, O., Bastiaansen, M., & Boode, W. (2022). If You're Happy, I'm Happy: Emotion Contagion at a Tourist Information Center. In R. Augusto Costa, F. Brandão, Z. Breda, & C. Costa (Eds.), *Planning and Managing the Experience Economy in Tourism* (pp. 122-140). IGI Global. https://doi.org/10.4018/978-1-7998-8775-1.ch007

Mnjama, N. M. (2017). Preservation of Recorded Information in Public and Private Sector Organizations. In Jain, P., & Mnjama, N. (Eds.), *Managing Knowledge Resources and Records in Modern Organizations* (pp. 149–167). Hershey, PA: IGI Global. DOI: 10.4018/978-1-5225-1965-2.ch009

Mokoqama, M., & Fields, Z. (2017). Principles of Responsible Management Education (PRME): Call for Responsible Management Education. In Fields, Z. (Ed.), *Collective Creativity for Responsible and Sustainable Business Practice* (pp. 229–241). Hershey, PA: IGI Global. DOI: 10.4018/978-1-5225-1823-5.ch012

Monaghan, C. H., & Boboc, M. (2017). (Re) Defining Leadership in Higher Education in the U.S. In Wang, V. (Ed.), *Encyclopedia of Strategic Leadership and Management* (pp. 567–579). Hershey, PA: IGI Global. DOI: 10.4018/978-1-5225-1049-9.ch040

Monteiro, A., Lopes, S., & Carbone, F. (2021). Academic Mobility: Bridging Tourism and Peace Education. In J. da Silva, Z. Breda, & F. Carbone (Eds.), *Role and Impact of Tourism in Peacebuilding and Conflict Transformation* (pp. 275-301). IGI Global. https://doi.org/10.4018/978-1-7998-5053-3.ch016

Morall, M. B. (2021). Reimagining Mobile Phones: Multiple Literacies and Digital Media Compositions. In C. Moran (Eds.), *Affordances and Constraints of Mobile Phone Use in English Language Arts Classrooms* (pp. 41-53). IGI Global. https://doi.org/10.4018/978-1-7998-5805-8.ch003

Mthethwa, V. (2022). Student Governance and the Academic Minefield During COVID-19 Lockdown in South Africa. In Alaali, M. (Ed.), *Assessing University Governance and Policies in Relation to the COVID-19 Pandemic* (pp. 255–276). IGI Global. https://doi.org/10.4018/978-1-7998-8279-4.ch015

Muniapan, B. (2017). Philosophy and Management: The Relevance of Vedanta in Management. In Ordóñez de Pablos, P. (Ed.), *Managerial Strategies and Solutions for Business Success in Asia* (pp. 124–139). Hershey, PA: IGI Global. DOI: 10.4018/978-1-5225-1886-0.ch007

Murad, S. E., & Dowaji, S. (2017). Using Value-Based Approach for Managing Cloud-Based Services. In Turuk, A., Sahoo, B., & Addya, S. (Eds.), *Resource Management and Efficiency in Cloud Computing Environments* (pp. 33–60). Hershey, PA: IGI Global. DOI: 10.4018/978-1-5225-1721-4.ch002

Mutahar, A. M., Daud, N. M., Thurasamy, R., Isaac, O., & Abdulsalam, R. (2018). The Mediating of Perceived Usefulness and Perceived Ease of Use: The Case of Mobile Banking in Yemen. *International Journal of Technology Diffusion*, 9(2), 21–40. DOI: 10.4018/IJTD.2018040102

Muthee, J. M., & Murungi, C. G. (2018). Relationship Among Intelligence, Achievement Motivation, Type of School, and Academic Performance of Kenyan Urban Primary School Pupils. In M. Khosrow-Pour, D.B.A. (Ed.), *Encyclopedia of Information Science and Technology, Fourth Edition* (pp. 1540-1547). Hershey, PA: IGI Global. https://doi.org/DOI: 10.4018/978-1-5225-2255-3.ch133

Naidoo, V. (2017). E-Learning and Management Education at African Universities. In Baporikar, N. (Ed.), *Management Education for Global Leadership* (pp. 181–201). Hershey, PA: IGI Global. DOI: 10.4018/978-1-5225-1013-0.ch009

Naidoo, V., & Igbinakhase, I. (2018). Opportunities and Challenges of Knowledge Retention in SMEs. In Baporikar, N. (Ed.), *Knowledge Integration Strategies for Entrepreneurship and Sustainability* (pp. 70–94). Hershey, PA: IGI Global. DOI: 10.4018/978-1-5225-5115-7.ch004

Naranjo, J. (2018). Meeting the Need for Inclusive Educators Online: Teacher Education in Inclusive Special Education and Dual-Certification. In Polly, D., Putman, M., Petty, T., & Good, A. (Eds.), *Innovative Practices in Teacher Preparation and Graduate-Level Teacher Education Programs* (pp. 106–122). Hershey, PA: IGI Global. DOI: 10.4018/978-1-5225-3068-8.ch007

Naumov, N., & Costandachi, G. (2021). Creativity and Entrepreneurship: Gastronomic Tourism in Mexico. In Soares, J. (Ed.), *Innovation and Entrepreneurial Opportunities in Community Tourism* (pp. 90–108). IGI Global. https://doi.org/10.4018/978-1-7998-4855-4.ch006

Nayak, S., & Prabhu, N. (2017). Paradigm Shift in Management Education: Need for a Cross Functional Perspective. In Baporikar, N. (Ed.), *Management Education for Global Leadership* (pp. 241–255). Hershey, PA: IGI Global. DOI: 10.4018/978-1-5225-1013-0.ch012

Nedelko, Z., & Potocan, V. (2017). Management Solutions in Non-Profit Organizations: Case of Slovenia. In Potocan, V., Üngan, M., & Nedelko, Z. (Eds.), *Handbook of Research on Managerial Solutions in Non-Profit Organizations* (pp. 1–22). Hershey, PA: IGI Global. DOI: 10.4018/978-1-5225-0731-4.ch001

Nedelko, Z., & Potocan, V. (2017). Priority of Management Tools Utilization among Managers: International Comparison. In Wang, V. (Ed.), *Encyclopedia of Strategic Leadership and Management* (pp. 1083–1094). Hershey, PA: IGI Global. DOI: 10.4018/978-1-5225-1049-9.ch075

Nedelko, Z., Raudeliūnienė, J., & Črešnar, R. (2018). Knowledge Dynamics in Supply Chain Management. In Baporikar, N. (Ed.), *Knowledge Integration Strategies for Entrepreneurship and Sustainability* (pp. 150–166). Hershey, PA: IGI Global. DOI: 10.4018/978-1-5225-5115-7.ch008

Nguyen, H. T., & Hipsher, S. A. (2018). Innovation and Creativity Used by Private Sector Firms in a Resources-Constrained Environment. In Hipsher, S. (Ed.), *Examining the Private Sector's Role in Wealth Creation and Poverty Reduction* (pp. 219–238). Hershey, PA: IGI Global. DOI: 10.4018/978-1-5225-3117-3.ch010

Nkabinde, Z. P. (2017). Multiculturalism in Special Education: Perspectives of Minority Children in Urban Schools. In Keengwe, J. (Ed.), *Handbook of Research on Promoting Cross-Cultural Competence and Social Justice in Teacher Education* (pp. 382–397). Hershey, PA: IGI Global. DOI: 10.4018/978-1-5225-0897-7.ch020

Nkabinde, Z. P. (2018). Online Instruction: Is the Quality the Same as Face-to-Face Instruction? In Keengwe, J. (Ed.), *Handbook of Research on Digital Content, Mobile Learning, and Technology Integration Models in Teacher Education* (pp. 300–314). Hershey, PA: IGI Global. DOI: 10.4018/978-1-5225-2953-8.ch016

Nugroho, A., & Albusaidi, S. S. (2022). Internationalization of Higher Education: The Methodological Critiques on the Research Related to Study Overseas and International Experience. In Magd, H., & Kunjumuhammed, S. (Eds.), *Global Perspectives on Quality Assurance and Accreditation in Higher Education Institutions* (pp. 75–89). IGI Global. https://doi.org/10.4018/978-1-7998-8085-1.ch005

Nulty, Z., & West, S. G. (2022). Student Engagement and Supporting Students With Accommodations. In Bull, P., & Patterson, G. (Eds.), *Redefining Teacher Education and Teacher Preparation Programs in the Post-COVID-19 Era* (pp. 99–116). IGI Global. https://doi.org/10.4018/978-1-7998-8298-5.ch006

O'Connor, J. R.Jr, & Jackson, K. N. (2017). The Use of iPad® Devices and "Apps" for ASD Students in Special Education and Speech Therapy. In Kats, Y. (Ed.), *Supporting the Education of Children with Autism Spectrum Disorders* (pp. 267–283). Hershey, PA: IGI Global. DOI: 10.4018/978-1-5225-0816-8.ch014

Obicci, P. A. (2017). Risk Sharing in a Partnership. In *Risk Management Strategies in Public-Private Partnerships* (pp. 115–152). Hershey, PA: IGI Global. DOI: 10.4018/978-1-5225-2503-5.ch004

Obidallah, W. J., & Raahemi, B. (2017). Managing Changes in Service Oriented Virtual Organizations: A Structural and Procedural Framework to Facilitate the Process of Change. *Journal of Electronic Commerce in Organizations*, 15(1), 59–83. DOI: 10.4018/JECO.2017010104

Ojo, O. (2017). Impact of Innovation on the Entrepreneurial Success in Selected Business Enterprises in South-West Nigeria. *International Journal of Innovation in the Digital Economy*, 8(2), 29–38. DOI: 10.4018/IJIDE.2017040103

Okdinawati, L., Simatupang, T. M., & Sunitiyoso, Y. (2017). Multi-Agent Reinforcement Learning for Value Co-Creation of Collaborative Transportation Management (CTM). *International Journal of Information Systems and Supply Chain Management*, 10(3), 84–95. DOI: 10.4018/IJISSCM.2017070105

Okolie, U. C., & Yasin, A. M. (2017). TVET in Developing Nations and Human Development. In Okolie, U., & Yasin, A. (Eds.), *Technical Education and Vocational Training in Developing Nations* (pp. 1–25). Hershey, PA: IGI Global. DOI: 10.4018/978-1-5225-1811-2.ch001

Olivera, V. A., & Carrillo, I. M. (2021). Organizational Culture: A Key Element for the Development of Mexican Micro and Small Tourist Companies. In Soares, J. (Ed.), *Innovation and Entrepreneurial Opportunities in Community Tourism* (pp. 227–242). IGI Global. DOI: 10.4018/978-1-7998-4855-4.ch013

Ossorio, M. (2022). Corporate Museum Experiences in Enogastronomic Tourism. In R. Augusto Costa, F. Brandão, Z. Breda, & C. Costa (Eds.), *Planning and Managing the Experience Economy in Tourism* (pp. 107-121). IGI Global. https://doi.org/DOI: 10.4018/978-1-7998-8775-1.ch006

Ossorio, M. (2022). Enogastronomic Tourism in Times of Pandemic. In Fernandes, G. (Ed.), *Challenges and New Opportunities for Tourism in Inland Territories: Ecocultural Resources and Sustainable Initiatives* (pp. 241–255). IGI Global. https://doi.org/10.4018/978-1-7998-7339-6.ch014

Özekici, Y. K. (2022). ICT as an Acculturative Agent and Its Role in the Tourism Context: Introduction, Acculturation Theory, Progress of the Acculturation Theory in Extant Literature. In Ramos, C., Quinteiro, S., & Gonçalves, A. (Eds.), *ICT as Innovator Between Tourism and Culture* (pp. 42–66). IGI Global. https://doi.org/10.4018/978-1-7998-8165-0.ch004

Pack, A., & Barrett, A. (2021). A Review of Virtual Reality and English for Academic Purposes: Understanding Where to Start. *International Journal of Computer-Assisted Language Learning and Teaching, 11*(1), 72–80. https://doi.org/10.4018/IJCALLT.2021010105

Pal, K. (2018). Building High Quality Big Data-Based Applications in Supply Chains. In Kumar, A., & Saurav, S. (Eds.), *Supply Chain Management Strategies and Risk Assessment in Retail Environments* (pp. 1–24). Hershey, PA: IGI Global. DOI: 10.4018/978-1-5225-3056-5.ch001

Palos-Sanchez, P. R., & Correia, M. B. (2018). Perspectives of the Adoption of Cloud Computing in the Tourism Sector. In Rodrigues, J., Ramos, C., Cardoso, P., & Henriques, C. (Eds.), *Handbook of Research on Technological Developments for Cultural Heritage and eTourism Applications* (pp. 377–400). Hershey, PA: IGI Global. DOI: 10.4018/978-1-5225-2927-9.ch018

Papadopoulou, G. (2021). Promoting Gender Equality and Women Empowerment in the Tourism Sector. In F. Brandão, Z. Breda, R. Costa, & C. Costa (Eds.), *Handbook of Research on the Role of Tourism in Achieving Sustainable Development Goals* (pp. 152-174). IGI Global. https://doi.org/DOI: 10.4018/978-1-7998-5691-7.ch009

Papp-Váry, Á. F., & Tóth, T. Z. (2022). Analysis of Budapest as a Film Tourism Destination. In R. Baleiro & R. Pereira (Eds.), *Global Perspectives on Literary Tourism and Film-Induced Tourism* (pp. 257-279). IGI Global. https://doi.org/10.4018/978-1-7998-8262-6.ch014

Pashollari, E. (2019). Building Sustainability Through Environmental Education: Education for Sustainable Development. In L. Wilson, & C. Stevenson (Eds.), *Building Sustainability Through Environmental Education* (pp. 72-88). IGI Global. https://doi.org/10.4018/978-1-5225-7727-0.ch004

Patiño, B. E. (2017). New Generation Management by Convergence and Individual Identity: A Systemic and Human-Oriented Approach. In Baporikar, N. (Ed.), *Innovation and Shifting Perspectives in Management Education* (pp. 119–143). Hershey, PA: IGI Global. DOI: 10.4018/978-1-5225-1019-2.ch006

Patro, C. S. (2021). Digital Tourism: Influence of E-Marketing Technology. In M. Dinis, L. Bonixe, S. Lamy, & Z. Breda (Eds.), *Impact of New Media in Tourism* (pp. 234-254). IGI Global. https://doi.org/10.4018/978-1-7998-7095-1.ch014

Paulson, E. N. (2017). Adapting and Advocating for an Online EdD Program in Changing Times and "Sacred" Cultures. In I. Management Association (Ed.), *Educational Leadership and Administration: Concepts, Methodologies, Tools, and Applications* (pp. 1849-1876). Hershey, PA: IGI Global. https://doi.org/DOI: 10.4018/978-1-5225-1624-8.ch085

Pawliczek, A., & Rössler, M. (2017). Knowledge of Management Tools and Systems in SMEs: Knowledge Transfer in Management. In Bencsik, A. (Ed.), *Knowledge Management Initiatives and Strategies in Small and Medium Enterprises* (pp. 180–203). Hershey, PA: IGI Global. DOI: 10.4018/978-1-5225-1642-2.ch009

Pejic-Bach, M., Omazic, M. A., Aleksic, A., & Zoroja, J. (2018). Knowledge-Based Decision Making: A Multi-Case Analysis. In Leon, R. (Ed.), *Managerial Strategies for Business Sustainability During Turbulent Times* (pp. 160–184). Hershey, PA: IGI Global. DOI: 10.4018/978-1-5225-2716-9.ch009

Perano, M., Hysa, X., & Calabrese, M. (2018). Strategic Planning, Cultural Context, and Business Continuity Management: Business Cases in the City of Shkoder. In Presenza, A., & Sheehan, L. (Eds.), *Geopolitics and Strategic Management in the Global Economy* (pp. 57–77). Hershey, PA: IGI Global. DOI: 10.4018/978-1-5225-2673-5.ch004

Pereira, R., Mira da Silva, M., & Lapão, L. V. (2017). IT Governance Maturity Patterns in Portuguese Healthcare. In De Haes, S., & Van Grembergen, W. (Eds.), *Strategic IT Governance and Alignment in Business Settings* (pp. 24–52). Hershey, PA: IGI Global. DOI: 10.4018/978-1-5225-0861-8.ch002

Pérez-Uribe, R. I., Torres, D. A., Jurado, S. P., & Prada, D. M. (2018). Cloud Tools for the Development of Project Management in SMEs. In Perez-Uribe, R., Salcedo-Perez, C., & Ocampo-Guzman, D. (Eds.), *Handbook of Research on Intrapreneurship and Organizational Sustainability in SMEs* (pp. 95–120). Hershey, PA: IGI Global. DOI: 10.4018/978-1-5225-3543-0.ch005

Petersen, A. J., Elser, C. F., Al Nassir, M. N., Stakey, J., & Everson, K. (2017). The Year of Teaching Inclusively: Building an Elementary Classroom for All Students. In Curran, C., & Petersen, A. (Eds.), *Handbook of Research on Classroom Diversity and Inclusive Education Practice* (pp. 332–348). Hershey, PA: IGI Global. DOI: 10.4018/978-1-5225-2520-2.ch014

Petrisor, I., & Cozmiuc, D. (2017). Global Supply Chain Management Organization at Siemens in the Advent of Industry 4.0. In Saglietto, L., & Cezanne, C. (Eds.), *Global Intermediation and Logistics Service Providers* (pp. 123–142). Hershey, PA: IGI Global. DOI: 10.4018/978-1-5225-2133-4.ch007

Pfannenstiel, K. H., & Sanders, J. (2017). Characteristics and Instructional Strategies for Students With Mathematical Difficulties: In the Inclusive Classroom. In Curran, C., & Petersen, A. (Eds.), *Handbook of Research on Classroom Diversity and Inclusive Education Practice* (pp. 250–281). Hershey, PA: IGI Global. DOI: 10.4018/978-1-5225-2520-2.ch011

Phan, A. N. (2022). Quality Assurance of Higher Education From the Glonacal Agency Heuristic: An Example From Vietnam. In Magd, H., & Kunjumuhammed, S. (Eds.), *Global Perspectives on Quality Assurance and Accreditation in Higher Education Institutions* (pp. 136–155). IGI Global. https://doi.org/10.4018/978-1-7998-8085-1.ch008

Pierce, J. M., Velliaris, D. M., & Edwards, J. (2017). A Living Case Study: A Journey Not a Destination. In Silton, N. (Ed.), *Exploring the Benefits of Creativity in Education, Media, and the Arts* (pp. 158–178). Hershey, PA: IGI Global. DOI: 10.4018/978-1-5225-0504-4.ch008

Pipia, S., & Pipia, S. (2021). Challenges of Religious Tourism in the Conflict Region: An Example of Jerusalem. In E. Alaverdov & M. Bari (Eds.), *Global Development of Religious Tourism* (pp. 135-148). IGI Global. https://doi.org/10.4018/978-1-7998-5792-1.ch009

Poulaki, P., Kritikos, A., Vasilakis, N., & Valeri, M. (2022). The Contribution of Female Creativity to the Development of Gastronomic Tourism in Greece: The Case of the Island of Naxos in the South Aegean Region. In Valeri, M. (Ed.), *New Governance and Management in Touristic Destinations* (pp. 246–258). IGI Global. https://doi.org/10.4018/978-1-6684-3889-3.ch015

Preast, J. L., Bowman, N., & Rose, C. A. (2017). Creating Inclusive Classroom Communities Through Social and Emotional Learning to Reduce Social Marginalization Among Students. In Curran, C., & Petersen, A. (Eds.), *Handbook of Research on Classroom Diversity and Inclusive Education Practice* (pp. 183–200). Hershey, PA: IGI Global. DOI: 10.4018/978-1-5225-2520-2.ch008

Radosavljevic, M., & Andjelkovic, A. (2017). Multi-Criteria Decision Making Approach for Choosing Business Process for the Improvement: Upgrading of the Six Sigma Methodology. In Stanković, J., Delias, P., Marinković, S., & Rochhia, S. (Eds.), *Tools and Techniques for Economic Decision Analysis* (pp. 225–247). Hershey, PA: IGI Global. DOI: 10.4018/978-1-5225-0959-2.ch011

Radovic, V. M. (2017). Corporate Sustainability and Responsibility and Disaster Risk Reduction: A Serbian Overview. In Camilleri, M. (Ed.), *CSR 2.0 and the New Era of Corporate Citizenship* (pp. 147–164). Hershey, PA: IGI Global. DOI: 10.4018/978-1-5225-1842-6.ch008

Raghunath, K. M., Devi, S. L., & Patro, C. S. (2018). Impact of Risk Assessment Models on Risk Factors: A Holistic Outlook. In Strang, K., Korstanje, M., & Vajjhala, N. (Eds.), *Research, Practices, and Innovations in Global Risk and Contingency Management* (pp. 134–153). Hershey, PA: IGI Global. DOI: 10.4018/978-1-5225-4754-9.ch008

Raman, A., & Goyal, D. P. (2017). Extending IMPLEMENT Framework for Enterprise Information Systems Implementation to Information System Innovation. In Tavana, M. (Ed.), *Enterprise Information Systems and the Digitalization of Business Functions* (pp. 137–177). Hershey, PA: IGI Global. DOI: 10.4018/978-1-5225-2382-6.ch007

Randolph, K. M., & Brady, M. P. (2018). Evolution of Covert Coaching as an Evidence-Based Practice in Professional Development and Preparation of Teachers. In Bryan, V., Musgrove, A., & Powers, J. (Eds.), *Handbook of Research on Human Development in the Digital Age* (pp. 281–299). Hershey, PA: IGI Global. DOI: 10.4018/978-1-5225-2838-8.ch013

Rao, Y., & Zhang, Y. (2017). The Construction and Development of Academic Library Digital Special Subject Databases. In Ruan, L., Zhu, Q., & Ye, Y. (Eds.), *Academic Library Development and Administration in China* (pp. 163–183). Hershey, PA: IGI Global. DOI: 10.4018/978-1-5225-0550-1.ch010

Ravasan, A. Z., Mohammadi, M. M., & Hamidi, H. (2018). An Investigation Into the Critical Success Factors of Implementing Information Technology Service Management Frameworks. In Jakobs, K. (Ed.), *Corporate and Global Standardization Initiatives in Contemporary Society* (pp. 200–218). Hershey, PA: IGI Global. DOI: 10.4018/978-1-5225-5320-5.ch009

Rell, A. B., Puig, R. A., Roll, F., Valles, V., Espinoza, M., & Duque, A. L. (2017). Addressing Cultural Diversity and Global Competence: The Dual Language Framework. In Leavitt, L., Wisdom, S., & Leavitt, K. (Eds.), *Cultural Awareness and Competency Development in Higher Education* (pp. 111–131). Hershey, PA: IGI Global. DOI: 10.4018/978-1-5225-2145-7.ch007

Rezaie, S., Mirabedini, S. J., & Abtahi, A. (2018). Designing a Model for Implementation of Business Intelligence in the Banking Industry. *International Journal of Enterprise Information Systems*, *14*(1), 77–103. DOI: 10.4018/IJEIS.2018010105

Richards, M., & Guzman, I. R. (2020). Academic Assessment of Critical Thinking in Distance Education Information Technology Programs. In I. Management Association (Ed.), *Learning and Performance Assessment: Concepts, Methodologies, Tools, and Applications* (pp. 1-19). IGI Global. https://doi.org/10.4018/978-1-7998-0420-8.ch001

Richards, V., Matthews, N., Williams, O. J., & Khan, Z. (2021). The Challenges of Accessible Tourism Information Systems for Tourists With Vision Impairment: Sensory Communications Beyond the Screen. In Eusébio, C., Teixeira, L., & Carneiro, M. (Eds.), *ICT Tools and Applications for Accessible Tourism* (pp. 26–54). IGI Global. https://doi.org/10.4018/978-1-7998-6428-8.ch002

Riel, J., Lawless, K. A., & Brown, S. W. (2017). Defining and Designing Responsive Online Professional Development (ROPD): A Framework to Support Curriculum Implementation. In Kidd, T., & Morris, L.Jr., (Eds.), *Handbook of Research on Instructional Systems and Educational Technology* (pp. 104–115). Hershey, PA: IGI Global. DOI: 10.4018/978-1-5225-2399-4.ch010

Roberts, C. (2017). Advancing Women Leaders in Academe: Creating a Culture of Inclusion. In Mukerji, S., & Tripathi, P. (Eds.), *Handbook of Research on Administration, Policy, and Leadership in Higher Education* (pp. 256–273). Hershey, PA: IGI Global. DOI: 10.4018/978-1-5225-0672-0.ch012

Rodgers, W. J., Kennedy, M. J., Alves, K. D., & Romig, J. E. (2017). A Multimedia Tool for Teacher Education and Professional Development. In Martin, C., & Polly, D. (Eds.), *Handbook of Research on Teacher Education and Professional Development* (pp. 285–296). Hershey, PA: IGI Global. DOI: 10.4018/978-1-5225-1067-3.ch015

Rodrigues de Souza Neto, V., & Marques, O. (2021). Rural Tourism Fostering Welfare Through Sustainable Development: A Conceptual Approach. In Perinotto, A., Mayer, V., & Soares, J. (Eds.), *Rebuilding and Restructuring the Tourism Industry: Infusion of Happiness and Quality of Life* (pp. 38–57). IGI Global. https://doi.org/10.4018/978-1-7998-7239-9.ch003

Romano, L., Grimaldi, R., & Colasuonno, F. S. (2017). Demand Management as a Success Factor in Project Portfolio Management. In Romano, L. (Ed.), *Project Portfolio Management Strategies for Effective Organizational Operations* (pp. 202–219). Hershey, PA: IGI Global. DOI: 10.4018/978-1-5225-2151-8.ch008

Romanowski, M. H. (2017). Qatar's Educational Reform: Critical Issues Facing Principals. In I. Management Association (Ed.), *Educational Leadership and Administration: Concepts, Methodologies, Tools, and Applications* (pp. 1758-1773). Hershey, PA: IGI Global. https://doi.org/ DOI: 10.4018/978-1-5225-1624-8.ch080

Rubio-Escuderos, L., & García-Andreu, H. (2021). Competitiveness Factors of Accessible Tourism E-Travel Agencies. In Eusébio, C., Teixeira, L., & Carneiro, M. (Eds.), *ICT Tools and Applications for Accessible Tourism* (pp. 196–217). IGI Global. https://doi.org/10.4018/978-1-7998 -6428-8.ch009

Rucci, A. C., Porto, N., Darcy, S., & Becka, L. (2021). Smart and Accessible Cities?: Not Always – The Case for Accessible Tourism Initiatives in Buenos Aries and Sydney. In Eusébio, C., Teixeira, L., & Carneiro, M. (Eds.), *ICT Tools and Applications for Accessible Tourism* (pp. 115–145). IGI Global. https://doi.org/10.4018/978-1-7998-6428-8.ch006

Ruffin, T. R., Hawkins, D. P., & Lee, D. I. (2018). Increasing Student Engagement and Participation Through Course Methodology. In M. Khosrow-Pour, D.B.A. (Ed.), *Encyclopedia of Information Science and Technology, Fourth Edition* (pp. 1463-1473). Hershey, PA: IGI Global. DOI: 10.4018/978-1-5225-2255-3.ch126

Ruhi, U. (2018). Towards an Interdisciplinary Socio-Technical Definition of Virtual Communities. In M. Khosrow-Pour, D.B.A. (Ed.), *Encyclopedia of Information Science and Technology, Fourth Edition* (pp. 4278-4295). Hershey, PA: IGI Global. DOI: 10.4018/978-1-5225-2255-3.ch371

Ryan, L., Catena, M., Ros, P., & Stephens, S. (2021). Designing Entrepreneurial Ecosystems to Support Resource Management in the Tourism Industry. In Costa, V., Moura, A., & Mira, M. (Eds.), *Handbook of Research on Human Capital and People Management in the Tourism Industry* (pp. 265–281). IGI Global. https://doi.org/10.4018/978-1-7998-4318-4.ch013

Sabina, L. L., Curry, K. A., Harris, E. L., Krumm, B. L., & Vencill, V. (2017). Assessing the Performance of a Cohort-Based Model Using Domestic and International Practices. In I. Management Association (Ed.), *Educational Leadership and Administration: Concepts, Methodologies, Tools, and Applications*(pp. 913-929). Hershey, PA: IGI Global. https://doi.org/DOI: 10.4018/978-1-5225-1624-8.ch044

Sabuncu, I. (2021). Understanding Tourist Perceptions and Expectations During Pandemic Through Social Media Big Data. In Demir, M., Dalgıç, A., & Ergen, F. (Eds.), *Handbook of Research on the Impacts and Implications of COVID-19 on the Tourism Industry* (pp. 330–350). IGI Global. https://doi.org/10.4018/978-1-7998-8231-2.ch016

Safari, M. R., & Jiang, Q. (2018). The Theory and Practice of IT Governance Maturity and Strategies Alignment: Evidence From Banking Industry. *Journal of Global Information Management*, 26(2), 127–146. DOI: 10.4018/JGIM.2018040106

Sahoo, J., Pati, B., & Mohanty, B. (2017). Knowledge Management as an Academic Discipline: An Assessment. In Gunjal, B. (Ed.), *Managing Knowledge and Scholarly Assets in Academic Libraries* (pp. 99–126). Hershey, PA: IGI Global. DOI: 10.4018/978-1-5225-1741-2.ch005

Saini, D. (2017). Relevance of Teaching Values and Ethics in Management Education. In Baporikar, N. (Ed.), *Management Education for Global Leadership* (pp. 90–111). Hershey, PA: IGI Global. DOI: 10.4018/978-1-5225-1013-0.ch005

Sambhanthan, A. (2017). Assessing and Benchmarking Sustainability in Organisations: An Integrated Conceptual Model. *International Journal of Systems and Service-Oriented Engineering*, 7(4), 22–43. DOI: 10.4018/IJSSOE.2017100102

Sambhanthan, A., & Potdar, V. (2017). A Study of the Parameters Impacting Sustainability in Information Technology Organizations. *International Journal of Knowledge-Based Organizations*, 7(3), 27–39. DOI: 10.4018/IJKBO.2017070103

Samkian, A., Pascarella, J., & Slayton, J. (2022). Towards an Anti-Racist, Culturally Responsive, and LGBTQ+ Inclusive Education: Developing Critically-Conscious Educational Leaders. In Cain-Sanschagrin, E., Filback, R., & Crawford, J. (Eds.), *Cases on Academic Program Redesign for Greater Racial and Social Justice* (pp. 150–175). IGI Global. https://doi.org/10.4018/978-1-7998-8463-7.ch007

Sánchez-Fernández, M. D., & Manríquez, M. R. (2018). The Entrepreneurial Spirit Based on Social Values: The Digital Generation. In Isaias, P., & Carvalho, L. (Eds.), *User Innovation and the Entrepreneurship Phenomenon in the Digital Economy* (pp. 173–193). Hershey, PA: IGI Global. DOI: 10.4018/978-1-5225-2826-5.ch009

Sanchez-Ruiz, L., & Blanco, B. (2017). Process Management for SMEs: Barriers, Enablers, and Benefits. In Vemić, M. (Ed.), *Optimal Management Strategies in Small and Medium Enterprises* (pp. 293–319). Hershey, PA: IGI Global. DOI: 10.4018/978-1-5225-1949-2.ch014

Santamaría, A. P., Webber, M., & Santamaría, L. J. (2017). Effective School Leadership for Māori Achievement: Building Capacity through Indigenous, National, and International Cross-Cultural Collaboration. In I. Management Association (Ed.), *Educational Leadership and Administration: Concepts, Methodologies, Tools, and Applications* (pp. 1547-1567). Hershey, PA: IGI Global. https://doi.org/DOI: 10.4018/978-1-5225-1624-8.ch071

Santamaría, L. J. (2017). Culturally Responsive Educational Leadership in Cross-Cultural International Contexts. In I. Management Association (Ed.), *Educational Leadership and Administration: Concepts, Methodologies, Tools, and Applications* (pp. 1380-1400). Hershey, PA: IGI Global. https://doi.org/DOI: 10.4018/978-1-5225-1624-8.ch064

Sanz, L. F., Gómez-Pérez, J., & Castillo-Martinez, A. (2018). Analysis of the European ICT Competence Frameworks. In Ahuja, V., & Rathore, S. (Eds.), *Multidisciplinary Perspectives on Human Capital and Information Technology Professionals* (pp. 225–245). Hershey, PA: IGI Global. DOI: 10.4018/978-1-5225-5297-0.ch012

Sarvepalli, A., & Godin, J. (2017). Business Process Management in the Classroom. *Journal of Cases on Information Technology, 19*(2), 17–28. DOI: 10.4018/JCIT.2017040102

Saxena, G. G., & Saxena, A. (2021). Host Community Role in Medical Tourism Development. In Singh, M., & Kumaran, S. (Eds.), *Growth of the Medical Tourism Industry and Its Impact on Society: Emerging Research and Opportunities* (pp. 105–127). IGI Global. https://doi.org/10.4018/978 -1-7998-3427-4.ch006

Saygili, E. E., Ozturkoglu, Y., & Kocakulah, M. C. (2017). End Users' Perceptions of Critical Success Factors in ERP Applications. *International Journal of Enterprise Information Systems, 13*(4), 58–75. DOI: 10.4018/ IJEIS.2017100104

Saygili, E. E., & Saygili, A. T. (2017). Contemporary Issues in Enterprise Information Systems: A Critical Review of CSFs in ERP Implementations. In Tavana, M. (Ed.), *Enterprise Information Systems and the Digitalization of Business Functions* (pp. 120–136). Hershey, PA: IGI Global. DOI: 10.4018/978-1-5225-2382-6.ch006

Schwaiger, K. M., & Zehrer, A. (2021). The COVID-19 Pandemic and Organizational Resilience in Hospitality Family Firms: A Qualitative Approach. In Zehrer, A., Glowka, G., Schwaiger, K., & Ranacher-Lackner, V. (Eds.), *Resiliency Models and Addressing Future Risks for Family Firms in the Tourism Industry* (pp. 32–49). IGI Global. https://doi.org/10.4018/ 978-1-7998-7352-5.ch002

Scott, N., & Campos, A. C. (2022). Cognitive Science of Tourism Experiences. In R. Augusto Costa, F. Brandão, Z. Breda, & C. Costa (Eds.), *Planning and Managing the Experience Economy in Tourism* (pp. 1-21). IGI Global. https://doi.org/DOI: 10.4018/978-1-7998-8775-1.ch001

Segredo, M. R., Cistone, P. J., & Reio, T. G. (2017). Relationships Between Emotional Intelligence, Leadership Style, and School Culture. *International Journal of Adult Vocational Education and Technology, 8*(3), 25–43. DOI: 10.4018/IJAVET.2017070103

Seidenstricker, S., & Antonino, A. (2018). Business Model Innovation-Oriented Technology Management for Emergent Technologies. In M. Khosrow-Pour, D.B.A. (Ed.), *Encyclopedia of Information Science and Technology, Fourth Edition* (pp. 4560-4569). Hershey, PA: IGI Global. DOI: 10.4018/978-1-5225-2255-3.ch396

Selvi, M. S. (2021). Changes in Tourism Sales and Marketing Post COVID-19. In Demir, M., Dalgıç, A., & Ergen, F. (Eds.), *Handbook of Research on the Impacts and Implications of COVID-19 on the Tourism Industry* (pp. 437–460). IGI Global. DOI: 10.4018/978-1-7998-8231-2.ch021

Senaratne, S., & Gunarathne, A. D. (2017). Excellence Perspective for Management Education from a Global Accountants' Hub in Asia. In Baporikar, N. (Ed.), *Management Education for Global Leadership* (pp. 158–180). Hershey, PA: IGI Global. DOI: 10.4018/978-1-5225-1013-0.ch008

Sensuse, D. I., & Cahyaningsih, E. (2018). Knowledge Management Models: A Summative Review. *International Journal of Information Systems in the Service Sector*, *10*(1), 71–100. DOI: 10.4018/IJISSS.2018010105

Seth, M., Goyal, D., & Kiran, R. (2017). Diminution of Impediments in Implementation of Supply Chain Management Information System for Enhancing its Effectiveness in Indian Automobile Industry. *Journal of Global Information Management*, *25*(3), 1–20. DOI: 10.4018/JGIM.2017070101

Seyal, A. H., & Rahman, M. N. (2017). Investigating Impact of Inter-Organizational Factors in Measuring ERP Systems Success: Bruneian Perspectives. In Tavana, M. (Ed.), *Enterprise Information Systems and the Digitalization of Business Functions* (pp. 178–204). Hershey, PA: IGI Global. DOI: 10.4018/978-1-5225-2382-6.ch008

Shalev, N. (2017). Empathy and Leadership From the Organizational Perspective. In Nedelko, Z., & Brzozowski, M. (Eds.), *Exploring the Influence of Personal Values and Cultures in the Workplace* (pp. 348–363). Hershey, PA: IGI Global. DOI: 10.4018/978-1-5225-2480-9.ch018

Shaqrah, A. A. (2018). Analyzing Business Intelligence Systems Based on 7s Model of McKinsey. *International Journal of Business Intelligence Research*, *9*(1), 53–63. DOI: 10.4018/IJBIR.2018010104

Sharma, A. J. (2017). Enhancing Sustainability through Experiential Learning in Management Education. In Baporikar, N. (Ed.), *Management Education for Global Leadership* (pp. 256–274). Hershey, PA: IGI Global. DOI: 10.4018/978-1-5225-1013-0.ch013

Shetty, K. P. (2017). Responsible Global Leadership: Ethical Challenges in Management Education. In Baporikar, N. (Ed.), *Innovation and Shifting Perspectives in Management Education* (pp. 194–223). Hershey, PA: IGI Global. DOI: 10.4018/978-1-5225-1019-2.ch009

Siamak, M., Fathi, S., & Isfandyari-Moghaddam, A. (2018). Assessment and Measurement of Education Programs of Information Literacy. In Bhardwaj, R. (Ed.), *Digitizing the Modern Library and the Transition From Print to Electronic* (pp. 164–192). Hershey, PA: IGI Global. DOI: 10.4018/978-1-5225-2119-8.ch007

Sinthupundaja, J., & Kohda, Y. (2017). Effects of Corporate Social Responsibility and Creating Shared Value on Sustainability. *International Journal of Sustainable Entrepreneurship and Corporate Social Responsibility*, 2(1), 27–38. DOI: 10.4018/IJSECSR.2017010103

Siu, K. W., & García, G. J. (2017). Disruptive Technologies and Education: Is There Any Disruption After All? In I. Management Association (Ed.), *Educational Leadership and Administration: Concepts, Methodologies, Tools, and Applications* (pp. 757-778). Hershey, PA: IGI Global. https://doi.org/DOI: 10.4018/978-1-5225-1624-8.ch037

Škarica, I., & Hrgović, A. V. (2018). Implementation of Total Quality Management Principles in Public Health Institutes in the Republic of Croatia. *International Journal of Productivity Management and Assessment Technologies*, 6(1), 1–16. DOI: 10.4018/IJPMAT.2018010101

Skokic, V. (2021). How Small Hotel Owners Practice Resilience: Longitudinal Study Among Small Family Hotels in Croatia. In Zehrer, A., Glowka, G., Schwaiger, K., & Ranacher-Lackner, V. (Eds.), *Resiliency Models and Addressing Future Risks for Family Firms in the Tourism Industry* (pp. 50–73). IGI Global. DOI: 10.4018/978-1-7998-7352-5.ch003

Slagter van Tryon, P. J. (2017). The Nurse Educator's Role in Designing Instruction and Instructional Strategies for Academic and Clinical Settings. In Stefaniak, J. (Ed.), *Advancing Medical Education Through Strategic Instructional Design* (pp. 133–149). Hershey, PA: IGI Global. DOI: 10.4018/978-1-5225-2098-6.ch006

Slattery, C. A. (2018). Literacy Intervention and the Differentiated Plan of Instruction. In *Developing Effective Literacy Intervention Strategies: Emerging Research and Opportunities* (pp. 41–62). Hershey, PA: IGI Global. DOI: 10.4018/978-1-5225-5007-5.ch003

Smith, A. R. (2017). Ensuring Quality: The Faculty Role in Online Higher Education. In Shelton, K., & Pedersen, K. (Eds.), *Handbook of Research on Building, Growing, and Sustaining Quality E-Learning Programs* (pp. 210–231). Hershey, PA: IGI Global. DOI: 10.4018/978-1-5225-0877-9.ch011

Smuts, H., Kotzé, P., Van der Merwe, A., & Loock, M. (2017). Framework for Managing Shared Knowledge in an Information Systems Outsourcing Context. *International Journal of Knowledge Management*, *13*(4), 1–30. DOI: 10.4018/IJKM.2017100101

Souders, T. M. (2017). Understanding Your Learner: Conducting a Learner Analysis. In Stefaniak, J. (Ed.), *Advancing Medical Education Through Strategic Instructional Design* (pp. 1–29). Hershey, PA: IGI Global. DOI: 10.4018/978-1-5225-2098-6.ch001

Sousa, M. J., Cruz, R., Dias, I., & Caracol, C. (2017). Information Management Systems in the Supply Chain. In Jamil, G., Soares, A., & Pessoa, C. (Eds.), *Handbook of Research on Information Management for Effective Logistics and Supply Chains* (pp. 469–485). Hershey, PA: IGI Global. DOI: 10.4018/978-1-5225-0973-8.ch025

Spremic, M., Turulja, L., & Bajgoric, N. (2018). Two Approaches in Assessing Business Continuity Management Attitudes in the Organizational Context. In Bajgoric, N. (Ed.), *Always-On Enterprise Information Systems for Modern Organizations* (pp. 159–183). Hershey, PA: IGI Global. DOI: 10.4018/978-1-5225-3704-5.ch008

Spring, K. J., Graham, C. R., & Ikahihifo, T. B. (2018). Learner Engagement in Blended Learning. In M. Khosrow-Pour, D.B.A. (Ed.), *Encyclopedia of Information Science and Technology, Fourth Edition* (pp. 1487-1498). Hershey, PA: IGI Global. DOI: 10.4018/978-1-5225-2255-3.ch128

Steenkamp, A. L. (2018). Some Insights in Computer Science and Information Technology. In *Examining the Changing Role of Supervision in Doctoral Research Projects: Emerging Research and Opportunities* (pp. 113–133). Hershey, PA: IGI Global. DOI: 10.4018/978-1-5225-2610-0.ch005

Stipanović, C., Rudan, E., & Zubović, V. (2022). Reaching the New Tourist Through Creativity: Sustainable Development Challenges in Croatian Coastal Towns. In Valeri, M. (Ed.), *New Governance and Management in Touristic Destinations* (pp. 231–245). IGI Global. https://doi.org/10.4018/978-1-6684-3889-3.ch014

Storey, V. A., Anthony, A. K., & Wahid, P. (2017). Gender-Based Leadership Barriers: Advancement of Female Faculty to Leadership Positions in Higher Education. In Wang, V. (Ed.), *Encyclopedia of Strategic Leadership and Management* (pp. 244–258). Hershey, PA: IGI Global. DOI: 10.4018/978-1-5225-1049-9.ch018

Stottlemyer, D. (2018). Develop a Teaching Model Plan for a Differentiated Learning Approach. In *Differentiated Instructional Design for Multicultural Environments: Emerging Research and Opportunities* (pp. 106–130). Hershey, PA: IGI Global. DOI: 10.4018/978-1-5225-5106-5.ch005

Stottlemyer, D. (2018). Developing a Multicultural Environment. In *Differentiated Instructional Design for Multicultural Environments: Emerging Research and Opportunities* (pp. 1–27). Hershey, PA: IGI Global. DOI: 10.4018/978-1-5225-5106-5.ch001

Swagerty, T. (2022). Digital Access to Culturally Relevant Curricula: The Impact on the Native and Indigenous Student. In Reeves, E., & McIntyre, C. (Eds.), *Multidisciplinary Perspectives on Diversity and Equity in a Virtual World* (pp. 99–113). IGI Global. https://doi.org/10.4018/978-1-7998-8028-8.ch006

Swami, B. N., Gobona, T., & Tsimako, J. J. (2017). Academic Leadership: A Case Study of the University of Botswana. In Baporikar, N. (Ed.), *Innovation and Shifting Perspectives in Management Education* (pp. 1–32). Hershey, PA: IGI Global. DOI: 10.4018/978-1-5225-1019-2.ch001

Swanson, K. W., & Collins, G. (2018). Designing Engaging Instruction for the Adult Learners. In M. Khosrow-Pour, D.B.A. (Ed.), *Encyclopedia of Information Science and Technology, Fourth Edition* (pp. 1432-1440). Hershey, PA: IGI Global. DOI: 10.4018/978-1-5225-2255-3.ch123

Swartz, B. A., Lynch, J. M., & Lynch, S. D. (2018). Embedding Elementary Teacher Education Coursework in Local Classrooms: Examples in Mathematics and Special Education. In Polly, D., Putman, M., Petty, T., & Good, A. (Eds.), *Innovative Practices in Teacher Preparation and Graduate-Level Teacher Education Programs* (pp. 262–292). Hershey, PA: IGI Global. DOI: 10.4018/978-1-5225-3068-8.ch015

Tabach, A., & Croteau, A. (2017). Configurations of Information Technology Governance Practices and Business Unit Performance. *International Journal of IT/Business Alignment and Governance, 8*(2), 1–27. DOI: 10.4018/IJITBAG.2017070101

Talaue, G. M., & Iqbal, T. (2017). Assessment of e-Business Mode of Selected Private Universities in the Philippines and Pakistan. *International Journal of Online Marketing, 7*(4), 63–77. DOI: 10.4018/IJOM.2017100105

Taliadorou, N., & Pashiardis, P. (2017). Emotional Intelligence and Political Skill Really Matter in Educational Leadership. In I. Management Association (Ed.), *Educational Leadership and Administration: Concepts, Methodologies, Tools, and Applications* (pp. 1274-1303). Hershey, PA: IGI Global. https://doi.org/DOI: 10.4018/978-1-5225-1624-8.ch060

Tam, G. C. (2017). Project Manager Sustainability Competence. In *Managerial Strategies and Green Solutions for Project Sustainability* (pp. 178–207). Hershey, PA: IGI Global. DOI: 10.4018/978-1-5225-2371-0.ch008

Tambo, T. (2018). Fashion Retail Innovation: About Context, Anteced-ents, and Outcome in Technological Change Projects. In I. Management Association (Ed.), *Fashion and Textiles: Breakthroughs in Research and Practice* (pp. 233-260). Hershey, PA: IGI Global. https://doi.org/DOI: 10.4018/978-1-5225-3432-7.ch010

Tandoh, K. A., & Ebe-Arthur, J. E. (2018). Effective Educational Lead-ership in the Digital Age: An Examination of Professional Qualities and Best Practices. In Keengwe, J. (Ed.), *Handbook of Research on Digital Content, Mobile Learning, and Technology Integration Models in Teacher Education* (pp. 244–265). Hershey, PA: IGI Global. DOI: 10.4018/978-1-5225-2953-8.ch013

Tantau, A. D., & Frăţilă, L. C. (2018). Information and Management Sys-tem for Renewable Energy Business. In *Entrepreneurship and Business Development in the Renewable Energy Sector* (pp. 200–244). Hershey, PA: IGI Global. DOI: 10.4018/978-1-5225-3625-3.ch006

Teixeira, N., Pardal, P. N., & Rafael, B. G. (2018). Internationalization, Financial Performance, and Organizational Challenges: A Success Case in Portugal. In Carvalho, L. (Ed.), *Handbook of Research on Entrepreneurial Ecosystems and Social Dynamics in a Globalized World* (pp. 379–423). Hershey, PA: IGI Global. DOI: 10.4018/978-1-5225-3525-6.ch017

Teixeira, P., Teixeira, L., Eusébio, C., Silva, S., & Teixeira, A. (2021). The Impact of ICTs on Accessible Tourism: Evidence Based on a Systematic Literature Review. In Eusébio, C., Teixeira, L., & Carneiro, M. (Eds.), *ICT Tools and Applications for Accessible Tourism* (pp. 1–25). IGI Global. DOI: 10.4018/978-1-7998-6428-8.ch001

Tobin, M. T. (2018). Multimodal Literacy. In M. Khosrow-Pour, D.B.A. (Ed.), *Encyclopedia of Information Science and Technology, Fourth Edition* (pp. 1508-1516). Hershey, PA: IGI Global. DOI: 10.4018/978-1-5225-2255-3.ch130

Torres, K. M., Arrastia-Chisholm, M. C., & Tackett, S. (2019). A Phe-nomenological Study of Pre-Service Teachers' Perceptions of Completing ESOL Field Placements. *International Journal of Teacher Education and Professional Development*, *2*(2), 85–101. https://doi.org/10.4018/IJTEPD .2019070106

Torres, M. C., Salamanca, Y. N., Cely, J. P., & Aguilar, J. L. (2020). All We Need is a Boost! Using Multimodal Tools and the Translanguaging Strategy: Strengthening Speaking in the EFL Classroom. *International Journal of Computer-Assisted Language Learning and Teaching*, *10*(3), 28–47. DOI: 10.4018/IJCALLT.2020070103

Torres, M. L., & Ramos, V. J. (2018). Music Therapy: A Pedagogical Alternative for ASD and ID Students in Regular Classrooms. In Epler, P. (Ed.), *Instructional Strategies in General Education and Putting the Individuals With Disabilities Act (IDEA) Into Practice* (pp. 222–244). Hershey, PA: IGI Global. DOI: 10.4018/978-1-5225-3111-1.ch008

Toulassi, B. (2017). Educational Administration and Leadership in Fran-cophone Africa: 5 Dynamics to Change Education. In Mukerji, S., & Tripathi, P. (Eds.), *Handbook of Research on Administration, Policy, and Leadership in Higher Education* (pp. 20–45). Hershey, PA: IGI Global. DOI: 10.4018/978-1-5225-0672-0.ch002

Trad, A., & Kalpić, D. (2018). The Business Transformation Framework, Agile Project and Change Management. In M. Khosrow-Pour, D.B.A. (Ed.), *Encyclopedia of Information Science and Technology, Fourth Edition* (pp. 620-635). Hershey, PA: IGI Global. https://doi.org/DOI: 10.4018/978-1-5225-2255-3.ch054

Trad, A., & Kalpić, D. (2018). The Business Transformation and Enterprise Architecture Framework: The Financial Engineering E-Risk Management and E-Law Integration. In Sergi, B., Fidanoski, F., Ziolo, M., & Naumovs-ki, V. (Eds.), *Regaining Global Stability After the Financial Crisis* (pp. 46–65). Hershey, PA: IGI Global. DOI: 10.4018/978-1-5225-4026-7.ch003

Trengereid, V. (2022). Conditions of Network Engagement: The Quest for a Common Good. In R. Augusto Costa, F. Brandão, Z. Breda, & C. Costa (Eds.), *Planning and Managing the Experience Economy in Tourism* (pp. 69-84). IGI Global. https://doi.org/10.4018/978-1-7998-8775-1.ch004

Turulja, L., & Bajgoric, N. (2018). Business Continuity and Information Systems: A Systematic Literature Review. In Bajgoric, N. (Ed.), *Always-On Enterprise Information Systems for Modern Organizations* (pp. 60–87). Hershey, PA: IGI Global. DOI: 10.4018/978-1-5225-3704-5.ch004

Umair, S., & Sharif, M. M. (2018). Predicting Students Grades Using Artificial Neural Networks and Support Vector Machine. In M. Khosrow-Pour, D.B.A. (Ed.), *Encyclopedia of Information Science and Technology, Fourth Edition* (pp. 5169-5182). Hershey, PA: IGI Global. DOI: 10.4018/978-1-5225-2255-3.ch449

Vargas-Hernández, J. G. (2017). Professional Integrity in Business Management Education. In Baporikar, N. (Ed.), *Management Education for Global Leadership* (pp. 70–89). Hershey, PA: IGI Global. DOI: 10.4018/978-1-5225-1013-0.ch004

Varnacı Uzun, F. (2021). The Destination Preferences of Foreign Tourists During the COVID-19 Pandemic and Attitudes Towards: Marmaris, Turkey. In Demir, M., Dalgıç, A., & Ergen, F. (Eds.), *Handbook of Research on the Impacts and Implications of COVID-19 on the Tourism Industry* (pp. 285–306). IGI Global. https://doi.org/10.4018/978-1-7998-8231-2.ch014

Vasista, T. G., & AlAbdullatif, A. M. (2017). Role of Electronic Customer Relationship Management in Demand Chain Management: A Predictive Analytic Approach. *International Journal of Information Systems and Supply Chain Management, 10*(1), 53–67. DOI: 10.4018/IJISSCM.2017010104

Vettraino, L., Castello, V., Guspini, M., & Guglielman, E. (2018). Self-Awareness and Motivation Contrasting ESL and NEET Using the SAVE System. In M. Khosrow-Pour, D.B.A. (Ed.), *Encyclopedia of Information Science and Technology, Fourth Edition* (pp. 1559-1568). Hershey, PA: IGI Global. DOI: 10.4018/978-1-5225-2255-3.ch135

Vieru, D., & Bourdeau, S. (2017). Survival in the Digital Era: A Digital Competence-Based Multi-Case Study in the Canadian SME Clothing Industry. *International Journal of Social and Organizational Dynamics in IT*, 6(1), 17–34. DOI: 10.4018/IJSODIT.2017010102

Vijayan, G., & Kamarulzaman, N. H. (2017). An Introduction to Sustainable Supply Chain Management and Business Implications. In Khan, M., Hussain, M., & Ajmal, M. (Eds.), *Green Supply Chain Management for Sustainable Business Practice* (pp. 27–50). Hershey, PA: IGI Global. DOI: 10.4018/978-1-5225-0635-5.ch002

Vlachvei, A., & Notta, O. (2017). Firm Competitiveness: Theories, Evidence, and Measurement. In Vlachvei, A., Notta, O., Karantininis, K., & Tsounis, N. (Eds.), *Factors Affecting Firm Competitiveness and Performance in the Modern Business World* (pp. 1–42). Hershey, PA: IGI Global. DOI: 10.4018/978-1-5225-0843-4.ch001

Wang, C., Schofield, M., Li, X., & Ou, X. (2017). Do Chinese Students in Public and Private Higher Education Institutes Perform at Different Level in One of the Leadership Skills: Critical Thinking?: An Exploratory Comparison. In Wang, V. (Ed.), *Encyclopedia of Strategic Leadership and Management* (pp. 160–181). Hershey, PA: IGI Global. DOI: 10.4018/978-1-5225-1049-9.ch013

Wang, J. (2017). Multi-Agent based Production Management Decision System Modelling for the Textile Enterprise. *Journal of Global Information Management*, 25(4), 1–15. DOI: 10.4018/JGIM.2017100101

Wiedemann, A., & Gewald, H. (2017). Examining Cross-Domain Alignment: The Correlation of Business Strategy, IT Management, and IT Business Value. *International Journal of IT/Business Alignment and Governance*, 8(1), 17–31. DOI: 10.4018/IJITBAG.2017010102

Wiemelt, J. (2017). Critical Bilingual Leadership for Emergent Bilingual Students. In I. Management Association (Ed.), *Educational Leadership and Administration: Concepts, Methodologies, Tools, and Applications* (pp. 1606-1631). Hershey, PA: IGI Global. DOI: 10.4018/978-1-5225-1624-8.ch074

Wolf, F., Seyfarth, F. C., & Pflaum, E. (2018). Scalable Capacity-Building for Geographically Dispersed Learners: Designing the MOOC "Sustainable Energy in Small Island Developing States (SIDS)". In Pandey, U., & Indrakanti, V. (Eds.), *Open and Distance Learning Initiatives for Sustainable Development* (pp. 58–83). Hershey, PA: IGI Global. DOI: 10.4018/978-1-5225-2621-6.ch003

Wolf, R., & Thiel, M. (2018). Advancing Global Business Ethics in China: Reducing Poverty Through Human and Social Welfare. In Hipsher, S. (Ed.), *Examining the Private Sector's Role in Wealth Creation and Poverty Reduction* (pp. 67–84). Hershey, PA: IGI Global. DOI: 10.4018/978-1-5225-3117-3.ch004

Woodley, X. M., Mucundanyi, G., & Lockard, M. (2017). Designing Counter-Narratives: Constructing Culturally Responsive Curriculum Online. *International Journal of Online Pedagogy and Course Design*, 7(1), 43–56. DOI: 10.4018/IJOPCD.2017010104

Yablonsky, S. (2018). Innovation Platforms: Data and Analytics Platforms. In *Multi-Sided Platforms (MSPs) and Sharing Strategies in the Digital Economy: Emerging Research and Opportunities* (pp. 72–95). Hershey, PA: IGI Global. DOI: 10.4018/978-1-5225-5457-8.ch003

Yaşar, B. (2021). The Impact of COVID-19 on Volatility of Tourism Stocks: Evidence From BIST Tourism Index. In Demir, M., Dalgıç, A., & Ergen, F. (Eds.), *Handbook of Research on the Impacts and Implications of COVID-19 on the Tourism Industry* (pp. 23–44). IGI Global. https://doi.org/10.4018/978-1-7998-8231-2.ch002

Yell, M. L., & Christle, C. A. (2017). The Foundation of Inclusion in Federal Legislation and Litigation. In Curran, C., & Petersen, A. (Eds.), *Handbook of Research on Classroom Diversity and Inclusive Education Practice* (pp. 27–52). Hershey, PA: IGI Global. DOI: 10.4018/978-1-5225-2520-2.ch002

Yusoff, A., Ahmad, N. H., & Halim, H. A. (2017). Agropreneurship among Gen Y in Malaysia: The Role of Academic Institutions. In Ahmad, N., Ramayah, T., Halim, H., & Rahman, S. (Eds.), *Handbook of Research on Small and Medium Enterprises in Developing Countries* (pp. 23–47). Hershey, PA: IGI Global. DOI: 10.4018/978-1-5225-2165-5.ch002

Zacher, D., & Pechlaner, H. (2021). Resilience as an Opportunity Approach: Challenges and Perspectives for Private Sector Participation on a Community Level. In Zehrer, A., Glowka, G., Schwaiger, K., & Ranacher-Lackner, V. (Eds.), *Resiliency Models and Addressing Future Risks for Family Firms in the Tourism Industry* (pp. 75–102). IGI Global. https://doi.org/10.4018/978-1-7998-7352-5.ch004

Zanin, F., Comuzzi, E., & Costantini, A. (2018). The Effect of Business Strategy and Stock Market Listing on the Use of Risk Assessment Tools. In *Management Control Systems in Complex Settings: Emerging Research and Opportunities* (pp. 145–168). Hershey, PA: IGI Global. DOI: 10.4018/978-1-5225-3987-2.ch007

Zgheib, P. W. (2017). Corporate Innovation and Intrapreneurship in the Middle East. In Zgheib, P. (Ed.), *Entrepreneurship and Business Innovation in the Middle East* (pp. 37–56). Hershey, PA: IGI Global. DOI: 10.4018/978-1-5225-2066-5.ch003

Zinner, L. (2019). Fostering Academic Citizenship With a Shared Leadership Approach. In Zhu, C., & Zayim-Kurtay, M. (Eds.), *University Governance and Academic Leadership in the EU and China* (pp. 99–117). IGI Global. https://doi.org/10.4018/978-1-5225-7441-5.ch007

About the Author

Christina Chin M.M. is an Associate Professor with the University of Nottingham Malaysia in the Department of Mechanical, Materials & Manufacturing Engineering. She is also the departmental Undergraduate Course Director overseeing, managing and providing strategic lead all the undergraduates programmes. She has a wide range multi and interdisciplinary knowledge in project engineering management for sustainability & environmental impact industries, energy management related aspect including green technology, energy trading, security and storage capacity and efficiency. She has earned her Professional Technologist (Ts.) and Graduate Technologist from Malaysia Board of Technology recently accrediting her skills and experiences. With over 50 publications to date in internationally refereed journals, technical papers, congress/ conference proceedings, and book chapters, she is also an active reviewer for international journals, conferences, books and invited guest speakers for lectures and webinars based on well-established academic-industrial collaboration partnership in various countries globally.

Index